CAN ROBOTS INFLUENCE WORKING

AND CONSUMPTION DECISION TIME

JOHN LOK

Contents

Preface

Nowadays, many businessmen or marketing research professional hope to apply different methods to predict consumer behaviors in order to know what will be future market activities and market changes to help them to choose to implement what kinds of marketing strategies more accurately. The methods include economic environmental change prediction method, consumer individual psychological change prediction method, micro or macro behavioral economic environmental change prediction method, marketing environmental change prediction method etc. different kinds of methods which can be applied to predict how consumer behavioral changes to influence whose behavioral consumption to the manufacturer products sale within one to two years short term or three to five years middle term, even above five years long term business plans. Hence, if the product manufacturers can apply the most suitable consumer behavioral prediction method to predict how consumers' choice will be changed to influence their products sale easily. It will have more beneficial intangible and tangible advantages to achieve the their product easier sale aim to ensure their businesses' future market share to be increased more easier to their countries' choice target sale markets. Otherwise, if they applied the inaccurate consumer behavioral prediction methods to predict how their consumers' behavioral changes wrongly. Then, it will influence their market shares to be same level, even it will decrease their market shares, when their consumer behavioral prediction inaccurately.

How AI technology influence productivities and service performance ? Whether it can raise productivities and improve service performance?This book aims to explain why and how future artificial intelligent technology (big data gathering method) can be applied to assit businesses to predict why and when and how consumer behavior changes. I shall explain why traditional psychological and statistic and marketing methods are applied to predict consumer behaviors, human's judgement and analytical effort will be worse to compare AI machine's judgement and analytical effort. Also, I shall indicate different business organizations why they apply AI big data gathering method to help them to design any questionnaires (surveys) questions which will be more valid and useful to conclude human's questionnaires (surveys) design questions method. This book has these two research questions need to be answered? Can apply (AI) learning machine predict consumer behaviors? Can (AI) learning machine replace human marketing research method, e.g. survey or human psychological and micro and macro economic methods to predict consumer behaviors more accurate?

In my this book first part, I concentrate on indicate whether any artificial intelligence (AI) tools will be one kind of good consumer behavioral prediction method to be choose to apply to predict consumer behaviors. I shall indicate some examples, cases to give reasonable evidences to analyze whether (AI) tools will be one kind suitable tool to be applied to predict when and how consumer behavioral changes. If (AI) can be one kind tool to attempt to be applied to predict when and how consumer behavioral changes. Will it replace other kinds of methods to predict consumer behaviors? Does it have weaknesses to be applied to predict consumer behaviors, instead of strengths? Can it be applied to predict consumer behaviors depending on any situations of only some situation? Finally, I believe that any readers can find answers to answer above these questions in this book.

In my this book second part, I shall explain why and how human can possible apply (AI) tool to predict consumer individual emotion. I shall indicate case studies to explain how consumer individual better or worse emotion how to influence whose consumption behavior in different situation. Finally, I shall indicate evidences to conclude how and why (AI) tool that can be used to predict consumer individual emotion and it will have direct relationship to influence consumption behavior, as well as how (AI) tool can assist businessmen to judge whether what reasons case the customer does not choose to buy its product, it is possible because the product high price factor, poor product quality or poor staff service performance or attitude etc. different factors to influence the consumer decides to choose to buy the other product consequently, when the (AI) tool can confirm consumer has good or bad emotion to judge what factors are the causes his decision making at the moment.

Readers can understand why and how (AI) tool can be attempt to be applied to predict customer emotion and it can influence positive or negative consumption behavior to the product clearly in this part.

This book third part has these two research questions need to be answered? Can apply (AI) learning machine as well as micro and macro economic methods predict consumer behavioral changing?Can (AI) learning machine replace human marketing research method, e.g. survey or human psychological and micro and macro economic methods to predict consumer behaviors more accurate? The part indicates whether micro and macro economic methods can be attempted to apply to predict when, how and why consumer behavioral changing for every kind of different business. The second part indicates whether artificial intelligence can be attempted to apply to predict when, how and why consumer behavioral changing for every kind of different business.

Whether can businessmen apply micro and macro-economic methods to assist them to analyze how marketing will change, what marketing trend will develop next month or next half year, even more than one year marketing development trend in possible?

In my this book final part, I shall considerate on businessmen and customers both beneficial view point to explain how to apply behavioral economic concept to predict how their specific industries marketing development trend or consumer behavioral changing trend in these micro economic (individual consumer psychological shopping change trend) and macro-economic (global every specific industry marketing changing trend) environment. This third part researches this two questions: Has it relationship between macro and micro economic environment change factors to influence marketing development change trend? Can businessmen apply macro and micro economic methods to predict future marketing development change trend in their specific industries?

I shall indicate some specific cases industry to attempt to explain whether it has really relationship between macro and micro economic environment change factors to influence marketing development change trend as well as whether businessmen can apply micro and macro-economic methods to predict future marketing development change trend in these specific industries.

In my this part, I concentrate on indicate whether any artificial intelligence (AI) tools will be one kind of good consumer behavioral prediction method to be choose to apply to predict consumer behaviors. I shall indicate some examples, cases to give reasonable evidences to analyze whether (AI) tools will be one kind suitable tool to be applied to predict when and how consumer behavioral changes. If (AI) can be one kind tool to attempt to be applied to predict when and how consumer behavioral changes. Will it replace other kinds of methods to predict consumer behaviors? Does it have weaknesses to be applied to predict consumer behaviors, instead of strengths? Can it be applied to predict consumer behaviors depending on any situations of only some situation? Finally, I believe that any readers can find answers to answer above these questions in this book. In my analysis, I conclude marketing development or marketing change trend will be influenced by consumer behavioral change model or attitude factor. Finally, I hope my readers can give opinions to make judgement to evaluate my opinions whether is right or wrong in this research topic. In part four, I shall indicate sample case study to judge whether it is possible to apply (AI) tool to attempt to help businesses to predict consumer behaviors in different business environment.

Prologue

(AI) -driven automation industry development
1.1 (AI) - driven automation industry development how to influence work nature change p.86-110
1.2 How (AI) influences labor market
Redefining management in the workforce of artificial intelligence
2.1 Change management
2.2 How (AI) influences organizational
change
Future works change: Automation, employment and productivity
3.1 How (AI) influences employment
3.2 What occupations will be influenced by
(AI) technology
3.3 Whether (A) technology machine labor
will replace human worker more or assist
human worker more
reference
3.4 Robot society advantages and disadvantage
Part two Robots how improve efficiency

Chapter 7 How robots shorten working and consumption decision time
Employee psychological rational
work behavior
Reference

Long time working hours how influence
marketing consultant team
cooperation

Long time working hours how influence
nuclear factory team cooperation
Long time working hours how influence
electronic assemblies factory team
cooperation

● Developing countries labors abnormal long time
● working hours influences
● What is abnormal working hours Economic
Problem

● Hypotheses Testing And Data Analysis
● What is difference benefits between normal working hours and abnormal working hours
● Can abnormal working hours raise productivity and economic growth in long term
●
● Bibliography p.111-120

Behavioral economy
method predicts organizational
behavioral changes and marketing

behavioral changes.
· How to apply behavioral economy
theory to predict marketing
behavioral changes more accurate?
· How to apply behavioral economy
theory to understand and manage
people within organizations?
Bibliography
Behavioral economic method
predicts stable basic income
consumer individual spending
behavior
· How to apply behavioral
economic method to
contribute to the stable basic
income target consumer group's
consumption prediction?
· How to apply behavioral
economic method to
predict labor market changing
behavior ?

How can apply behavioral
economy method raises basic
stable income consumer
consumption desire
1. Basic stable income consumption
great of small amount desire
2. Life-cycle advertisement method prediction of consumer behavior
3. Raising electricity consumption
from electricity user individual habit
Consumer confidence is as a
predictor of consumption spending
· What is confidence in consumption survey ?
· What is a confidence indicator ?
How to apply behavioral
economy methods influence employee individual psychology to achieve
raise productivity of long term
incentive intention?
· Increasing salary is short term incentive productivity method
· How to improve the design of
incentive structures to encourage productivities organizations?
· Building employees and managers
kindly co-operational relationship
method
· Can bonus method encourage
service performance to be raised ?
· Economic views of human

motivation nature

Under-level productive efficiency
and low-consumption desire
behavioral economic influences p.121-130
    How robots shorten consumption decision time and manufacturing time
    How and why time limiting pressure
influences consumer choice
    How the time consumption pressure
factor influences irrational
consumption decision making

Time pressure consumption decision
making process characteristics

Reducing time pressure consumption
methods

What are the in-store and out-store
factors influence supermarket
fast moving consumer decision

What consumption is most
influenced in preference choice
by time pressure

Time pressure impacts consumer
behavioral effect
    · The reasons cause consumers
feel time pressure

May time dominate consumption
final purchase decision making

Methods avoid consumers
feel time pressure

Time press how influences
video playing game consumer
purchase behavior

Time pressure consumption or
production situation explanation p.131-140
    How robots shorten working time and
consumption decision time

Human Behavioral network job brings social
economic benefits

What does human network job mean
Why human network job behavior may influence economy

Robots take our jobs behavioral and economy influences
Robot job behavior brings economy influences

Intellectual human economic behaviors
What does intellectual human economic behaviors
mean ?
The relationship between social change and human
behavior
How human productive behavior may influence economic development
● New Zealand farmer individual wine productive behavior
● America high technological productive behavior
● China share market investing behavior
Why has any individual country have many people invest share behavior which can influence the country's macro consumption desire?
Can technology influence human shopping behavioral change?
Why and how human behavior may influence the country's economic growth or recession?
Technology how impacts human behavior changing?
How and why employees behaviors may influence economy development?
Robots invention whether they can help organizations to raise efficiencies or inefficiencies? p.141-169

Robots How Improve Performance

CHAPTER ONE

(AI) PREDICTION CONSUMER BEHAVIOR TOOL

1.1 How can artificial intelligent tools predict consumer behavior in vehicle market

What is (AI) consumer behavioral prediction tool? How any why will (AI) tool assist manufactures to attempt to predict consumer behavior before and after consumption occurrence? First, I shall indicate how to apply (AI) tool to predict vehicle product consumer behavior case example.

Nowadays, many vehicle manufacturers hope their vehicles can attract to vehicle buyers to choose to buy their vehicles. However, there are many different brands of vehicles to provide to them to choose, so the vehicle market competition is very serious.

How to judge their different kinds of vehicle price which is reasonable acceptance to attract vehicle buyers to choose to buy the brand of vehicle manufacturers' any kinds of vehicles, e.g. fast speed sport style vehicles, comfortable and slow speed common cars, for four passengers common small size or more than four passengers common large car size? How to evaluate the vehicle prices issue is important factor to influence vehicle buyers' choices. Either if the brand of vehicle price is too high to compare brands, it will influence many vehicle buyers choose to buy other brands' vehicles or if the brand of vehicle price is too low, it will influence vehicle buyers feel this brand's vehicle's quality is worse to compare to other vehicle brands' similar vehicle products.

Thus, if the brand of vehicle manufacturers can predict how to design vehicles which can attract many vehicle buyers to choose to buy whose any vehicle products. What are future vehicle buyers' favorable vehicle styles? Then, the vehicle manufacturer can concentrate on manufacturing the kind style of vehicle products to sell already. It will reduce its vehicle manufacturing investment risk.

How to apply (AI) tools to predict vehicle buyers' behavioral consumption model? Whether artificial intelligent tools can predict automotive buyers' behavioral consumption model and predict future trend. In fact, automotive brands and dealerships are facing an increasingly competition when attempting to manually gathering the vast quantities of data required to create customer focused programs that increase retention, ultimately new sales and service automotive business. Building a based on that client's intrinsic needs and interests to any kinds of automotive vehicles at any given time. This is especially true in the automotive industry where the time span between purchases is measured in years. Because vehicle buyers would not like often to change their old vehicle to another new one. So, their decisions to buying another new vehicle, the time is usually after one year, even longer time. Hence, it seems any vehicles won't be frequent consumption products to the owned at least one vehicle family consumers (vehicle buyers).

Hence, how to predict vehicle consumers' taste or preferable which styles of vehicle choices issues is very important. If the vehicle manufacturers can not manufacture any attractive vehicles to sell easily in this year. Then, it will lose time, money in this year because it won't know when the owned least one vehicle users or non-owned any vehicle users who will decide to buy one new vehicle or change another new vehicle ensure. The different brand vehicle dealers will possible wait more than one year to attract them to buy their vehicles if their styles are not attractive to compare other brands of vehicle competitors.

However, artificial intelligence and machine learning can help any vehicle manufacturers to find solution to solve patterns in highly to solve patterns in highly complex data-sets that are beyond the capability of a human brain, and then building and automatically acting on the customer insights it generates.

Given the automotive customer need for individualized communications, this technology is positioned to become a critical component of any successful vehicle retailer's domestic or/and overseas vehicle markets. How can vehicle manufacturers and retailers use (AI) to enhance their vehicle marketing campaigns? How will (AI) affect their vehicle sale marketing strategy? What criteria would they use when selecting on (AI) solution?

Vehicle consumers today are able to quickly access different brands of vehicle information, research vehicle products and reviews, negotiate prices and compare one vehicle brand or retailer to another resulting of the brands of vehicle customers. At the same time, the rise of " big -data mining", wearable devices that track user's every move and preference and greater contextualization in advertising and social media has resulted in consumer expectations of individualized. Thus, it seems that (AI) tools can be used to gather " big-data" and then they can make human's mind to analyze how to design kinds of vehicles to satisfy vehicle buyers' needs.

As automotive vehicle marketers can apply (AI) tools to achieve messaging strategies to meet the needs of this new generation of informed vehicle consumers, using data from a variety of sources to move from a variety of sources to move from mass- messaging to more personalized messages aimed at particular vehicle buyer segments, e.g. fast speed sport vehicle buyer segment, slow speed comfortable small size or large size of buyer segment. However, when 90% of vehicle marketers believe having a single vehicle buyer view is important, only 6% have achieved it.

However, one of the main issues vehicle marketers facing is the lack of capacity to efficiently sift through and analyze the massive vehicle buyer amounts of data required to create vehicle buyer individualized vehicle customer experiences easily. This is especially difficult for automotive dealers, the long periods between purchase cycles, and the highly considered nature of the vehicle purchase means that each vehicle dealer needs to not only track a large number of potential vehicle customers for an extremely long period of time, but each of those vehicle customers will generate a huge amount of different kinds of vehicle behavioral consumption data as they research their next vehicle purchase. However, by choosing the right (AI) technological tools and programs , vehicle dealers can solve this big data gathering challenge into a major advantage.

For Forrester vehicle brand example, vehicle consumers have more power over the Forrester vehicle brand's reputation than ever before. Mayne, L. (2014) indicated that Forrester calls this new (AI) tools is the " age of the vehicle customer", a 20 year business cycle in which the most successful vehicle enterprises will reinvent themselves to systematically understand and serve increasingly powerful vehicle consumers. To win in this new age, Forrester declares companies must become vehicle customer obsessed and the only sustainable competitive advantage is knowledge and engagement with customers, such as (AI) gathering data knowledge.

Thus, the biggest challenge vehicle businesses currently face is not the collection of a large quantity of vehicle consumer data, but what to do with that data once they have it. Even at a large vehicle data research firm, the data sets are often too big for a single analyze, or even a team of analysts to sort through and draw conclusion from. However, enter artificial intelligence and machine learning , an efficient technology solution that can continuously find patterns in highly complex data sets that are way beyond the capacity of a human brain and then automatic drive action based on the customer insights is generated.

What is (AI) machine learning tool? Machine learning is a type of (AI) that learns from data and is not explicitly program. Think Amazon, face book. Machine learning serves up relevant content based on an individual vehicle purchase behavior and experiences. More simply, machine learning is a computer program that can learn relationships between data, subject those learnings to errors functions, and then learn from its errors. The program in effect, trains itself.

Lee, T. (2016) explained that "Thus, (AI) tools can learn deep a more advanced branch of machine learning inspired by how our brain's nervous function, has also been found to be especial effective in identifying patterns from data."

When this way sound is complicated from a vehicle dealer perspective, the implementation of a marketing program driven by artificial intelligence can take care of these tasks in an automatic vehicle fashion with little to no manual intervention required from the staff at time vehicle stores.

In practice at a vehicle dealership, the program will continue track vehicle customer behavior online, merging that data with any offline source (like CRM or DMS data) and then analyze this aggregated vehicle buyer data set to predict what vehicle customer may be shopping for and what information they might like to relevance from different kinds style of vehicle design photos.

1.1 Why can (AI) be applied to predict consumer behaviors?

Artificial intelligence refers to complex in vehicle market, machine learning that posses the same characteristics of human intelligence and that have all our sense, all our reason and think just like human do. Besides, machine learning is the practice of using algorithms to collect and examine data, learn from it, and then make a determination or prediction about something in the world.

The machine is " trained" using large amounts of data and algorithms that give it the ability to learn how to automatically perform a task with increasing accuracy. Otherwise, deep learning is primarily based on artificial neural networks inspired by our understanding of the biology of human's brains.

Deep learning breaks down tasks in ways that enables machines to assist us with increasingly complex tasks, driverless cars, better preventive healthcare and more accurate product recommendation (including vehicle recommendations). So, such as why (AI) technology can be applied to predict how vehicle consumer behavior changes to bring to judge whether vehicle consumer will like what kinds of vehicle styles next year. Then, vehicle manufacturers can gather overall vehicle consumer data to analyze and conclude the more accurate vehicle design direction for next year any new design vehicle manufacturing products.

Thus, (AI) machine learning can help vehicle manufacturers to solve how to design any new vehicle products challenge. A vehicle is both one of the most important and carefully considered purchases the majority of people will ever make in their lifetime. It is also a purchase that tends to be fundamentally tied to a person's identify and view of themselves. As the same time, vehicle consumers changing lifestyles result in changing vehicle needs, e.g. the young sport car enthusiast matures into the family driver.

Automotive dealers need to remember that vehicle customers and prospects are individual human beings with risk, complex and ever-changing lives factors, these factors will influence every vehicle consumer why who feels has vehicle purchase need, and how who choose to buy the first vehicle if who decided to buy the first vehicle.

The (AI) technological customer behavioral prediction tool seems to be the best vehicle salespeople in the world are those that know every one of their vehicle customers. Their likes and dislikes which style of vehicle design, preferences and changing tastes to vehicle choices. The capacity of the human brain, however, limits us from achieving this type of vehicle sales and frequent turnover at vehicle dealerships often results in the further loss of vehicle salespeople along with their vehicle customer relationships and knowledge. In this competitive vehicle environment, machine learning enables platforms to assist the vehicle sales team by tracking the vehicle consumer behaviors of each vehicle customer, learning and memorizing their preferences and predicting their future vehicle purchase needs.

Finally, I recommend that for a vehicle dealerships marketing platform to make their customer engagement efficient and fully-functional, I should be able to: applying (AI) tools to track every vehicle customer behavior across the web, connecting to a society of data sources, CRM, DMS, third-party, web vehicle brands, social email, click etc., aggregating and accurately cross-reference data from a variety of sources, leveraging this data to drive insights on a mass scale, as well as on an individualized basis, driving actions and automatically direct customer engagement via multiple channels based on where each customer is in their individual lifecycle.

1.2 How can (AI) provide businesses with better-informed decisions

I shall explain how (AI) technology can provide businesses with better-informed decisions to drive top-line growth, deliver meaningful experience for customers and smooth their path along the consumer journey. The widely understood definition of (AI) involves the ability of machines or computers to learn human thinking, reasoning and decision-making abilities.

A Narrative science study in 2015 year identified that (AI) was being used primarily in voice recognition, machine learning virtual assistants and decision support. This study also highlighted the many branches of (AI) and that techniques and their definition are used interchangeably. It is possible that (AI) can be used to gather big data , then to analyze to help businesses to predict consumer behaviors. For example, one of the most common techniques is machine learning, where algorithms are used to perform tasks by learning from historical data. Another growth branch of (AI) is natural language procession.

However, during 2017 year, search engines will begin to factor additional behavioral data into prediction of customer behavioral results, such as the user's history of searches and locations and previously captures conservations. Artificial intelligence will use this information to power predictive search results, e.g. predictive future consumer's choice behavioral processing for any kinds of businesses.

Predictive search will improve the quality of search results, and provide new insights into consumers' behavior and the moments which matter to them. Search will give recommendation into tailored how consumer individual choice in consumption process. Several of the largest online platforms already use machine learning to improve predictive consumer behavioral search results.

For example, Google's rank brain technology adds research by understanding the context in which the consumer has entered it. Over time, rank brain will learn further from user behaviors Amazon's DSSTNE (pronouned destiny) learns from shoppers' purchasing habits and consumption behavior to offer better product recommend actions, which Amazon can offer before a consumer has entered anything into the search bar. However, this technology is not independent of human input. For example, Google engineers will periodically retain the rank brain system to improve the models it uses. For another example, in 2016 year , Apple computer revamped its photos app to allow consumers to search for specific items in the phots, they want to find, not just dates and locations. Each photo that an intelligent phone or intelligent pad user takes goes through 11 billion computations, so that photos can understand exactly what is the photography.

It seems that in future, (AI) machine learning will allow search to evolve even further. Search engineers will deliver refined recommendations to their business users and use less human input to predict consumers' needs. For IBM computer example, it indicated 90% of the data that exists today has been created in the last two years. This huge explosion of data gives brands the opportunity to quickly spot and react to the latest trends, fashion and fads among its clients and potential clients. This will allow companies to better engage with younger consumers, who gain influence access to the latest trends, and use the brands. They associate with to help define who they are as individuals. Thus, brands have to identify and make use of them before consumers move on, but the vast quantity of data available makes. This a resource-intensive task. For next example, Lesara, a based online clothes store, uses this machine learning to inform its product decision often gathering information from internal and external sources. When its trends -spotting shoes. Lesara has a range of over 20 styles and sells hundreds of pairs a day. It focus on giving consumers, the very latest trends allow Lesara to develop on average of 50,000 new items each year. It compared to 11,000 old items each year. Thus, (AI) brain seems to human brain to own analytical ability to predict consumer behaviors.

For another example, Lesara is one online clothes store, uses machine learning decisions after gathering information from internal and external sources. One of its most popular products, shoes with LED started life when its trend spotting software flagged up a blogger wearing similar shoes. Now Lesara has a range of over 20 styles and sells hundreds of pairs a day. Its focus on giving consumers the very latest trends allows Lesara to develop an average of 50,000 new items each year, compared to 11,000 for its competitor Lara. it seems (AI) machine learning can help Lesara business to predict what kinds of shoes design or style that shoe consumers will prefer choose to buy in future shoe market trend. Thus, Lesara can predict shoe consumers' taste successfully and it can manufacture many attractive style of shoes. (AI) machine learning can gather global past shoe consumer's shoe shopping experiences, then analyzes to make conclusion to give lesara recommendation successfully. This will make the experience more enjoyable for shoe consumers and allow Lesara to advert whose different new style or design of shoes to deliver them move relevant messages by understanding the context of the experience.

However, (AI) machine learning will have this risk who manufacturers need to concern if they applied this technology to predict consumer behavior. It is on sample consumers' privacy issue, in order to avoid complaint chance occurrence. However, machine learning can tie this data together to identify which f the billions of devices are being used by individual consumers. This helps brands understand how consumer engagement and actions can be attributed to different messages in different contexts and at different time. So, machine learning can help brands to build confidence to promote their products by any advertisement channels. When, this new (AI) machine learning technology can conclude how to design their products to be the most attractive, due to it has more accurate to predict consumer behaviors to compare human themselves prediction judgement effort. It seems that (AI) machine judgement effort is more accurate to compare to human judgment effort.

For example, google is moving away from cookies and using logged in data to track and make to users. It plans to expand the scope of the brand lift tool from online video. Thus, consumers are responded will to shippable context, finding it persuasive and easy to navigate by (AI) machine learning decision. For example, fashion brands can aggregate their You tub videos and blogs into a mobile context marketing experience, such as brand centric context into a personal shopping activity gives the shopper an experience, who are likely to remember and tell their friends about any new style of products design promotion from these internet advertisement channels after (AI) machine learning tools' styles of product design recommendation.

WHAT IS (AI) DEEP LEARNING TECHNIQUES TO FORECAST ENVIRONMENT BEHAVIORAL CONSUMPTION

The (AI) deep-learning technology leads to performance enhancement and generalization of artificial intelligent technology. It influences the global leader in the field of information technology has declared its intention to utilize the deep-learning technology to solve environmental problems, such as climate change. So, it will help agriculture farming businesses can raise any plant food: vegetable, fruit, rice which grow up very easily if farmers can apply (AI) deep-learning technology to solve environment problems to influence their plant food grow. If the whole year seasonal change is very good and it is suitable for any plant food to grow in farming land easily, e.g. rain is enough and soil is enough for any plant food to grow in the farm lands. Then, fruit, rice, vegetable etc. agriculture businesses will have much beneficial attribution to global farmers.

The question is how to use deep-learning technologies in the environmental field to predict the status of pro-environmental consumption. We predicted the pro-environmental consumption index based on Google search query data, using a recurrent neural network (RNN model). To certify the accuracy of the index, we compared the prediction accuracy of the RNN model with that of the ordinary least square and artificial necessary network models. For example, the RNN model predicts the pro-environmental consumption index better than any other model. we expect the RNN model to perform still better in a big data environment because the deep-learning technologies would be increasingly as the volume of data grows. So, deep-learning technologies could be useful in environmental forecasting to prevent damage caused by climate change to influence any rice, vegetable, tomato, potato, fruit etc. different plant food grow in any countries' farming land easily.

For South Korea example, over 800 government agencies spent 2.2 trillion Korea won on eco-products in 2014 year. However, green products are rarely purchased outside these agencies. This phenomenon occurs because there is a gap between consumer attitudes and behavior , that is environmental attitude is a major factor in decision making vis-a-vis the consumption of " green" food and services (Jorea Ministry of Environment, 2015). Therefore, it is necessary to understand those consumer attitude, that will lead to sustainability-conductive behavior and consumption.

2.1 Environmental consumption prediction

Recently, many researchers have studied pro-environmental consumption and household indexes as well as suicide rate predictions using messages posted by internet users on Google trend, Tweets etc. channel. Whether can environmental consumption be predicted by (AI) deep-learning technological internet channel? How can impact the pro-environmental consumption attitudes of green policies? Korea scientists estimated pro-environmental attitudes using search query data provided by Google trend and confirmed through regression analysis, that pro-environmental attitude has a positive correlation with the pro-environmental attitude index. They also explained that environment-friendly attitude of residents plan an important role in policy making. In the past, most household consumption indexed were calculated through surveys, but (AI) deep-learning technological tool " big data" have recently gained research attention (Lee et al. 2016).

It seems that (AI) deep-learning technology can help agricultural export countries' farmers , e.g. US, UK, Canada, New Zealand, Australia, Japan, China, India etc. they can predict environmental behavioral consumption to any rice, tomato, potato , fruit, vegetable etc. plant food consumers. The beneficial advantages to them include as below:

(a) Assuming they know their countries' weather, when it has less rain to cause drought or when it has more rain in any seasonal time in the year. They can choose not to grow any kinds of above these plant food to avoid loss.

(b) They can make any kinds of above these plant food price raising after their prediction of these bad seasonal time to cause their plant food shortage supply challenge. Because these plant food consumers' demand number is more, but the supply of these above plant food supply number is less. However, due to they had predicted when the bad seasonal time can not allow them to grow these above plant food before. So, they have enough time to grow many these above plant food number in predictive good seasonal time to prepare to supply to their plant food import countries' plant food consumers to eat. Thus, these predictive environmental consumption plant food export countries can raise their plant food price to sell to them. When, the other non-pre-predictive environmental consumption plant food export countries can not supply any one of those plant food to them to eat, due to the bad climate to cause them can't grow any one of these plant food to export to sell.

Thus, (AI) deep-learning technology can be applied to predict how to raise the plant food supply number in order to raise price to the import plant food countries consumers to eat, due to they feel difficult to buy these plant food to eat in the bad climate seasonal time in whole year.

(c) (AI) deep-learning technology can help climate scientists to find what reasons cause their countries; rain sudden increases or cause their countries' rain sudden decreases. After its gathering data analysis, it can assist climate scientists to find solution methods to attempt to control the rain level can be right falling down level to let agricultural export farmers who can grow their plant food to sell to agricultural import countries in whole year.

(d) The agricultural export countries' farmers can apply (AI) deep-learning technology to help them to choose whether growing which kinds of plant food in that whether climate time to earn more plant food consumption number more easily.

Due to the agricultural countries climate will often change, for example, tomato, potato, rice, fruit etc. plant food can be adapt to grow in more rain time, but vegetable can not be adapt to grow in more rain time. If farmers can apply this technology to predict when it will have move rain or when it will have less rain to fall down in their countries. Then, they can choose to grow which kinds of plant food number more, in the suitable seasonal climate time in order to raise plant food growing number productivities to supply to sell to satisfy any agricultural food import countries' demand effectively.

(e) (AI) deep-learning technology can help agricultural import countries to solve agricultural food shortage challenge in long term. When this technology can be popular to base applied by the agricultural plant food export countries. It will solve global agricultural food shortage challenge. For example, when one agricultural export countries' farmers can popular accept to apply this technology to predict when to grow which kinds of plant food more to rise number productivities to sell. e.g. vegetable, fruit, rice Besides another agricultural export countries' farmers can also accept to apply this technology to predict when to grow plant food, e.g. potato, tomato to raise number productivities to sell. Then, they can concentrate on growing the specific kinds of plant food in order to raise the specific plant food number productivities in every seasonal change time every month. Then, global agricultural plant food supply must be raised, due to these predictive environmental change farmers can know who ought grow which kinds of plant food to sell to raise number productivities.

2.2 How can apply (AI) digital channel to predict consumer behaviors?

(AI) digital channel can be applied to help businesses to evaluate whether how much the product price is the most attractive to persuade consumers feel it is the most reasonable price to sell. It helps consumers to feel which brands of products which ought change the price to let consumers to choose to buy the brand of product. It can be applied to predict whether how many consumer numbers can be increased or decreased when the brand of product's price is variable. It aims to give opinions to help any brand of product manufacturers or sellers to judge whether which price is the most reasonable to let consumers to accept to choose to buy the brand of product in popular.

Thus, (AI) price measurement technology can be preference to be applied online communication ecommerce and mobile phone internet platform aspect. As businesses can enter their past products prices data and past customer number data into computer or mobile. Then, (AI) price measurement technology can gather these data to analyze these product prices and past customer number to compare their prices variable changing range level to find their price variable difference to measure to make conclusion about every product's price variable changing will influence how many customer number increase or decrease changing to choose to sell their different kinds of products more accurate. Then, (AI) price measurement software will help them to analyze all past price variable changing data to compare whether which price range can let customers to feel it is more reasonable and attractive to influence them to choose to buy the product among different brands of product choice.

Because any product's price is one important factor to influence consumers to choose to buy the product, instead of quality, durability, shape, appearance, color, brand familiarity etc. factors. Any online businesses with a focus on Asia should considerate (AI) customer care, and virtual shopping experience, whereas is Europe and North America still value face-to-face and/or real human interaction over (AI) or virtual worlds.

For example, Amazon publish has applied (AI) price measurement technology to help authors to decide how much every different topic of e-book or paper book price, it can attract the largest number of readers to buy. Any one author only needs to type whose book name to Amazon publish author himself/herself Amazon website. Amazon publish (AI) price measurement learning machine will help them to auto-calculate and judge how much e-book or paper book price is the most attractive and the most reasonable in order to increase reader number to buy their e-books or paper books to read. So, (AI) online price measurement machine will gather past similar book names and past every similar book readers' reading times and the number of readers to give opinions to let every author to judge whether his/her very new e-book or paper book ought charge how much price to the e-book or paper book which can attract many readers to choose to buy. Although, it is not ensure that the e-book or paper book price must let readers to feel it is the most reasonable price to choose to buy in reader's view point. However, it has other factors to influence readers' choice to buy the e-book or paper book, e.g. whether the book content is attractive to public, the author's familiarity, the book's page is enough or not to satisfy readers to read etc. factors. But, instead of all these extra factors to influence readers to choose to buy the book to read. (AI) price measurement learning machine can real give opinions to every author to let them to judge the e-book or paper book different price range whether is too high to influence readers to choose to buy to read or tool low to influence readers feel it is possible poor content book to compare other similar content books. Thus, (AI) price measurement machine can help authors to predict every reader's reading behaviors or reading experience and reading habit from online channel in short time easily. The author only enter the book name to let Amazon publish price measurement machine to check, it will follow past reader's reading habit and reading experience to judge whether the similar all book topic sale record to judge how much price is the reasonable price to attract many readers to buy the book.

Hence, (AI) can be applied to digital channel to help businesses to predict consumer behavior in the future. In the future, mobile/smartphone, laptop, desktop will be most frequent used ecommerce channels to develop online business. So, (AI) can be also applied to these platforms to gather data to make analysis to help businesses to predict consumer purchase behaviors popularly. Due to , ecommerce is popular to global, so digital online and instore channels can be one good channel to let (AI) learning machine to make platform to gather past every online consumer purchase (buying) experience data to help businesses to build brand personality and having a responsible, positive impact on society.

To apply (AI) learning machine technology to understand customer online purchase behavior, it will raise business e-commerce successful chance: For example, (AI) learning machine can help businesses to gather data to analyze to determine whether short-term or long-term signals in the online consumer behavior that indicate higher purchase intents to let every online business to know. (AI) learning machine can find that online users with long-term purchasing intent tend to save and click through on more content.

However, as online users approach the time of purchase their activity becomes more topically focused and actions shift from saves to searches from online consumption channel. Then, (AI) learning machine will further find that the brand product purchase signals in online behavior can exist weakness before an online purchase is made and can also be traced across different online purchase categories. Finally, (AI) learning machine synthesize these insights in predictive models of online user purchasing intent to the brand of product. Taken together, it's work identifies a set of general principles and signals that can be used to model online user purchasing intent across many online content discovery applications. Thus, (AI) learning machine can help online businesses to gather any online users' click online behaviors data to judge whether there are how many online users will choose to find their online business websites to make final decisions to buy their products from online channels. Then, it will give opinions to help the online businesses to let it to judge whether what are the important website factors will help its online business to attract many online consumers, e.g. designing unattractive website issue, online unattractive product photos issue, unclear website color issue, unclear website advertisement message, contents and words impressions issue, lacking image movement frequent attractive seeing issue etc. different website factors. Thus, online digital channel will be one good choice to apply (AI) learning machine to help businesses to predict consumer behaviors.

2.3 Can apply artificial intelligent learning machine " big data" gathering method to predict manufacturers' behavioral performance ?

In consumer view point, can they apply (AI) learning machine to predict manufacturers' behavioral performance to judge whether whose products are value to buy. Nowadays, (AI) and big data are reshaping the risk in consumer privacy. For example, consumers want to hide their willingness to pay just as firms want to hide their real marginal cost, and buyers have less favorable information, say a low credit shore, prefer to withhold it just as sellers want to conceal poor product quality. So, it implies that it is possible (AI) learning machine can help customers to gather any manufacturers' past sale performance, e.g. how many complaints or appreciation from clients, product quality etc. sale data to let consumers to make judgement whether it is value to buy to compare other competitors. So, it has risk to the poor product quality of manufacturers. Otherwise, it has benefits to the good product quality of manufacturers. It also implies all manufacturers' privacy is not protected or secret when (AI) learning machine is popular to be used to predict manufacturers' behaviors by consumers.

Information economists suggest that both buyers and sells have an incentive to hide or reveal private information, and these incentives are crucial for market efficiency. Data technology that reveals consumers type could facilitate a better match between product and consumer type, and data technology that helps buyers to assess product quality could encourage high quality production.

Thus, (AI) big data technology can also assist consumers to gather different manufacturers' data to compare what their advantages and disadvantages of their products are. Then, consumers can make comparison to choose which brand of product is the suitable to whom to buy in these more choice consumption market. (AI) learning machine will gather similar brand their products' data to analyze to make conclusion to let consumers know or feel to make final judge to find what advantages or disadvantages of these sample brands of similar products' comparison from internet. On the other hand, it means that manufacturers can gather consumers' past purchase behaviors or purchase experience from (AI) big data gathering method to record and analyze to give opinions to let manufacturers to know what reasons or factors influence consumers choose not to buy their products from internet.

(AI) big data gathering consumer behavior prediction method can give these benefits to manufacturers and consumers both, such as: New concerns arise because (AI) technological advance which have enables reducing cost of collecting, storing, processing and using data in mass quantities extend information beyond a single transaction. These advances are often summarized by the big data, it means charge volume of transaction-level data that could identify individual consumers by itself or in combination with the datasets.

The popular (AI) takes big data as in input in order to understand, predict and influence consumer behavior. Modern (AI) is used by legitimate companies, could improve management efficiency motivate innovations and better match demand and supply. But (AI) in the wrong hand, also allows the mass production of fraud and deception. Since , data can be stored, traded and used long after the transaction. Future data use is likely to grow with data processing technology, such as (AI) big data gathering consumer and manufacturer behavioral prediction method from internet channel.

Thus, future (AI) big data learning machine can also help consumers to choose the best brand of manufacturer's products among different brands of manufacturers products choice to compare their past sale performance from internet. They can apply (AI) big data statistic method to gather all different manufacturers' similar products past sale data to compare their advantages and disadvantages to make the best decision to choose to buy which brand of product is the most suitable to them to buy to use. It seems (AI) big data can also help consumers to predict any manufacturers' manufacturing behaviors or manufacturing performance whether they are improving their product quality or are deteriorating their product quality. Thus, (AI) big data tool is also important to help customers to predict future the different brands of manufacturer performance will have improvement in possible.

Thus, I believe that artificial intelligent "big data" gathering method can be suggested to be applied to attempt to predict consumer behavioral changes in global business environment, the reasons are as below:

On the consumer's beneficial hand, Consumers can apply this method to attempt to gather any global manufacturers data to be analyzed by this artificial intelligent learning system. Then, it analyzed all the different brands of specific similar product manufacturer' data to compare what are the range of the best past manufacturing history and sale data to the group of best manufacturers, and what are the range of the better past manufacturing history and sale data, and what are the range of the good past manufacturing history and sale data, and what are the range of the common past manufacturing history and sale data. Finally, the (AI) learning system will compare all the specific similar product, e.g. mobile phone or computer, television, car etc. different kinds of specific products of global manufacturers to conclude the result is such as whether which brands will be the best manufacturers to let the consumer to buy the television or mobile phone or computer or car etc. different kinds of products. It can make more accurate judgement to compare general human's phone or questionnaire surveys investigation method, newspapers, television, radios, internet searches etc. different manufacturing news or data gathering channels to find which brands are the most worth confidence to consumers to choose to buy the specific product in the global consumption market.

On the manufacturers' beneficial hand, manufacturers can apply (AI) data gathering method to predict consumer emotion and buying behavioral changes more accurate. For example, the vehicle manufacturer, it plans to gather data to predict potential driving fast speed sport vehicle consumers' preferences trends in order to make the accurate judgement how to design its sport vehicles to attract many sport vehicle buyers who will choose to buy it's brand of any driving fast speed sport vehicles. It can attempt to apply (AI) intelligent learning system to gather global different brands of sport vehicle data concerns that all past driving fast speed sport vehicle buyer's preference of sport vehicle design. Then, the (AI) intelligent learning system gather global different brands of driving fast speed sport vehicle which had ever been purchased by the different country's driving fast speed sport vehicles consumers. After, it can compare divide the range of similar driving fast speed sport vehicle design and similar price to be different groups. The (AI) intelligent learning system can attempt to follow the past number of different brands of driving fast speed sport vehicle buyers to calculate how many driving fast speed sport vehicle buyers who choose to buy the brand of driving fast speed sport vehicle as well as it will analyze and make judgement to find whether the cheaper price reason attracts the different countries sport vehicle buyers choose to buy the brand of driving fast speed sport vehicle or the attractive design reason attracts the different countries sport vehicle buyers choose to buy the brand of sport vehicle or fast speed reason attracts the sport vehicle buyers choose to buy the brand of sport vehicle.

For example, although some brands of driving fast speed sport vehicle manufacturers' prices are very high, but they can still attract global many sport vehicle consumers to buy. Whether all sport vehicle's attractive design is the main factor to influence them to buy or whether it's fast speed is the main factor to influence them to buy or whether it's safe confidence it the main factor to influence them to buy or it's familiarity brand is the main factor to influence them to buy. (AI) intelligent learning system will attempt to make judgement and analysis to conclude whether the attractive design factor is the main factor to influence many sport vehicle consumers to choose to buy the brand of sport vehicles.

Otherwise, for another example, although some brands of driving fast speed sport vehicle manufacturer's prices are low, but they can not still attract many global many sport vehicle consumers to buy. Whether all vehicle's unattractive design is the main factor to influence them choose not to buy their fast speed driving sport vehicles or whether the unsafe factor is the main factor to influence them choose not to buy their fast speed driving sport vehicles or whether unfamiliarity brand is the main factor to influence many consumers choose not to buy their fast speeding sport vehicles.

Thus, when (AI) learning system had helped the fast speed sport vehicles manufacturer to gather all different brands of fast speed driving sport vehicle's past sale data and price data, design of different sport vehicle, e.g. color choice, method of style, comfortable chair styles and chair sizes and what kinds of steel material to manufacture the sport vehicles data and driving safe and accident occurrence data and the data concerns what reasons of the past complaint to brand of sport vehicle manufacturer from its sport vehicle buyers. Then, it can make more conclusion to give more accurate opinions whether which brands of fast speed driving sport vehicle manufacturer(s) whose sport vehicle design is the main factor to attract consumers choose to buy its any driving fast speed sport vehicle products really. Thus, it seems that it can make more accurate judgement to compare television survey, questionnaire survey to gather data concerns how to design the fast speed sport vehicle to attract consumers to choose to buy the sport vehicle manufacturer's planning sport vehicle products. I believe that (AI) learning system can help the sport vehicle manufacturer to make more accurate conclusion or judgement how to design its fast speed driving sport vehicles to attract it's consumers more easily.

(AI) TOOL PREDICTS CONSUMER IMMEDIATE AND EXPECTED EMOTION HOW TO INFLUENCE CONSUMPTION DECISION

If (AI) tool can be confirmed to apply to predict consumer behavior, then I can conclude that it can be attempted to apply to predict what the factor(s) of the product itself can cause the consumer has positive or negative emotion, so the manufacturer can attempt to avoid the bad factors cause to bring negative emotion to influence the consumer chooses not to buy the product more easily, such as vehicle product case.

Economists refer to the consumption desirability is as " utility" and the product or service consumption decision making is arose

influenced by maximizing utility only. However, they neglect consumer individual immediate emotion change will also influence the consumer individual consumption decision consequently. Expected emotions are those that are anticipated to occur as a result of the outcomes associated

with different possible courses of action. For example, if a potential investor, were deciding whether to purchase a stock, who might imagine the disappointment who would feel if who ought it and it reduced its price. Otherwise, whose emotion would experience , such as regret if it increased in price, but who does not buy it before the stock rise its price. However, I believe nowadays technology, in the future one day, (AI) tool can be attempted to assist consumer psychology profession or marketing research profession to assist them to find what are the bad factors to influence consumers choose not to buy any manufacturers' products. Then, when the manufacturer

can discover what are the bad factor(S) cause(S) consumers who do not choose to buy their products, then the manufacturer can raise whose product of consumption desirability or " utility" to raise whose product's consumption decision making is influenced by maximizing utility. Hence, (AI) tool will be possible to find what the bad factor(S) to cause consumers do not choose to buy the manufacturer's product in order to raise the product's utility to bring consumer positive emotion to choose to buy its product in possible. SO, (AI) tool will be one consumer psychological emotion prediction tool to assist any manufacturers

to help their products to build positive emotion to any consumers in possible.

The key feature of expected emotions is that they are experienced when the outcomes of a decision materialize, but not at the moment of choice, at the moment of choice, they are only feel about future emotion. Such as consumption case, if the consumer chose to buy the product or consume the service before it's price is increased. Then, the consumer will feel happy and it is worth to purchase or consumer the service as well as the consumer's expected emotion is positive before who decides to buy the product or consume the service, because who believes or feels the product or service's price will be raised in short term, e.g. after one month, one week. Thus, it means that if the consumer does not believe or feel or predict the product or service's price either it will increase or decrease in short term, whose emotion will be negative, those negative emotion will influence who does not decide to buy the product or service, it is possible that who feel it is not worth to buy the product or consume the service immediately. He She will choose to consume the service or buy the product to wait it's price is decreased later. it seems that the consumer's positive or negative emotion will influence who decides to buy the product or consume the service later or earlier. Thus, it has close relationship between the consumer individual immediate purchase or consumption decision and positive emotion or negative emotion (either expected emotion or immediate emotion influences).

Consequently, if (AI) tool can help any manufacturers
to predict when its product price ought to be increased or decreased in order to attract consumer to choose to buy its product. Then, it can help any manufacturers to build positive expected emotion to attract consumers to choose to buy its product more easily. For example, when the (AI) tool can predict when the consumer expects the product price will fall down, then it can give ideas to the manufacturer to raise up the product price in the month, then it predicts many consumers expect the product price will fall down after six months. So, the product price will not be fall down after six months. So, many consumers will feel disappointment and they will choose to buy the product if the manufacturer
decided to raise the product price after six months. Then, the higher product price will cause many consumers worry about the product price will continue rise up, so they will prefer to choose to buy the product immediately after six months because they afraid the product price will continue to rise up in the year. Then, I assume that (AI) tool has effort to predict when consumers feel the product will rise up or fall down, then it can give ideas to the manufacturer when to rise up or fall down the product price in order to attract or persuade many consumers choose to buy the product in different period in the year.

1.1 What does (AI) tool predict immediate emotion mean?

Psychologists indicate that immediate emotions, by contrast, are experienced at the moment of choice and fall into one of two categories. Integral emotion, like expected emotions, arise from thinking about the consequences of one's decision, but " integral emotion", unlike expected emotions are experienced at the moment of choice. Such as purchase stock case, the share buyer might experience immediate fear at the thought of the stock's losing value. " Incidental emotions" are also experienced at the moment of choice, such as a consumer predicts the product or service price whether it will be risen up or fallen down. If he/she feels the product or service price will fall down after next month and he/she will choose to buy the product or consume the service. But consequently, after next month, the product or service's price won't fall down absolutely.

Then, he/she will have incidental emotion to influence whom to choose whether he/she ought buy the product or consume the service, due to the product or service price is not still fall down. Otherwise, he/she is fear the product or service will not fall down in short term. Even, it will increase price later. Hence, whose incidental emotion will have possible to influence whom to choose to buy the product or consume the service after one month, if the product or service's price is still not increased absolutely. So, (AI) tool can be attempted to apply to predict when the product price ought need to be raised or fallen down in order to attract consumers to choose to buy the manufacturers' product in different period.

Economists indicate utility an individual consumption with an outcome might arise from a prediction of emotion: For example, a dinner eater might choose a higher utility to an Italian restaurant dinner than a French restaurant dinner because who anticipates being happier at the former, even the former's dinner price is higher than the French restaurant.

So, such as this restaurant dinner case, if one (AI) tool can assist the French restaurant owner to find what factor(S) cause(S) the dinner consumers do not choose to go to its restaurant to eat its food, e.g. high price factor, bad taste factor, bad wait service performance factor, bad cooker's cooking skill factor, poor advertisement promotion factor, poor familiar factor, poor location or poor eating environment etc. different factors. Then, the French restaurant owner can find methods to avoid the bad factor(S) cause(S) many dinner consumers do not choose to go to whose French restaurant to eat dinner more easily.

The question is that whether the positive emotion factor can influence the consumer changes whose mind to choose to consume the more expensive service or buy the more expensive product. To answer this question. it depends on whether the consumer has an imperfect understanding of whose own tastes or the consumer has a perfect understanding of whose own tastes to the product or the service.

It means the consumer will choose to buy the product or consume the service, even it's price is higher than other general similar products or services if who has a perfect understanding of whose own tastes to the product or service. Otherwise, who won't choose to buy the product or consume the service, due to it's price is higher than other general similar products or services if who has an imperfect understanding of whose own tastes to the product or service. So, it seems that the consumer's negative or positive emotion arise will be influenced by whose perfect or imperfect understanding of whose own tastes to the product or service factor.

It concludes that whether how much degree of the consumer's utility to the product or service. It is not the only one important factor to influence the consumer to choose to buy the product or consume the service. Otherwise, the consumer's imperfect or perfect understanding own tastes to the product or service factor will influence the consumer to arise positive or negative emotion to make final purchase or consumption decision immediately. It will be one more consumption influential factor to lead the consumer to make the final consumption decision making immediately. So, future (AI) tool ought to be innovate to own how to judge good taste or bad taste for any food in order to predict food consumers to choose to buy the food manufacturer's any foods more attractively.

(AI) tool technical innovation in cruise tourism
immediate positive emotion influence to
cruise travelling consumers

Can apply (AI) tool to cause positive emotion to cruise tourism consumers? Cruise tourism industry is the most influential emotion industry example to influence cruise travelling consumers' travelling entertainment choice. I shall indicate some evidences how it's innovation will influence cruise travelling consumers' emotion to be changed to positive from negative immediately as well as to prove how the cruise traveler higher utility feeling to the cruise tourism provider is not the main factor to influence whom to choose the cruise provider to consume whose cruise journey service arrangement.

Nowadays, cruising has become one of the fastest growing sectors within tourism, cruise service providers need have themselves unique different entertainment service arrangement to satisfy every cruise travelling consumer individual needs in order to attract every one to choose whose cruise arrangement easily, e.g. meals, activities, entertainment and varied destinations create one-stop holiday shop, reasonable competitive ticket fare. Hence, it seems it is one exciting emotion industry. If the cruise service provider can bring positive emotion to influence many cruise travelling consumers immediately. The, even it change higher service fare to compare other similar cruise service providers. I believe it won't influence them to choose other similar cruise service providers if it can often bring immediate positive emotion to its cruise clients during they are staying in its cruises or during they have left its cruises, but they will often remember or won't forget to enjoy their cruise service provider's happing time forever. Hence, if (AI) tool can be attempted to help cruise entertainment providers to arrange different cruise journeys for varied destinations , to arrange different entertainment facilities, to arrange the different taste food to satisfy different countries age cruise consumers' needs. Then, the (AI) tool will assist the cruise providers to bring positive emotion to let every different countries age cruise consumers to feel satisfactory in order to choose to the cruise providers' cruise entertainment service more attractively.

2.1 How can apply (AI) tool to predict cruise service providers bring positive emotion to their clients?

Future, (AI) tool can help any cruise providers to design these kinds of any one entertainment service arrangement to satisfy the cruise provider's customers' needs.

There are different special interests cruising , such as wellness at sea, freighter cruises, river cruises. It has increased the attractiveness of cruising: Romance is for lover cruise traveler target, luxury is for rich cruise traveler target, exotica is for enjoyment exciting feeling traveler target. So, every kind of cruise traveler target will have different kind of cruise entertainment service to satisfy their needs. If the cruise service provider can provide the right and attractive cruise entertainment service to satisfy the specific cruise target. Then, it will bring the positive emotion to the specific cruise target consumers more easily.

Cruise travel was shaped for mass tourism. Prices have been very differently segmented. There are basically four types of markets (Biederman, 2008):

● Contemporary market: On board fun and amenities are playing important role and destinations have secondary importance.

● Premium market: This category is more expensive than the contemporary category and where the destination has same importance as on board amenities.

● Luxury market: It was once dominant type of cruise tourism, but now it has only a small portion of the industry. Generally, it is the most expensive cruise category and usually it takes longer than average cruise days.

● Adventure/exploration: It refers relatively long cruises with special and exotic places where the destination is the main purpose of the trip.

● European cruise travel: Duration takes more five days than worth American travel duration. There is a tendency on European market during the years that duration of travel is getting shorter. This short demand of is explained with the strong demand of customers (Hensen, 2003). Beside this, it is most likely that cruise companies try to convince tourists with short haul travels instead of long term cruise trips for more expenditure.

Thus, I believe that even, the cruise service provider charges higher ticket which won't influence cruise consumers who do not choose its entertainment service on its cruises. If it can arrange the attractive cruise entertainment facilities and destination journey arrangement, staying days arrangement to satisfy different specific cruise target market needs absolutely in order to bring whose emotion to be positive to it's service provision. Then, the cruise service provider will attract many potential cruise clients to choose its cruise service absolutely. Otherwise, if it only bring negative emotion to its cruise clients, it will not attract many potential cruise clients to choose it or loses its old cruise clients, even, its cruise ticket price is needed to decreased in order to raise competitive effort.

In conclusion, I believe that future (AI) tools need to learn how to bring cruise consumers to arise individual immediate or expected positive emotion, this positive emotion consideration is more important to compare to how to reduce cruise ticket price in order to attract cruise clients in global cruise competitive cruise industry.

2.2 Differentiation through the characteristics of cruising route method from (AI) tool route judgement

Future, (AI) tool can attempt to help any cruise entertainment service providers to judge how to design different route to attract different countries age cruise clients' choices to satisfy their cruise journey entertainment needs. The determinants of the cruising route's characteristics (functional, social, and emotion) is important factor to influence the cruise service provider's success. Cruising product is no longer selected primarily for the cruising service, but for the content of cruising route. So, the cruising route will influence the cruise consumer individual emotion, because it is the main service need for every cruise consumer.

The approach called the " land sea cruising in product development" is increasingly becoming an area of interest, e.g. determining the direction of the effects of the individual cruising route characteristics on service value's perception , and providing an evaluation model of the route's perception , and indicating significance variables of attraction.

The questions that cruise planners need to know: How does each of the identified determinants affect the overall perceived value of the cruise route? How the overall perceived value of the cruise route affects customer behavior intentions?

Because different routes factor will influence cruise consumer individual emotion changing seriously. It means the ship has become only a tool, when the offered route whose attractiveness highly influences the impression of the guests has become crucial.

Consumer behavior in cruising segment includes all the activities and influences in the selection of the specific cruise route. There activities result in decisions and actions related to a defined price, selection and reselection of cruising company (Cannot, Brink and Brijball, 2006).

2.3 How to apply (AI) tool to arrange cruise route planning have close relationship to influence cruise consumer emotion?

Firstly, use value of cruising routes is based on the subjective experience, and shows how individuals assess the route during, or immediately after sailing. It is affiliated with the benefits that cruising guest realize by choosing a route , and it is subjective because it depends on the individual assessment (photo taken on the route for one guest presents just a family souvenir, and for professional photographers are embodied financial capital).

Secondly, the utilitarian value is also subjective-oriented and is tied on the point where the inner and us ability of cruising routes are compared with the sacrifice of the client (money and time). Finally, the value is considered as the outcome of the comparison of scarifies and personal benefits, which is resulted in essentially utilitarian nature.

Hence, route design is the main value of cruising tourism and it is primarily determined and analyzed from the aspect of observed customers. Otherwise, the cruise is only one tool to be caught for the cruise passengers, whether the cruise can let whom to sleep comfortable , providing what kind of food to them to eat, what kind of entertainment facilities are provided to them to play, these issues are not more important to compare how to design route to bring them to travel to anywhere to enjoy in this cruise journey factor. Because how to design the route factor can bring each cruise passenger to influence them to feel either negative or positive emotion directly. The whole route journey planning is the most influential factor to influence the cruise passengers to feel whether they ought choose it's service again or not in the future.

(AI) tool judges the difference between utility factor and emotion to influence consumer decision making

In economic utility or immediate (expected) emotion aspects, whether which is more influential to excite consumption. To analyze whether it is economic utility or immediate (expected) emotion more influential to excite consumption. It depends on the consumer individual consumption choice is in which situations. For example, if the industry's general consumer individual consumption decision is concentrate on emotion influential aspect, such as cruise entertainment industry, hospital care service industry, theme park entertainment industry, movie watching entertainment industry etc. Above all these industries have same nature, it is service. So, it seems that service industry's main influential factor is immediate (expected) emotion influence, it is not economic utility influence. Otherwise, product sale industry's main influential factor is utility.

3.1 (AI) judges consumer utility factor

For this toy choice situation example, parent choose to buy one toy to give whose child to play. They usually considerate which kind of toy is attractive to their child whom like to play. In many different kinds of toys choice, if the child likes to choose the kind of toy to play. After the child's parents had purchased the kind of toy to let whose child to play one period time, e.g. six month. Then, when the child feel that who has need to buy another new toy to play, due to he/she feels bored to play this toy. So, it seems that the child feels this toy has less utility or it's utility is decreased. So, he/she expects whose parent can buy another new kind of toy to let whom to play. It also implies that it is not emotion factor to influence the child to feel boredom and unfunny to play this kind of old toy after six months. It is the product's utility factor which can not attract the child to play it any more. So, this old toy's utility is decreased when this child spends six months to play it. This toy's value is only six month utility to this child to play. Otherwise, if this kind of toy is bought by another parent. It is possible that the another child like to play this kind of toy one year or more. So, it's utility to another child is one year or more period. So, product's utility period is difference, it depends on how long time of the user's satisfactory time.

As this toy case, the child's decision will influence whose parent choose which kind of toy to buy to whom to play. Usually toy price is not difference too much. Parent won't consider when the toy price will be increase or will be decreased to influence their emotion to decide not to buy the toy immediately. So, when the child like to play the kind of toy, even the product's price is more than other kind of toys, and the parent feel it is possible that the kind of toy's price will be fallen down later. They will still choose to buy the kind of toy to let their child to play, they won't be influenced not to buy this kind product by later cheap price factor. So, immediate emotion is not the main factor to influence this parent does not choose buy this toy at this moment. Otherwise, utility factor will influence when the parent will buy another new kind of toy to provide to this child to play. If the child enjoy to play it only three months, after he/she will feel bore and he/she will tell whose parent to buy another new kind of toy to let whom play when the fourth month is beginning. So, it implies that if the kind of toy product can have more attractive utility time, then it can attract many parent to choose to buy it among different kind of toys. Thus, when this kind of toy's utility time is longer time. Then, it is possible that it can influence many parents choose to buy it's different style or design of similar kind of toys to let their children to play. In general, when many parents accept to buy this kind of different style or design of similar toys to give their children to play. Due to it's popular long time utility factor, it will influence children like to play it longer time to compare other kind of toys. Consequently, it will influence parents do not need often spend too much money to buy other kinds of toys to give their children to play. So, longer time utility factor to the product can attract many consumers to choose to buy the kind of product to compare lesser time utility factor to the product. Hence, it proves the explanation why utility factor is the main influential factor to influence the consumer choose to buy the product.

3.2 (AI) judgement tool of Medical care and utility case

Medical care is an input in producing health, it is subject to law of diminishing marginal productivity. Health yields utility to the consumer. It is subject to law of diminishing marginal utility. It bring this question: Does either the patient's emotion or the medical care service or medical care product utility which one can influence the patient's hospital choice more?

To answer this question: We need to know medical care is one kind of nursing care service in hospitals or clinics and medical care product is one kind of medical care product sale from merchants, e.g. medicine or medical equipment. So, in medical industry which has different kind of medical care services to provide to patients in hospitals or clinics as well as which has different kind of medical care products sale, e.g. medicine or wheelchairs, heart health measurement equipment etc. different medical care products in medical health industry.

In medical care aspect, it is one kind of any medical care service to patients from hospitals or clinics. So, medical care is an input in producing health service to patients from hospitals or clinics. When the patient is admitting to hospital or clinic, who needs to see doctor and the doctor need to give the right medicine to the patient to eat to ill whose illness. Even, if the doctor feels the patient whom needs to live hospital for one time period. Then, the hospital nurses must need to take care the patient during he/she is living in the hospital period. Consequently, if the patent can be health in short time, e.g. within one week leaving time, then he/she will be shortened time to leave the hospital in next weak. Otherwise, if the patent can not be health in short time, e.g. within on week, then he/she needs to live the hospital more than one week, even, one month, three months or more. So, the staying hospital time will influence the patent's emotion to feel whether the doctor's effort. If he/she needs to live the hospital long time, he/she will bring negative emotion to feel the doctor's medical effort is not good. The doctor's medical effort can not achieve or satisfy whose expected emotion during whose staying hospital time.

Thus, medical care is an input service in producing health, it is subject to law of diminishing marginal productivity. When the patient does not need to live the hospital longer time, the patient will feel more satisfactory to the hospital's doctor and nurses' care effort as well as the patient can give less money to spend the expenditure to live the hospital. So, the law of diminishing marginal health productivity will explain the hospital will shorten time to the staying days of the hospital to the patent as well as the patient's care expenditure will be decreased when he/she only needs to live to the hospital in short time. Otherwise, the patient needs to live longer time in the hospital, it means that the diminishing marginal health productivity to the hospital, the patient's staying hospital days will be increased and the patient's medical expenditure to the hospital will also be increased. It will bring negative emotion to patient and why this negative emotion factor will influence the patient would choose another hospital to live or find other doctors to see if he/she felt illness in future one day.

In medical care product aspect, health yields utility to the consumer. It is subject to law of diminishing marginal utility. Because patient needs to buy different kind of medical equipment to use or medicine to eat to attempt to cure whose illnesses. So, if the patent can choose the right medicine to eat from the doctor's recommendation or if the patent can choose the right medical equipment to use from the doctor's recommendation. When the patient buy less number of medicine to eat, then he/she can be health or when he/she buy the medical equipment to use, then he/she can be health. Then, he/she will spend less money to buy medicine to eat or medical equipment to use and he/

she can be health in short time. Then, the medical consumer will feel the medicine or medical equipment has good utility to satisfy whose medical needs. So, good medicine and good medical equipment can only need short time and less money to let the medical patient to be health.

3.3 Immediate (expected) emotion factor

As cruise entertainment case, every cruise journey must provide fixed stay days on the cruise to let every cruise passenger to play to every cruise journey. So, cruise passenger can not change or extend whose fixed stay day choice in every cruise journey, when they had caught the cruise to go to sea on the day. Is implies that cruise entertainment has none longer time utility factor which can influence each cruise passenger's choice to each different design of cruise journey arrangement.

If the cruise passenger feels very satisfactory and enjoyable to the last time of specific cruise journey arrangement, e.g. five days and four nights New Zealand and Australia cruise journey. Due to this cruise journey can bring positive emotion to let the cruise passenger to let whom feel that he/she can not forget or remember this happy cruise journey forever.

It is possible that this time happy five days and four nights New Zealand and Australia cruise journey will bring positive emotion to influence this cruise passenger to choose to find this cruise service provider to help whom to arrange this same cruise journey or another similar cruise journey again after one month, or three month, or six month or one year or more. Due to this cruse passenger felt this cruise service providers' cruise journey design arrangement can satisfy whose needs and it can achieve whose expected emotion to be positive. So, this cruise entertainment industry must be immediate (expected) emotion influential factor more than time utility factor to influence the cruise consumer's cruise service provider and cruise journey choices.

In conclusion, it is not only utility factor can influence consumption decision. It is emotion factor can also influence consumption decision. It depends on situations whether the consumer is choosing to buy one product or consume one service. If the consumer is choosing to buy one product, how long time of the product's utility factor which will influence the consumer choose to buy which product. If the consumer feels the product can give longer utility time among other similar products, then he/she will have more chance to choose to buy the product. Otherwise, if the consumer feels the product can give lesser utility time among other similar products, then he/she will have less chance to choose to buy the product. If the consumer is choosing to consume one service, emotion factor will influence the consumer choose to find which service provider to consume the same service or similar service. If the service provider can provide excellent service to the consumer, then it will bring positive immediate or expected emotion to whom and it can attract the consumer to choose the service provider again. Otherwise, if the service provider can not provide excellent service to the consumer, then will bring negative immediate or expected emotion to whom and it can not attract the consumer to choose the service provider again.

Why and how (AI) judgement tool can judgement what utility factors are to influence consumer emotion

In emotion and utility both aspects, they include these situations. I shall explain how and why emotion and utility factors can influence consumption behaviors in these different situations as below:

(1) In the first situation is brand factor, the brand image, product quality, product knowledge , attitude and
(2) brand loyalty intangible factor will attract the consumer individual purchase.
For example, luxury
products, e.g. luxury fashion brands of clothing. Brands like Zara from Spain and H&M from Seweden began to produce catwalk-style fashion at low cost offering consumers of luxury fashion alternatives at low prices.

Nowadays, the luxury fashion sector is the fourth largest revenue generator in France, and one of the most remarkable sectors in Italy, Spain , the USA and the potential markets of China, Russia and India. The luxury industry has increased having a huge youth in demand. The luxury consumer have much choice in products, shopping channels and pricing of luxury products. It has possible relationship of age, gender, income and other demographic factors with purchasing intentions to influence the rational and emotional buying behavior regarding luxury fashion products.

(2) The second situation concerns the decision-making of make or female consumers are possible experience an emotional desires and cognitive (reasoning) mind in purchasing choice process. Their emotion includes negative or positive buying emotion and mood management and cognitive process components include cognitive deliberation, planning buying with the exception regard for the future.

University had been using analysis of variances tests, male and female students were found significantly different with respect
affective process components including positive buying emotion, and mood management and cognitive process components include planning buying.

Significant differences were also found between the following product categories: shirts/sweaters, skirts, coats, underwear, accessories, shoes, electronic hardware, computer software, music , CD or DVDs, sports, memorabilia, health /beauty products and magazines/books for pleasure reading. No differences were found in regard to suits/ business wear and entertainments.

The investigate proved that some products will have different emotion influence to cause female or male students whose final consumption decision to buy the kind of product. So, the difference od male and female students will have emotion influence to make purchase decision to buy the product in consuming choice process.

(3) The third situation concerns search advertising factor, e.g. online search to influence consumption behavior. Advertising is possible one method to persuade the consumer to choose to buy the product, even the consumer does not know the product exists. For example, proper cloth, a company based in New York, has a site on the social networking site Facebook.

Whenever the company posts a new photos of its clothes, all its face book " fans" automatically receive the information on their own face book pages. "We want to hear what our customers have to say." It seems online advertisement is a potential promotion method to promote any new attractive products to sell to let publicity to know to buy. Internet is one popular communication tool to be used by youth today. So, when one company can have one website to let any youth to find and enter to the website to discover any new things easily. It will cause many consumption chances to let online potential clients to attempt to choose any products to make purchase decision from online advertising tool easily.

How does the role of advertising influence the purchase decision process? Needs and motivations are the starting points of purchase decisions. In fact, advertising is a communication of photo image, sound image, and word advertisement image channel to persuade consumers to choose to buy the brand of product or consume the brand of service between the merchant and its consumers from television, radio, newspapers, magazine, movie etc. channels.

Why does advertisement influence consumer
choice? For this case example, when one buyer waits until more information is gathered before making a decision. The time, two types of cost are involved. First, there are psychological opportunity costs experienced by consumers who are deprived of the product who need and are consequently in a state of psychological tension.

As time elapses, this psychological tension becomes more frustration. Second, buyers experience costs with the information-gathering efforts. They must invest time and energy to visit several retailers, seek out and read advertisements, or inquire for other opinions about the best product to buy.

These delayed decision costs considerably increase as time elapses. The buyer must seek information until it is felt that a search for additional information will bring about more costs than benefits. So, an advertisement is reaching a potential buyer when who is seeking information will have a greater impact, since the buyer is spending time and effort needed to seek out this information himself and he is less likely to find other competing and advertisements to obtain the additional information.

In general, buyers are generally more responsive to different brand advertisements, when they are seeking information on these brands. This is why the becomes a choice target for the advertiser provided the advertiser can identify and locate them. Thus, a client has interested and is in an information-gathering stage is asked.

Then, the advertiser takes advantage of the consumer's having identified him or herself to send a series of informative and persuasive messages or to send a salesperson who will try to conclude a sale. Thus, advertisement gives a chance to let consumers to gather information to choose the best product to buy or the most excellent service to consume.

What of situations do merchants need advertisements promotion? The short purchase cycle markets are characterized by routine
purchase decision processes or by limited problem solving when a new brand is introduced on the market, e.g. coffee, bread , sugar, soft drinks, canned vegetables and household and beauty care products fall into this category. Another irregular purchase cycle markets are characterized by products that are purchased more or less regularly , e.g. cookies, cake mixes, wines, food products. Finally, long or unpredictable purchase cycle markets include all durable products, such as cars, household appliances and furniture (products from which occasions of purchase can't be predicted, which most consumers buy only occasionally). Hence, these kinds of products ought need advertisement promotion specially, due to advertisement can build brand image to let consumers to know. Especially , it is a new brand of product. In conclusion, advertisement will be one good channel to let new product to introduce its brand to let clients to remember in minds heart.

Consequently, future (AI) tool needs to learn how to design different kinds of advertisement to attract consumer attention to the product, needs to learn how to find what the bad factor(S) which cause(S) many consumers do not choose to buy the product, needs to learn when the product price needs to be raised up or fallen down in order to bring consumers' positive emotion to choose to buy the product immediately. SO, if (AI) tool can be invented to own itself effort to design different kinds of methods to predict consumer behavior in order to bring their positive emotion to the product successfully, then the manufacturer can earn positive consumer emotion advantage from the (AI) tool assistance for long term benefit to its product.

CHAPTER FOUR

PSYCHOLOGICAL METHOD PREDICTS CONSUMER BEHAVIOR

Can apply economic models solve marketing changing challenges?

Economists indicate economic modeling can provide a logical, data to help organize the analyst's thoughts. The model helps the economist logically isolate and sort out complicated chains of cause and effect and influence between the numerous interacting elements in an economy. There are four types of models used in economic analysis: Visual models, mathematical models, empirical models and simulation models. Visual models are simply pictures of an abstract economy: graphs will lines and curves that tell an economic story. It is one kind of micro or macro-economic method to predict consumer behavioral change. Some visual models are diagrammatic such as which flow the income thought the economy from one sector to another (micro economic environment). It is mathematical model, when it is presented the mathematics are explained what the data analysis is or not. The model does not normally require a knowledge of mathematics, but still allow the presentation of complex relationship between economic variable.

For example, the common supply-and demand model is meant to show the effect of inflationary expectations upon price and output. In this application, an increase in inflationary expectations causes demand to shift, raising prices and outputs (macro-economic environment). For another example, a very simple micro-economic model would include a supply function (explaining the behavior of products or those who supply commodities to the market), a demand curve (explaining the behavior of purchasers) and an equilibrium equation, specifying the simple conditions that must be met if the model's equilibrium is to be satisfied. So, the variables in a model like this represent a type of economic activity (such as demand) or data (information) that either determines or is determined by that activity (such as a price or interest rate variable change activity).

Dynamic models, in contrast, directly incorporate time into their structure. This is usually done in economic modeling by this mathematical systems of difference of differential equations. For example, it can use a difference equation from a business cycle model, investment now depends upon changes in income in the past. Time is incorporated into the model. Dynamic models, when they can be used, sometimes better represent the business cycles, because certainly behavioral response and timing strongly shape the character of a cycle.

For another example, if there is a delay between the time income is received and when it is spent. A model that can capture the delay is likely to those higher consumption desire to the consumer. It is a micro-personal behavioral consumption predict method. So, the user can experiment with an endless variety of values and assumptions to see whether results obtained are realistic or insightful. Since computers are now powerful and cheaper, the importance of dynamic simulation models should follow the future prediction time, when the consumer income receive and when it is spent to predict how much degree of the consumer's consumption desire in micro-economic view point.

Another model to be applied to predict consumption behavior. It is expectations and enhanced model, it includes one or more variables based upon economic expectations about future values. For example, if consumers for whatever reason, expect the inflation rate to be much higher next year, then this year, they are said to have formed inflationary expectations. If numerical values are being used in a model and the current inflation rate is 9%, if they expect inflation to be higher next year, the variable for inflationary expectations might be given be a value if 12% or more.

Normally, though general models used for instruction or analysis, it assumes an expectation value to be high. Where it will have an impact on the models result or " low" or " mot existent" where it will have no impact. In the simple supply - and demand to model presented earlier, inflationary expectations were high, shifting the equilibrium and causing higher prices and output. Hence, expectations and enhanced model as well as demand and supply model is a good predictive tool to predict when inflationary rate rises to the general unacceptable level to consumers to influence their consumption desires in societies in micro and macro-economic both view point.

What factors can reduce social consumption desire in general. The theory of rational expectations presumes that expectations are formed when economic agents see new developments in the economy and they logically deduce expectations based upon the information they have. For example, if the country's government central reserve system were to suddenly increase the money supply, according to the theory of rational expectations, consumers would immediately form inflationary expectations, not because prices are actually rising, but become they deduce that excessive money supply growth is likely to cause inflation. It presumes that a relatively high degree of raising consumption desire to people or people have access to, or even care about, information on the economy, such as the money supply growth rate, the rate of taxation etc. So, it's the government micro or macro-economic policy to attempt to raise consumption desire, due to people feel more money supply to society. So, it causes the feel salary increase. Due to money is excessive supply, so they will accept to consume more. But in fact, their salaries growth, it is due money supply growth. Moreover, due to the social businessmen had not raise products price to sell, e.g. food price, entertainment price, school fee etc. Different kinds of consumption price. So, it makes consumers feel their salaries growth and social consumption expenditure have no growth to influence them to feel they have more extra income to accept to buy any more things to consume in society. So, the government inflationary policy (supply more money to society) is one example of macro-economic method to persuade people to accept more consumption behaviors in this inflationary (increasing money supply to society) period. It aims to assist social businessmen have more consumption in order to avoid businesses failure risk in society.

1.2 Micro and macro-economic analysis methods solve Starbucks coffee shop faces marketing change challenges

This Starbucks case indicates how Starbucks coffee drinking business applies micro and macro-economic analysis methods to predict consumer behavior. Today, Starbucks has become world famous and brings high quality coffee and beverages to its clients over the world daily. Their well-known mission statements is: to inspire and nurture the human spirit, one person, one cup and one neighborhood at a time.

How does it apply macro and micro economic analysis methods to predict consumers' coffee taste more accurate? According to the following statistics, coffee market is large market potential in the world for this particular coffee service and production. Starbucks along with many competitors, such as Costa coffee and Mc-cafe have seized this opportunity and continue to indicate within this coffee market. It is no doubt that this coffee market can be profitable in 2012 year, the CEO of Starbucks was classified as the 8th best -paid CEO in the United States of America making $ 103 million dollars of profit (Rushe, 2013). Hence, the question concerns that how Starbucks can predict its coffee customer fast accurate.

Micro and macro-economic marketing environment analysis: It is crucial to be aware and understand environment in which a company is operating in order to implement their strategies successfully. The micro environment strategies can be analyzed using in SWOT analysis and further completed with a macro environment study by doing a PEST analysis.

As Starbucks background, it can apply micro environment " a SWOT analysis" method, it must focus on the external factors since internal factors are rather analyzed in the core marketing strategy and extended marketing strategy and extended marketing mix. However, macro environment refers to everything external to the organization. So, it seems Starbucks can't necessarily fully control, only influence. Such as PEST analysis indicates political, economic, social and technological external environment factors. Such as certain political issues can raise since coffee beans are grown in developing countries and this could raise questions about the working conditions and child labor. Tariffs and import taxes could also influence the prices in stores as well as the country's economic recession or exchange rates change could threaten Starbuck's profits.

However, Starbucks internal strengths include that the development of new technologies and user friendly machines, such as home coffee machines, quality of beverages in other restaurants served are increasing and Starbucks should create Starbucks experience at home by manufacturing their own capsules machine with their coffee and tea. The emergence of social media is already used by Starbucks especially via Twitter where gift cards can be purchased and sent to friends (Starbucks, 2014). There are Starbucks internal strengths to win its competitors, although, it can not control external environment factors to threaten its business.

Coffee drinking sale industry is a service marketing, positioning has received little attention from marketers, but is very useful in defining and modifying the tangible characteristics of the different kind of taste coffee product and its intangible perceptions.

As Starbucks, customers are buying an expensive product high quality (tangible) every cup of different kind of taste coffee, but they also have the personalized in-store drinking experience enhanced by the trained employees, for example, the customer's name is written on the plastic cup their beverage will be served in (tangible), this helps Starbucks obtains the premium brand status and win competition.

Due to coffee drinking industry is a competitive business. In micro economy analysis strategy (supply and demand). Nowadays, different coffee drinking service stores supply numbers are increasing. Although, it has limited supply numbers growth. Also, coffee drinkers' taste demand is changed quickly , who need to drink different kind of good taste coffees and they also considerate coffee stores' staffs service performance when they can let them to feel enjoyable to sit down the coffee shops to drink its coffee. Hence, Starbuck considers its employees' service performance issue. It concentrates on training its staffs to let its every coffee drinking client has unforgettable drinking coffee enjoyable experience in its any one coffee shop. It implies Starbucks employees' service behavioral performance can influence every coffee drinkers' positive or negative emotion to decide to choose to go to Starbuck to drink coffee again or choose another coffee shops to drink coffee. Hence, Starbucks employees' service behaviors must have relationship to influence its future coffee drinking client growth number. If it's employees can provide kindly service attitude to every coffee drinker, adds it can produce any kinds of good taste coffees, adds it can let coffee drinkers to feel it's every cup of coffee price is reasonable. Sum of all the factors, they can influence why Starbucks can earn more sale of its coffee shops in global different countries in short term successfully.

I conclude that Starbucks still needs to find different kinds of new taste coffee to satisfy different coffee taste clients' needs. Because coffee drinking market will have many clients who like to drink different kinds of coffee. If Starbucks can not increase to provide different kinds of new taste coffee to satisfy client individual drinking new coffee taste demand. Otherwise, other coffee shops can provide new unique different kinds taste of coffees to satisfy their drinking new taste coffee demands. Then, due to Starbucks limited supply of new taste coffee factor, it will have possible to influence its competitive ability in this competitive coffee drinking market.

In conclusion, it needs to consider how many coffee supply number is not the main factor to influence its success. Otherwise, how much different kinds of coffee taste supply is the main factor to influence its success because coffee drinkers can either choose to go to supermarkets to buy different brands of coffee to drink at home or choose to go to other coffee ships to drink the kinds of coffee taste which Starbucks can not provide to them to drink. So, satisfying coffee clients' different kinds of coffee taste demand will be one main successful key to Starbucks, it is not how many coffee number supply (enough coffee number supply) factor to influence its success. It needs to find different kinds of new taste coffee to let clients to know and to have more coffee choice to drink to satisfy their drinking new taste of coffee needs. It reflects the new taste of coffee supply and the new taste of coffee demand micro economic theory to influence coffee consumers' drinking behavioral needs in this coffee drinking industry.

Micro economic assess the influence on location choices and growth performance consumption prediction.

Some economists indicate idea that seen central to the development of regional science at large and to economic geography and international trade theory. In this terms of economies of specialization increase returns to scale and in the case of regional science and economic geography, economies of localization and urbanization.

The questions concern: Can choose the best business location to attract consumption growth performance? Does the best destination attract consumption growth?

" Two cities attract trade from an intermediate town in the vicinity of the breaking point, approximately in direct proportion to the population of the two cities, and in inverse proportion to the squares of the distances of the intermediate town" (Reggiani, 1998).

It implies some economists believe that geographic location choice factor can influence consumption growth. It is possible due to the location has many people are living. So, it brings many business chance, or the location is one the country's main in economic development location, it can attract many travelers choose to go to the location to travel. So, it has many travelling clients to prefer to consumer.

However, a smaller region can still attract consumption growth, if it had good transportation system. For example, a small region may not have its own university, but inhabitants may still have access to higher education. Elsewhere accessibility measures are also need in activity location models, where access ability is the way through which the quality of the transport system influences the land use.

So, it seems although the regional land is small size and far from cities, but if it can have good transportation system to provide any people to travel the small size regional land from outside cities. It is possible to bring consumption growth. However, some economists believe that distance influence relations in economics and economic geography in two ways: first, natural resources are distributed unevenly across space and second, distance separates various activities from each other. They apply " law of demand" to support their reasons.

In regional sciences, accessibility plays an important role for analyzing the distribution of economic cities and regional development. Within regional science, the attempt to predict and explain the distribution of economic activity has become known as economic geography. Research in economic geography attempt to answer the question: What forces cause geographic behavioral consumption? Some economists support the production function and into the interaction between transportation cost and plant level scale economies, this geographical factor will bring much geographical behavioral consumption. For example, accessibility of population is an indicator of market size for suppliers of products and services, whereas successful ability to GDP could be an indicator of the market size for suppliers of high level business services (Spiekermannn and Wegener, 2007).

However, some economists argue that market potential is not necessarily the actual market. For example, since a person can't make the same purchase at two different locations. Hence, they believe that is one person has make purchase in one location far from whose home. Then, if he/she find another location which is close to whose home. The, he/she must not choose to buy the same purchase again, even he/she believe the seller's shop is close to whose home location. It implies that far location is not one factor to influence consumers to choose to buy the product if the consumer lines to buy the product. Even, the seller's shop is far away from whose home, he/she will still choose to drive whose car or catch transportation tool to go to the seller's shop to buy the product far away from whose home. Otherwise, if the consumer does not like the product, even the product seller's shop is close to whose home. Although he/she can walk to the shop to buy the product in short time. He/she won't choose to buy the product, due to who dislike the product. Hence, even close whose home, the seller product price is cheaper than the far away whose home, the another seller product price is higher than the similar or same product.

In conclusion, we have been downward trend of transportation costs of people, product and information to influence any geographical consumer behaviors. It implies that firms and people become less to restricted in their locational choices, it should lead to a greater homogeneity across regions. However, there are still great variation across geographical space in terms of incomes, cost of living, regional structure of production etc. different locational factors to influence regional consumption behavior in different countries.

2.1 Media economic methods to predict readers' behaviors in publishing industry

Media economics the application of economic theories, concepts and principles to study the macroeconomics and microeconomic aspects of most media consumption and industries, for academic lecturers, policymakers, and industry analysts. Media economics methods include how to apply variety of methodological approaches both qualitative and quantitative methods and statistical analysis, as well as studies using financial, historical and policy driven data.

Some economists define land, labor, and capital as the three factors of production and the major contributors to a nation's wealth. Can land, labor and capital be as three main factors of production any books, newspapers, magazines etc. reading products in publishing industry? Some economists believed price was determined by the costs of production, whereas marginal economists equated prices with the level of demand can be any books, magazines, newspapers etc. reading products prices is either determined by the cost of printing production or equated any one kind of these reading products with the level of reader' demand more.

The marginal economists contributed the basic analytic tools of demand and supply, consumer utility and the use of mathematics as analytical tools to develop microeconomics. Can apply the basic analytic tools of reader demand and the any one kind of these reading products supply and reading consumer individual reading need, utility and the use of mathematics as analytical tools to predict any kind of reading consumer numbers and reading interesting topic choice in media industry?

However, some economists also demonstrated that given a free market economy, such as in free publish industry, the factors of production (land, labor and capital) were important in understanding the economic system. Can apply the factor of production , e.g. publishing book sale location (land); publishing book salespeople sale experience (labor); and attractive book printing quality (capital printing expense) to influence the publishing industry reading consumer reading habit or purchase book activities?

However, some economists suggested two important contributions: Analysis of monopoly and price discrimination and the market for labor will influence consumer number. Such as publishing case: Can analysis of which famous royalty publishing book sale firm to the most monopoly and then following its different topic of books sale price to evaluate whether how much every different topic of its similar book topic sale price to be higher to avoid reduce reader numbers, due to the not famous royalty book seller which similar topic book to the famous royalty book seller's prices are too higher than the famous royalty publishers' book prices?

Book salespeople individual sale experience and sale ability and book knowledge (labor supply) influence the book publishing shop's reading clients buying decisions, such as the more experience book sellers can persuade many readers to buy the book store's books. Otherwise, the less sale experience book sellers can not persuade many readers to buy the store's books.

As the found in the field of economics, it became more refined, scholars began investigate many different economic concepts and principles to predict consumers behaviors, such as media reading customer. Nowadays, the media industries provides all of the elements required for studying the economic process. Content providers can offer information and entertainment, education etc. different topic books, magazine reading products which became the media publishing suppliers. Whereas, reading consumers and media advertisers formed the demand side of the media market.

The macroeconomic market conditions and the relationship among any media publishing reading product suppliers in various industries created microeconomic market conditions , e.g. publishing suppliers need logistic transportation service suppliers to help them to deliver books or magazines or newspapers etc. different kinds of reading products to book shops or magazine shops to sell every day. It can bring the logistic transportation service business to contribute social economic development.

Early media economists apply microeconomic concepts to examine newspaper competition and radio competition media industry. They predicted advertisement can help these both media industry to earn advertisement income to help other businesses to promote their products to let radio listeners and newspapers readers to know from these two media channel effectively. So, they believed that newspapers and radio extra income source can be provided advertisement service for other businesses, instead of radio audience income or newspapers reader normal income source. In addition to a number of book and edited volumes have contributed to the development of media economics to help them to predict consumer reading psychology.

How to apply media economic methods to predict media consumer's psychology? Some media economists believe the market structure-conduct performance model is as a tool for analysis, it has been widely used in the study of media markets and industries, such as book publishing industry. How to choose the attractive topic for every book product structure? They believe attractive book structure will help book structure firm to grow reader numbers. So, book topic and content factor is more influential to raise reader number more than cheaper book price sale factor.

In its most simply for the industries organizational model indicates that of the structure of the market is known, it allows explanation of the likely conduct and performance among firms. For example, in terms of market structure, the variables used for analysis include the numbers of sellers/buyers, e.g. US publishing book market number of US book reading publishers/number of US book publishing sellers every year in US book publishing market; product differentiation, e.g. US different topic and content of electronic book or paper book product ; barriers to entry, e.g. economic recession, tariff book import tax, limitation of import book number etc. different external barriers factors to influence overseas (foreign) book publishing import to US to sell their paper books ; cost structures, e.g. US book publishing firms need to spend how much printing expenditure to print high quality paper production of every paper book to sell and the degree of vertical integration, e.g. US book publishing firms how to choose middlemen to help them to sell books, e.g. themselves book publishing shops, other book retailers, themselves electronic book publishing website online platform sale channel or other book publishing sellers' websites online platform sale channel etc. different channels to sell the paper of electronic books to US readers. Hence, predicting the country' book market structure, it will have more confidence to evaluate book publishing competitors' effort and book sale price and how to design book content and topic to raise reading quality to let readers to feel much attractive to choose to buy the books from the book publishing shop.

Media economics research is in the sense that many different types of methods are used to answer research questions and investigate hypotheses. However, many economists accept to choose to apply any one of methods to predict media reader behavior, such as trend studies, financial analysis, econometrics and case studies.

Trend studies compare and contrast data over a time series. In assessing media concentration. Most trend studies use annual data as the unit of analysis. Trend studies are useful, due to their descriptive nature and ease of presentation and they aid in analyzing the performance of media companies and industries, e.g. study of changes in newspaper pricing and subscription costs.

Financial analysis is another common methodological tool used in media economics research. Financial analysis can take many different forms and use different types of data. The most common data include information derived from financial statements and the use of various types of financial ratio.

Econometrics involves the use of statistical and mathematical models to verify and develop economic research questions, hypotheses and theory.

Case studies represent another useful method in media economics research. Case studies are popular because they allow a researcher to gather different types of data as well as different methods. Case studies in media economics research tend to be very targeted and focused examinations.

What are forces to influence media industry development? There four forces consist of technology, regulation, globalization and sociocultural can influence media industry development. I shall indicate why these forces will influence media industry change in order media industry businesses need to consider s below:

Technology force: Because media industries are heavily dependent on technology for the creation, distribution and exhibition of various forms of media contents, changes in technology affect economic processes between and within the media industries. For example, many publishing book businesses choose to apply internet technology to help authors to publish electronic books sale. Due to it is popular to let online readers to study from internet, even they choose to pay visa card to buy electronic or paper books to read from internet sale channel. So, technology brings electronic book digital content and text and graphics digitally soon led to digital audio and video files to let authors to download their files to change to electronic books to publish to sell to electronic book readers to read from online channel. So, internet builds electronic book web sites to attract reading consumers to read from internet channel. They do not need to bring paper book to read. They only need to bring mobile phone or laptops to go to anywhere to read electronic books any time conveniently.

Regulation: If regulation is eliminated in publishing or media industry to any countries, the cross ownership rules would give publishing companies. The opportunity to acquire broadcast stations able cable systems within the markets, they serve, leading to the development of multi-media based companies offering content and advertising across multiple mediums.

Globalization can influence media industry development. Media products are often created with global audiences in mind, which is why so much content contains sex and violence. However, globalization of media content began with motion pictures and magazines, but then expanded into another media channels, e.g. television programming, VHS and DVD sales and rentals. These media publishing products' income are influenced by global audience entertainment choice.

Finally, it is socio-cultural force factor which can influence reader or media entertainment consumer industrial consumption behavior. Socio-cultural, such as the country's young people accept to like to read electronic books more than paper books reading behaviors. Then, it is the country's socio-cultural factor to influence the country's book buyers who prefer to pay visa card to buy electronic books to read from book store online website platform channel. It is electronic book reading cultural trend to influence the country young people reading behavior change . They will change their traditional reading habits to choose to buy electronic books to read from internet reading channel. So, online reading of electronic book method will be popular to the country and the country's paper book publishing shops ought consider to apply internet technology to develop their electronic book publishing business to let young people electronic book buyers to read electronic books from online channel conveniently.

Finally, all media industry players ought consider any technology development in order to predict readers' or media entertainment players' whose consumption behavior changes to avoid themselves publishing media businesses encounter fail in future one day.

Can predict the real economic situation using liquidity of financial assets?

How about alternative ways of measuring liquidity? Can liquidity predict turning points of a business cycles or predict whether customer number will grow or reduce in next year? Is it a good consumer number predictive tool for alternative macroeconomic predictive results? Can liquidity predict real economy variables in macro-economic view point, i.e. such macro-economic aggregate ass economic growth (changes in GDP), investments direction changes etc.?

There are some analysis to support its possibility , such as: Most of the predictability is coming from changes in the liquidity of small stocks (presumably the least liquid ones). How about alternative ways of measuring liquidity? IS it real liquidity? If so, which aspect concerns to the liquidity to the company? So, the conclusion of question concern: Can liquidity method predict macroeconomic variable?

Consumer changing expectation to consume any things will be possible to influence macroeconomic variable. If it is true, calculating how many of the kind of businesses liquidity data that can predict whether the year macroeconomic variable is better or worse to compare last year. Can it use the current and past year kind of businesses liquidity data to predict next year macroeconomic variable situation whether it is suitable
to any businessmen choose to do the kind of business or not to do next year.

The resulting trading decisions reflects changing expectations about whether business cycles and consumers' taste or consumption desires whether they are changing or not to cause the kind of most businesses choose to liquidity finally. So, if one foresees a deteriorating economy , one wants to shift the portfolio into assets better predicted in that case. For example, when one foresee an upturn one will shift into materials as the demand for that industry's products is likely to be high when investments are increasing. Using the sector as explanatory variable, one may catch this kind of behavior, since order flow is increasing in the desire for that particular sector.

So, if liquidity of asset method can be attempted to predict whether next year which kind of businesses will have risk. Then, it brings these questions:

Which liquidity measures are the best for forecasting?

How does liquidity measures relate to alternative forecasting variables?

I shall assumes that it has relationship between stock market liquidity and cost of trading shares, with macroeconomic conditions. For example is that liquidity levels of local stocks are higher (lower) , when the local economy has performed well (poorly). The relation is stronger when local financing constraints are more binding, the local information environment is more better or worse, and local businessmen ownership levels and trading intensity are higher. More liquidity seems temporary relationship, due to short time economic recession factor to influence some kind of businesses , but still, linking the country local stock liquidity with local business cycle, it is possible that the country's different kinds of businesses will liquidate more than one year if the country's economy is recession long time. So, predicting many kind different kind of businesses liquidity choice in the country in the year. It will predict how long time the country economic recession will occur or find what factors cause the country economic recession occurrence in possible.

In conclusion, it seems that gathering the country's any kind of businesses whose past liquidity of financial assets data, it will possible to predict whether what kind(s) of businesses has(have) risk to do the kind of businesses next year. What factor(s) cause(s) the country's economic recession, economic recession situation will remain how long time, This liquidity of financial assets data gathering method will give opinions to let the country's businessmen to choose whether it is right time to set up their new businesses next year or close down their old businesses to be better next year.

3.1 Micro solution methods solve macro-economic problem

Nowadays, global financial crisis cause a slowdown in world trade growth. The recent great recession has important impacts on international trade. The international trade has changed from three factors: The evolution of global imbalances, trends in globalization and the structure of trade negotiations.

For example, new technologies in manufacturing, connectivity and energy efficiency in particular, have the potential to transform the global economic risk. From macroeconomic perspective these new technologies increase potential growth, allowing the economy to grow faster and it may also put downward pressure on energy price. The US seems as a likely beneficiary, where its competitive advantage in the production and deployment of information technology is widely recognized. Otherwise, some countries' development could be threatened by the substitution of cheaper and more efficient capital for (labor and by the shortening of global supply chains).

I believe new technologies have the potential to solve global macro economic development challenges from micro economic (every country technological firms cooperation development) method. The reason as below:

(1) Recent advances in information and communications technology new innovations in methods of manufacturing and fresh ways of exploiting energy could bring significant growth benefits for the world global economic technological development from different countries themselves technological firms research new (undiscovered) technological products development to influence future human life, water energy, solar energy, nuclear energy, vehicle battery energy new energy development technology. It aims to avoid global energy shortage challenge occurrence and new artificial intelligent cities development, it aims to let human feel to live in high technological development, artificial intelligent cities can let human to live more comfortable and more convenient in global cities from artificial intelligent assistance.

For another example, some of the new technologies allow companies earn higher quality of physical capital at lower prices. Enhanced energy storage, shale gas and oil techniques, and innovations in renewable energy are helping to drive down the price of energy relative to the trend that would have unfolded in their absence. In all cases, new energy development, these technologies have the potential to raise productivity growth sectors and countries, allowing faster, new energy supply growth and lower inflation, when human have different kind of energy to choose to use.

For another example, mobile communications technology can make the world economy more efficient and may also lead to significant dislocation. Mobile communications technology has the potential to bring 2 to 3 billion people into the world economy development. Additive manufacturing as 3 D printing, could remove up to 90% of the waste from some manufacturing processes. At the same time, advanced robots which can work as little as USD$4 per hour, may eventually display existing employment in manufacturing. So, on micro economic view point, technology will be one kind production of factor to global future manufacturing firms. Mckinsey Global Institute finds that our trend global growth could be 0.5 to 0.7 percentage points higher in 2025s than in the absence of technological change, it implies productivity gains comparable to apply only personal computer and internet revolutions of the 1990s.

(2) What is future these new technology? A new technology ought change the way the world economy operates in micro economic view point. A new technological change can shift the global economy's production function simply put, better technology allows the economy to produce more products and services at low prices. (production of factor). For example, potential efficiency gains include the widespread diffusion of mobile devices, easing access to

the internet, artificial intelligence machine learning and voice recognition as well as the " internet of things", big of data gathering method to be applied to manage supply chains better in any factories (production of factor).

(3) In manufacturing efficiency gains include the deployment of more advanced robotics making it more practice and profitable to substitute capital for human labor. Low-cost robots can change manufacturing by increasing precision and productivity without higher costs. Further efficiencies can be exploited with the use of 3 D printing, which reduces waste in manufacturing, improves precision of design and shortens complex supply chains (production of factor).

(4) Finally, energy efficiency opportunities range from the extraction of oil and gas reserves from shale rock formations to enhanced energy storage. US storage team's work suggests that shale extraction techniques alone may add o.5% points per year to US growth over the next 10 years (production of factor). New technologies may also put downward pressure on energy prices. Many of these technologies, such as waste -reducing , 3D printing, lower the energy intensity of global manufacturing and trade. By bringing product design and manufacturing closer to the end user, thus shortening supply chains, 3 D printing also reduces transport costs. The US department of energy anticipates that 3 D printing could save more than 50% of energy use compared to today's existing manufacturing.

(5) What new technologies influence global economy. Some economists predict new technologies will bring benefits to global economy development. They have conducted model simulations suggesting that global GDP growth could be 0.5 to 0.7 percentage points per annum higher as a result of the adoption and diffusion of these new technologies. the models also suggest that global inflation levels could be one percentage point lower than would otherwise have been the case.

However new technology can also bring some countries; labor marker change. Labor markets in manufacturing could be materially affected as capital in the form of robotics and 3D printing replace low and semi-skilled jobs. For some new technological global manufacturing and trading system countries. For example, in South Asia, the Middle East, Africa and parts of Latin America development could be threatened by the shortening of global supply chains and by the substitution of cheaper and more efficient capital for labor.

Hence new technological manufacturing development will bring disadvantages to these without effort development of new technological manufacturing and trading system countries to influence themselves labor unemployment, if their employers choose to buy other countries' new technological manufacturing system, e.g. robots replace the human labor to help them to manufacture their products. Hence, it seems new manufacturing technology will have negative impact to the without effort development new technological manufacturing countries' manufacturing labor. Due to the robots can raise productivities to shorten manufacturing time and no salary expenditure and robots efficiency is higher than human labor.

However, if these countries' labor can learn how to apply robots knowledge to control robots to help their employer to manufacture products. It is possible that they won't be dismiss, even employers will need them to assist them to control the new robots manufacturing machines to manufacture their products in factories. It depends on whether they choose to attempt to control manufacturing robots or not.

In conclusion, new technology can be one important production factor to influence global macro-economic growth from micro new technological manufacturing sectors development. So global manufacturers will concern how to apply new technology to help them to manufacture any products.

3.2 Economic science or economic art methods predict consumer behavior

Economic is both a science and art. Economic is considered as science because systematic knowledge derived from observation, study and experimentation. An art is the practical application of knowledge for achieving definition ends. A science teaches us to know a phenomenon and art traches us to do a thing.

How to apply economic science or art method to predict consumer behavior? for example, there is a inflation US this year. This information is derived from positive science. The government takes certain fiscal and monetary measures to bring down to general level of prices in the country. The study of the monetary measures to bring down inflation makes the subject of economics as an art. Hence, as this case, if US government applies economic science or art method to predict this year will have inflation in US, then US government will attempt to avoid social general product prices to be raised, due to inflation influence. It aims to avoid US consumers reduce consumption desire in this year.

For another example, nothing could be more useful than water. But in much of the world waste is plentiful enough that another glass more or less matters little to a fresh water supply agent businessman. So, water is chap. But, if any offices buy bottle of glass fresh water to let employees to drink. It will bring advantages that they do not spend time to buy water to drink when they are working in the office time in any offices as well as employees do not need to heat water to drink to waste time to work in offices. So, the bottle of fresh drinking water supply agent is one kind of drinking water product monopoly fresh drinking water supplier to supply fresh drinking water to satisfy office employees who do not need to spend time to heat water to drink in offices. Hence, it is possible that replace other different kind taste of drink or office employees themselves heat water drink in offices. It is general office employees' drinking habits and drinking choice in offices popularly. So, the bottle of fresh drinking water supply agents will concentrate on selling their fresh drinking water to office employee customers only in global fresh drinking water consumption target market. The office employees must be fresh drinking water companies' main target consumers. What is economic laws qualitative or quantitative method to predict consumer behavior? Law of economic are qualitative in nature. They are not exactly stated in quantitative terms. They tell the direction of change which is expected rather than the amount of change. For example, according to the law of consumer demand, the quantity demanded varies inversely with price, We don't say that 10% rise in price will lead to 30% fall in the customers' quantity demand.

What is economic merits of deduction method? This method is near to reality. It is less time consuming and less expensive. the use of mathematical techniques in deducing theories of economics brings exactness and clarity in economic analysis. The deductive method is highly abstract. It require a great deal of care to avoid bad logic or faulty economic reasoning. This method makes conclusions to predict consumer behavior, due to reliance on imperfect and correct assumptions.

It involves the process of reasoning from particular facts to general principle on the basic of experimentations, observations and statistical methods. In this method, data is collected about a certain economic phenomenon. There are systematically arranged and the general conclusions are drawn from them.

What are the advantages of inductive method to predict consumer behavior? It is based on facts as such the method is realistic. In order to test the economic principles, method makes statistical techniques. The inductive method is therefore more reliable, inductive method is dynamic. The changing economic phenomenon are analyzed and on the conclusions and solutions are drawn from them and this method also helps in future consumer behavioral investigations.

However, inductive method has weaknesses to predict consumer behavior, such as below:

It conclusions drawn from insufficient data, the generalizations obtained may be faulty. The collection of data itself is not easy task. The sources and methods employed in the collection of data differ from investigator to investigation. The result, therefore may differ even with the same problem and it is time-consuming and expensive to find data to predict consumer behavior changes.

How apply this method to predict general social consumer sources of income and consumption pattern when economic environment factor changes consumer behaviors? It should also be stressed that micro analysis plays other roles. First, it may serve to some macro data (any labor force by production sector or by skill category). Second, it can be used to estimate of key consumer behavioral consumption functions. For example, price and income elasticities can be estimated using data available in a typical householder budget survey. Third, in the case of tax reforms involving changes in exemptions or deductions is a model useful to estimate changes in effective tax rates changes how to influence consumer behavioral changes in society.

In conclusion, economists have proved macro and micro economic both methods have possible to be applied to predict consumer behavior when , how and why their consumption behavioral changing occurrence in order to manufacturers and product sellers or service providers can pre-make judgement to achieve the marketing strategies to avoid the number of client loss, due to marketing or economic environment changes to influence negative impact to consumer behavioral changes to influence the manufacturers' manufacturing products or the sellers' products or the service providers' service provision which number to be decreased.

Marketing communication strategy predicts
consumer behaviors
    4.1 What are marketing communication
strategy benefits?

Can marketing communication strategy help organizations to build brands, innovation, developing relationship, create good consumer service and communication benefit. Most marketing professionals believe effective communicaton strategy can help organizations to raise brand competition as well as to create and enhance relationship with consumers and other stakeholders. Marketing communication strategy is concept of communication through the promotional mix, with these better-educated, cost-conscious and demanding customers. Why do organizations need marketing communication strategies? Marketing communication strategy is concept used for sales promotion, product publicity, events sponsorships and direct marketing. It can help new brands to raise familiarity to let customers to know when the brand product plans to enter the marketing to sell in beginning.

Nowadays, organizations need promotional mix strategy to let consumers to familiar their new products, such as public relations, marketing, advertising, promotion and online media. Generally, organizations expect to achieve these aims. Otherwise, one effective marketing communication strategy can assist the organizations to drive forces for growth.

The driving forces include: Value of money means the organizations want to gain maximum value for money with maximum impact, resulting in raising value of money to different products in different departments and pressure on margins: Increasing pressure on organizations' bottom lines means organizations seek compensatory savings in all activities through saving, economic pressures and profitability, increasing client confidence means specially to understand retailers, cutomers and an increased confidence in using other marketing communication disciplines, a dissatisfaction with advertising means resulting in clients using other disciplines to improve consumer relations and sales, increasing mass media costs means where database costs decreased, mass-media costs (especially television, increased dramatically) and a reduction advertising agencies expenses in terms of strategic input and direction. Hence, one effective marketing communication strategy can be possible to assist the organizations to reduce advertising expense, raise brand familiarity, increase client number, raise product sale price for long term benefits.

Some marketing professional researches recommend marketing communication strategy ought have these several stages, they include as below:

Stage one is tactical coordination of marketing communication. It means to find what are the fails on function areas including advertising, promotion, direct response, public relation and special events. The tactical coordination of marketing communication strategy aims to find why a high degree of personal and cross-functional communications needed as formal policies and procedures are insufficient to achieve the organization marketing communication operation. It aims to find what the weaknesses are to cause the organization's internal communication between different departments and external communication to its clients inefficiency and ineffectiveness.

Stage two is refining the scope of marketing communication. The organization begins to examine communication from the consumer's viewpoint, include all contact and entry points between the organization and clients. The scope of communication activities also include internal marketing to employees, suppliers and other business partners.

The extensive information on consumers is gathered through primary and secondary market research as well as actual consumer behavior data and feedback channels are created to gather information about consumers. So, it aims to find what marketing communication challenges influence the organizations' internal and external communication difficulties to influence poor unsatisfactory customer behavior performance to seek valuable solution to raise the organization's internal and external marketing communication more efficient and effective to raise customer communication success.

Then, third stage concerns how to improve and apply skill to build good marketing communication channel. Due to the marketing communication strategy implementation organization will need to learn how to use data obtained through IT skill to provide a basis for the identification of values and to monitor the impact of integrated internal and external marketing communication program over time. So, IT must be incorporated effectively into communication planning development and execution.

The final stage is financial and marketing communication strategic integration. It emphasizes shifts from skills and data to driving corporate strategic planning using consumer information and insight. Financial measures should be adapted into the evaluation process based on return on consumer investment measures.

So, these stages will be the key component to raise or improve the external marketing communication efforts with the internal marketing communication efforts to raise the overall organizational corporate brand for long term effective and internal and external marketing communication channels to employees and consumers both stakeholders' benefits.

4.2 Marketing communication functions

Why do organizations need marketing communication? What are marketing communication functions to organizations? What kinds of challenges will encounter if the organization lacked an efficient marketing communication strategy? This chapter will be explained above these questions clearly.

Marketing communication seems to be gathered information and communication seems to be gathered information and communication technology, which will influence every aspect of consumer need in order to bring positive or negative emotions to the brand of product. Hence, if the organization had effective marketing communication tools and strategies, which will raise its competitive effort in nowadays business societies.

An effective marketing communication strategy or tool will help the brand of product to build good emotion to its consumers. The steps include: The organization needs have one good marketing plan. Then, it needs to design the right or suitable kind of marketing strategy to satisfy its products or services characteristics. Finally, if its marketing communication tools or methods are suitable to the organization to be used to promote. Then, it will either build good brand or remember or familiar as well as build either good (positive) or bad (negative) emotion to the customers. So, it seems an efficient and marketing communication tool or method will help the organization to increase customer familiarity and build positive emotion to its product or service. Otherwise, an inefficient marketing communication tool or method will not help the organization to increase customer familiarity build negative emotion to its product or service. So, it is one important function to any marketing communication strategy.

Why organizations ought need to spend time and human resource / communication tool resources to design the most right or the most suitable marketing communication strategy for its organization to promote its product or service? Before any organizations design any communication strategy , they need to know what is this marketing situation. In general, marketing is defined the establishment of mutually satisfying exchange relationships between the brand's product or/and service and its clients. It is managing profitable client relationships. It's goal of marketing is to attract new clients by promising superior value and to keep and grow current clients by delivering satisfaction.

Therefore, the marketing function is to identify client needs and to provide a product or service that meets some or all of those needs, accessibily and at an acceptable price to the target market. Hence, the organization's marketing communication strategy is only one part of its overall marketing strategy. A marketing strategy includes how to help the organization to promote its product or service, how to sell its product or provide its service, how to arrange the reasonable price strategy, how to help the organization to improve production and distribution efficiencies, how to focus on continue product improvement, how to focus on aggregative selling tactics, focuses on customer needs, applied on integrated marketing approach, how to give welfare of society.

How does the marketing communication strategy influence the overall marketing strategy success to the organization? An effective marketing communication strategy can create value for customers and build good customer relationship for the brand of product or service. It's function includes that is can let the organization understands market places and its customer needs and want more clearly, it can assist the organization how to design a customer-driven marketing strategy if the organization can build good relationship between them , it can also help the organization to construct a marketing communication strategy(program) that delivers superior value.

Then, when the organization has an efficient marketing communication strategy, it can help the organization to build relationship and create customer delight in long term. Finally, it can help the organization to achieve a superior capture value from its clients to create profits and client quality more easily.

Why do organizations need have an efficient marketing communication strategy? The reasons include that as below: In fact, customers have much choices, usually different product or service marketing places will have (excess) oversupply of product or service to influence consumers to make careful choices to buy which brand of product or consume service in whose choice processes. So, if the brand of product or service cn build good communication relationship between itself and customers. It can influence customers to have positive emotion to choose to buy its product or consume its service. So, any organizations needs have good price, location (place), people (staff) strategies, it also need have good promotion (communication) strategy in order to learn how to communicate to its customers to keep close relationship and build positive emotion to let them to feel.

However, the marketing communication must include these several tools for any organizations to choose which kind(s) of communication tool(s) is (are) the best tool(s) in order to be used to promote its clients efficiently. They include: Advertising, it means that controlled paid for communication, it consists of communication messages, initiated by a specific communicator in the mass media to a defined target audience. Personal selling involves interpersonal communication between sellers and buyers through personal interactions. Sales promotion concerns the free and favorable exposure of a product's benefits or value in the media, public relations can establish and maintain favorable relations between an entity and its stakeholders. So, any organization needs to choose either only use one kind of communication tool or more than one kind of communication tools in order to achieve an efficient marketing communication strategy to build positive emotion and good product or service image or familiar brand to let its potential customers to know by any above one media. Also, it implies that customers won't know or familiar to the brand more clearly if the organization had not implement any promotion tool(s) to promote its product or service to let clients to know whether its existing product or service can give what benefits to them.

How to achieve an efficient marketing communication strategy? To achieve an efficient marketing communication strategy to the organization. It includes this process: It needs to identify who are its target customers (main target customer) potential customer and prospects. Then, it needs to measure the valuation of its different groups of client (e.g. age, sex, shopping characteristics). Next, it needs to create and deliver the right or suitable or useful or persuasive messages and incentives to let its different group clients to know what its product or service existing in its country or global market places. Next, it needs to estimate how much it can earn return on its customer investment for its future possible reward. Because it if estimated that its marketing communication expenditure can not achieve its budget return in customer investment reward. Then, it needs revise its this (these) kind of marketing communication tool (s) whether it (they) is (are) useful to promote its product or service to let clients to know. Finally, it needs to implement its budgeting allocation and evaluation to review its every time marketing communication tool(s) whether is (are) achieved its original aim. If it believed or confirmed its slae result is not successful. Then, it needs to revise its marketing communication tool(S) whether they (it) is (are) the most suitable or useful one tool(s) t be used to promote to its clients in the future. Hence, the whole process of marketing communication strategy is very important to influence its sale number. Every product or service provider needs to spend enough time and human resource to marketing communication tool resources to decide how to design to implement in order to sell in failure finally.

For one integrated marketing communication model of brand contact delivery system case example: The brands customer (prospect exposure will include message and incentive both aspects. Message and incentive will bring promotion communication information concern relevance and receptivity to the brand's product or service to let its customers to know or remember or familiar by these any one or more than one delivery systems , such as product/ use of the package product message tool or directed marketer channel or undirected member channel or traditional media tools (accesses or unintentional , such as TV, radio, magazine, signage outdoor direct marketing tool or electronic media tools (wired or wireless) such as website second intranet or mobile phone engines GPS or special events promotion methods (natural or sponsored) , such as holiday events or sport cultural trade events. All any one of these media delivery systems will be one choice tool to let the product/ service providers to be chosen to find which tool is the most efficient delivery tool. Hence, one marketing communication strategy elements include the marketing communication source is the company/brand or agency, the brand message concerns (planned , unplanned, product or/and service) and the channel includes newspapers, TV, radio, magazine, e-mails, salespeople sale service, customer service, internet and the receiver is the target audience in the whole marketing communication process. Finally, the delivery system will bring feedback to the company/brand, agency and the target audience both. The feedback includes that purchase/not purchase, request information, visit store, sample product, repeat visit/ purchase.

Consequently, any marketing communication strategy will bring feedback to let the product/service provider to know in order to judge or predict whether its potential customers will have positive or negative emotion (attitude) to choose to buy its product or consume its service. Thus, feedback affect will be one important factor to influence the product or service providers success. If the product / service providers and clients both feedback trends to more negative emotion to its potential customers, then it can attempt to follow whose ideas to find what internet weaknesses or external threats to cause whose potential customers feel negative emotion to its product or/and service. Then, it can attempt to find solutions to avoid whose negative emotion is caused more easily. Thus, an efficient marketing communication strategy can help the product/service provider how to raise its potential clients' emotion to be trended more positive emotion for their product or service choices.

4.3 The possible sale of relationship marketing and communication in public utility service

What are the function of marketing communication to public utility service ? If the public utility service organization lacks an efficient communication channel between internal staffs and utility consumers, what kinds of challenges who will encounter. How to they make solution ? What are the negative attitude of the utility consumers will be if it lacked an efficient communication service between them?

In fact, many countries' public utility service is monopoly market. Their governments usually have a regulated prices to control their price to be charged to public utility consumers. Consumers have had affordable public utility access to these utility service, but they have been defense against the service providers . Hence , every government usually control utility service providers' price charged behavior in order to avoid their excess of charge. So, public utility service providers have realized that those is a competition on the utility service market.

Hence, an effective and efficient marketing communication channel will bring those benefits of advantages between the organization's internal staffs and every utility service consumer. I shall indicate the advantages as below:

Firstly, an efficient marketing communication channel can let utility service consumers to feel whether the public utility service is a real public service. Due to public utility service aims to provide any enough utility remains to consumers to use, such as electricity , water, gas, oil etc. is the field on non-business marketing because the public utility service providers do need aim on profit seeking . This is made characteristics as well by the fact that in many service field, e.g. higher education, public transport, public utility service. So , an efficient communication marketing channel can let the public service consumersm who can make easy to distinct between public and private as well as between profit and non profit , e.g. the students can judge whether their schools charge higher education fee or lower education fee in the general school fee charge level and judge whether the public transport charges higher or lower transport for general public transport service standard charge level and judge whether the gas, oil, water, electricity utility service charge is accepted to general public utility service charge standard level. Hence, an efficient marketing communication channel can let the public service consumers have more familiar and effort to judge whether the public service providers' charge is reasonable.

However, an efficient communication marketing channel is very important to assist the public utility service consumers to make a distinction as well . Every public utility service organization has responsibility to let public service consumers to know what are basic services to be provided to let them to judge whether the kind of possibility of public service substitution is small or large to let the public service consumers to choose in the country 's current public service market to let them to judge whether the public service quality is good or bad and whether the price conditions are reasonable. Hence, an efficient marketing communication channel can build the good relationship between the public service organization and its public service consumers.

Do public utility services have important characteristics from marketing communication channel? It is agreed that efficient marketing communication channel is needed to any public utility service industries. It has chose marketing and communication relationship to any public utility service organizations. It is to think in terms of back office organizations in most person to person contact based services, but in the case of the utility services, the situation is unique different. In fact, the role of back office is significant different in the case of public utility services. In general , public utility consumers do not assess the work of background staff as they are unseen and are not usually part of the service providing process. However, the result of the servicing activity depends on the work of the back office. So, it explains that why efficient internal department communication is very important between public utility service back office staffs. There is no effective public utility service without the tools, equipment and operating staff and the application of efficient and effective communication relationship marketing is challenges by this fact. For example, the role of power , heating, water and long distance telephone supply etc. customer service front office staff role is influential to their service efficiency by the back office staffs cooperation. If they have good communication channel to let them to work in order to achieve efficient communication effect. Then, the front office public utility service staffs can provide better consumer service to satisfy any public utility service consumer needs or build the high direct consumer service relationships between them.

Besides, efficient communication marketing strategy can assist the public utility service organization to promote its prices to let public utility service consumers to feel more acceptable to the price level charge range. It is often difficult for service providers to apply differentiating price strategies and to use prices as promotional devices. Even, when price incentives are allowed public utility service providers rarely use. There effectively with elements of the marketing mix or with effective segmentation program to an efficient communication marketing strategy can help any public utility service organizations to solve any tangible and/or intangible communication challenges, such as back office and front office staffs communication challenges, fron toffice customer service staffs poor or inefficient service performance challenge, who causes utility service consumers to feel emotion unsatisfactory or do behavioral complains. So, effective communication marketing strategy is important tool to influence any public utility service organizations successes.

4.4 Understanding food industry marketing communication (pull marketing communication strategy)

In food industry , it needs have an efficient marketing communication strategy in order to the food providers can persuade their food consumers to choose to buy their food easily. Firstly, the food provider needs to understand the global consumer's preference to find how any why to persuade they to choose to buy their food products. It is important to develop marketing communication strategies to solve challenges and find or seek opportunities in the communication process between the food providers (manufacturers) and its food retailers, food wholesalers (supermarkets , food stores). In its communication marketing strategy, it needs to consider two channels: The first channel is supply chain development and management channel. The food supplier (manufacturer) needs to learn how to manage its difference kinds of food supply chain, learn how to manage its food quality and food transportation logistics methods and learn how to communicate to its food retailers or food wholesalers how to help it to sell its different kinds of food to let consumers to buy attractively. The another channel is that it needs to learn how drive food consumer behavioral consumption and learn hoe to predict why whose consumption behavioral change. Hence, the food supplier (manufacturer) needs to learn how to communicate with its food retailers and food wholesalers to know how any why its food consumers' choices to but its foods behavioral change. It concerns that it needs to communicate with them to learn how and why its old food consumers' taste change, research and builds new food product brand development as well as learns how to achieve efficient marketing communication strategy and point of sale strategies. Finally, the food supplier) manufacturer) will gather all data from there both channels to brings all data together to implement strategy revisited and revised the weaknesses and keep strengths in order to find the most useful solvable method to attract new potential food consumers to choose to buy to food or keep its old consumers to continue to choose to buy its food. Hence, one efficient marketing communication strategy which can represent the " PROMOTION" element of the marketing mix. Such on this food industry case, food marketing is all about food selling and communicating ideas be they to buy a good taste of food or good food salespeople service or take notice of a public health appeal (e.g. eat fruit and vegetable). None of this is possible without a good and effective communication strategy between the food supplier (manufacturer) and its food retailers or food wholesalers.

In many food and agricultural markets, the food and agriculture suppliers (producers and supply chain/ channel partners, it has become increasingly difficult to differentiate between food or agricultural product offerings. So, the number of available and positioning opportunities also diminishes. So, it implies that efficient communication strategy can assist them to create long-life marketing communication opportunities to promote their any agriculture food success. Some of the key roles that promotion can play in food marketing include as below:

An efficient communication marketing strategy can help the agricultural food producers to build brand depth awareness. For example, when some food consumers ask the supermarket staffs concern which brands of chicken taste that they can choose to buy in the supermarket chilled meat sections. If the chicken food supermarket staffs can speak some brands of chicken food, e.g. steggles, lillydale, ingham etc. brands. Then, the supermarket staffs can help those chicken brand producers to promote the different chicken taste food to let the supermarket consumers to know. So, it means that the brand of chicken food producers can build good communication relationship to the supermarket . Then, the supermarket staff's promotin behavior , it seems to advertise the chicken food producers to let the supermarket customers to know or be familiar the brand of chicken's different chicken tastes.

So, good food taste marketing communication strategy can achieve good or physical availability , such as the food producers can arrange how much different food distribution to different wholesalers or retailers, such as supermarkets, food stores. Hence, if they had good communication relationship, whose middle sale agents, such as supermarkets or food stores will tell about how much different kinds of food will encounter food shortage or food excess perishable challenges in next month in order the food producers can predict who ought continue to increase supply the kind of food or reduce supply for every kind of food to the supermarkets or food stores to help them to sell next month. It aims to achieve all food will be fresh and good quality to provide to food buyers to eat. So, predicting food supply number will be one important solution to food perishable challenge.

In conclusion, an efficient marketing communication strategy can assist the agricultural food producer to avoid to supply the excess of different kinds of food number or the shortage of different kinds of food number challenge. If the agricultural foods producers can build good marketing communication relationship between itself and its food wholesalers/ food retailers, e.g. supermarkets, food stores. Then, the food producers will have goods notice about its different kinds of food sale number data every month or every week ,even every day in order to decide whether it ought increase or decrease how much accurate predictive number of the kind of food to its food retailers or wholesalers to sell every day to avoid the different kinds of food excess or shortage challenges. So, efficient marketing communication strategy is very serious to agriculture food producers.

4.5 The role of marketing communication strategy in theatre management

Why does theatre industry need communication media, e.g. combination of advertisement, publicity, and public relation, plus other marketing tools in promotional activities of theatre management strategy. If the theatre performance provider neglected to achieve efficient marketing communication strategy , it will bring what kinds of challenges to influence performance entertainment consumers' entertainment desires.

Theatre industry can be explained to refer to any structure or group of people (even non professional existing primarily for the preparation/presentation of theatrical performance, such as dance, music, song, movie, life show etc. performance for purpose of audience entertainment activities, such as movie is one kind of popular entertainment in theatre industry. It can provide entertainment activity to entertain audience to satisfy their visible enjoyable desires when they had bought tickets to choose any movies to watch in theatres.

What is the purpose of communication marketing management principles and strategies to theatrical procedures? Theatrical communication marketing management strategy consists planning, staffing, organizing , motivating, directing and controlling human and material resources in the arts of the theatre and their interaction in order to attain the predetermined objectives of guaranteeing satisfaction and maximizing profit. So , theatrical organization needs have efficient communication between its internal departments as well as itself and its any performance entertainment service providers . It aims to achieve every final entertainment performances which can be more attractive to let audiences enjoy to watch or listen any kinds of entertainment performances.

What role is a directing communication channel to theatre industry? Advertising is the structured and composed non-personal communication of information usually paid for and usually persuasive in nature about products, services and ideas by identified sponsors through various media. Advertising can be explained the techniques and practices used to bring products , services , opinions or causes to public notice for the purpose of persuading the public to respond what is advertised. It seems theatre industry needs have efficient communication to let internal departments or entertainment performance service providers to communicate to them to achieve to prepare any attractive advertisement before any entertainment performance implementation. Because if one entertainment performance provider can provide attractive advertisements can persuade and notify potential audiences to choose to buy tickets to enter theatres to watch the entertainment performance service provider's any entertainment performance event more easily. So, the theatre service provider and its entertainment performance service providers need have good communication in order to advertise every different kind of entertainment performance event more attractive to let its audiences to feel. So, theatre provider needs to concern this internal and external communication issue in order to apply advertisement promotive channel to attract potential audiences.

Other kind of promotion channel to theatre providers. It is publicity , it is difference to public relations or even advertisement. Although, publicity seems a tool of public relations, but the aim of publicity is to create awareness through the media by placing news information about on organization, such as the theatre provider and its enteretainment performance service providers. The major characteristic of publicity that differentiates it from other marketing tools is tat it is not be paid for by an identified . Otherwise, public relation serves mainly the create an understanding between the theatre entertainment performance service provider and its publics (audiences) , thereby creating awareness for its entertainment performances. A public relations campaign takes various forms. It can be through the theatre provider's sponsorship of program beneficial to the audiences or through the award of scholarships is through any music, song, movie, dance, life show etc. different kinds of entertainment performance projects that attempt to build better understanding between the theatre provider and its audiences . So, having taken a critical look of advertising , publicity and public relations will be the important part of communication or promotion tools in theatre industry.

The aim of every well communication methods to manage theatre , which can have much influential to impact audiences' emotions and their entertainment performance consumption desires to the theatre provider. However, the marketing communication channel of advertisement has weakness to theatre entertainment performance service provider, it depends on most printing spending times, as the printing of posters. This is not out of place because it has its role to play in marketing , but the fact, the electronic media advertisement does not need to print papers . Hence, this kind of promotion method will bring more economic benefit to the theatre service and entertainment performance service provider both.

A theatre entertainment performance provider will have different departments to cooperate efficiently in order to produces theatrical performances, such as drama, dance, movie, opera, music , life show etc. entertainment performances. So, one department of any theatre provider needs t make use of advertisement to create awareness about their any entertainment performance to any let audiences (entertainment consumers)to know. So, efficient communication is necessary between the theatre provider's departments.

In conclusion, in theatre entertainment performance industry, any theatre entertainment performance providers expect their every movie, song, music, dance, life show etc. art performances can be promoted from advertisement , publicity and public relations marketing tools successfully. In efficient marketing communication strategy is an essential facility available to every internal departments in order to strengthened cooperation how to design every advertisement, publicity and public relations channel to let every different kinds of art performance to be promoted to attract potential audiences to choose to admission tickets to watch or listen the theatre entertainment performances more easily.

4.6 Marketing communication function in clothing industry

What marketing communication tools are the most useful or suitable to clothing industry? I shall indicate mailings, telephones and personal interview marketing communication tools to reflect the useful function to clothing industry.

Nowadays, clothing fashion products total change of market had changed rapidly and its new trends which has changed too rapidly suddenly after 1950 year. So, the different brands of clothing products need to be designed unique to satisfy clothing buyer individual specific groups and / or lifestyle needs. Also, the different design of fashion clothing products can represent every different clothing brand's image. However, sufficient promotion will be one influential tool to help the clothing product designer to promote is any kinds of cloths to let potential cloth clients to know or help it to build familiar brand image in the clothing market.

Good fashion design can challenge conventional views. It should be recognized their consumers very in the conservation they have towards fashion styles and also speed and readiness with which change their opinions. So, an efficient marketing communication strategy will let the clothing products designer to gather whose cloth clients' opinions in order to predict how they ought to decide to design preferable fashion styles choices more easily in order to let it follow general clothing product buyers' fashion styles design choice to design many attractive fashion styles of clothing products to let them to persuade them to choose to buy its clothing products more easily.

So, clothing buyer personal interviews or telephone individual contact or posting mail questionnaire enquiry promotion method will be one suitable to be used to promote in clothing industry. Because these market communication tools can gather any clothing buyer individual opinions in order to help the designers to understand. Then, clothing market can enhance the clothing design creating process and marketing personnel appreciate that within the fashion industry design can lead as well as respond to customer requirements progress can be made more easily. Thus, telephone, clothing buyers individual interview or questionnaire researching or post mailing questionnaire researching marketing communication tools will have effort to help the brand of clothing designer to predict how to design its cloths styles which can persuade potential clothing buyers to choose to buy its brands of any kinds of styles clothing products to wear more easily in possible. So, any clothing designer needs have a fashion marketing concept and have demonstrated equal concern for design, customers and profits. Thus, any clothing designer's marketing communication strategy needs to concentrate on fashion design promotion. It means that when the clothing product provider has good different styles of clothing design products and the suitable place(clothing stores) and the reasonable price setting , then it needs have good promotion (communication tool) e.g. telephone, TV, radio, magazine etc. to its target audience (e.g. child, young , old age , expensive or cheap clothing product buyer group, traditional design or popular fashion design style clothing product preference cloth buyers.

Nowadays, clothing communication medias include broadcast advertisement (TV and radio), print advertisement (magazines and newspapers), brochures and booklets, posters and packaging, motion pictures, directories, display signs and symbols and logos. Any one of these communication medias can help any clothing designers to build its brand to be familiar to let its potential buyers to know. Instead of these communication media, sales promotion is usually connect closely with in clothing industry. The basic types of sales promotion include coupons, sampling , refunds and rebates, premiums and gifts , games, contexts. Any of these sale promotion will be one good communication method to persuade the clothing buyers to choose to attempt to buy the brand of any styles of clothing products to wear more easily. The primary communication objectives of these tools usually are: stimulation of clothing consume trials, increase of rebuy rates and reward of loyal customers in order to fasten he selling process. However, promotion should bot be used as an ongoing program, as it is only a short term taste. Otherwise, it can easily lower the price of the brand of clothing products.

The another kind communication tool is public relations, it means to build good relations with the clothing provider to public by obtaining favorable publicity. The " publics" are a the clothing provider's stakeholder, such as suppliers, employees, customers or governments, public relations activities can include press relationships, sponsorships, product placement, events management and crisis management. So, good public relation can help the clothing provider to build good brand image to let clothing buyers to know or familiar.

The final communication media is personal selling. It involves face-to-face activities, the clothing provider's clothing sales representatives of a particular clothing brand with the aim to inform, persuade or remind a clothing buyer to take appropriate action. The most common examples of personal selling include: sales presentations, sales meetings, incentive programs, samples, fairs and trade shows.

Consequently, any one of above communication medias will bring benefits to the clothing provider. However, the clothing provider needs to spend time and human resource and promotion communication tools resource to implement one effective marketing communication stragtegy to help its hw to promote its clothing products to let its potential clients to be familiar its different kinds of styles cloths more attractively. So, it seems on efficient communiation strategy can help the clothing provider to raise its different kinds of clothing design to attract its clothing buyers' consideration more easily.

CHAPTER FIVE

MAIN BARRIERS INFLUENCE ARTIFICIAL INTELLIGENCE CONSUMER BEHAVIORAL PREDICTION

In future, it is possible that these barriers will influence how to apply (AI technology) to predict consumer behavior in success. The barriers may include: Lacking of a (AI) digital data gathering vision and strategy, lacking of efficient workforce readiness, (AI) technology constraints., non reaching (AI) consumer behavioral prediction mature stage, time and money and resource constraints, law and regulations prohibition to develop (AI) consumer behavioral prediction bug data gather technology.

However, the recommendation of solutions to attack the barriers to influence artificial intelligence consumer behavioral prediction not success, it may include gaining employee buy in to participate and develop (AI) consumer behavioral prediction technology, making customer experience to a concern (AI) big data gather questionnaire investigation, providing compensation, training to employees in order to achieve (AI) consumer behavioral big data questionnaire investigation research digital technological goals and strategy, task senior leaders manage any (AI) digital big data gather technology changes, putting policies and (AI) big data gather digital technology in place to support a fully remote, flexible workforce in any (AI) digital big data gather questionnaires research projects, teaching all employees how to code/understand (AI) big data gather consumer behavioral prediction software development, appointing a chief (AI) officer to manage any (AI) big data gather customer behavioral prediction projects and automate everything and encourage customers to attempt experience to self-service and (AI) big data gather questionnaire research to earn beneficial consumption aim after they gave feedback to any (AI) digital questionnaire researches. So, in the future, the (AI) digital big data questionnaire researches can include these industries surveyed, such as automat m financial services, public healthcare, private healthcare, technology, telecoms, insurance, life sciences, manufacturing, media and entertainment , oil and gas, retail and consumer products etc.

Hence, in the future, any of these industries can attempt to apply (AI) digital big data gather technology to predict how and why consumer behaviors will change in order to avoid reducing consumer number threat occurrence.

5.1 (AI) digital data gather technology predicts food consumer behavior's main barriers

What are the main barriers to food industry? When the food manufacturer applies (AI) big data gather technology to predict food consumer behavior? The barriers include that the food manufacturer / provider needs to decide whether when the right time is applied to the right (AI) digital big data prediction tool channel to find the right food consumers to be chose to full food consumption satisfactory questionnaires, how to gather multi-class food consumption classifiers on real-world food consumers transactional data from the food sale domain consistently to show the critical numbers of different kinds of food items at which the predictive performance most accurate? So, any food manufacturer / provider's advanced in (AI) digital data gather warehousing and management technologies can provide that opportunities for food business to enhance long term relationship with the food providers' clients.

However, food industry's (AI) digital data gather aims to improve food customer product targeting, increase food customer loyalty and food purchase probability to the food supplier. To effective identify, understand and satisfy the needs of their food customers, the food suppliers need to develop the right (AI) digital questionnaire questions and find the right food customers to fill every right questions from every digital questionnaire at the right time through the right channel.

Above of all these, they will be the barriers when one food supplier expects its (AI) digital data gather questionnaires which can conclude the most accurate prediction concerns any kinds of consumer food product choices. So, such as (AI) digital data prediction model, it is needed to incorporate into the food market segmentation, food customer targeting, and food challenging decisions with the goal of maximizing the total food customer lifetime. For example, (AI) big data gather transaction data is reasonable and accurate for building predictive models. Transaction data can be electronically collected and readily made available for data mining in lot quantity at minimum extra costs.

Suggestion to apply (AI) prototypes of food customer profiles method to predict food customer behavioral changes. Prototypes of food customer profiles mean to be extracted from the discovered bins and multi-class classifies models are built using those prototypes. The learned models can than be used to predict the class of food customer profiles (e.g. restaurants, school canteens, supermarkets etc. food suppliers) based on their food purchases. The approach is validated on the case study of a food retail and food service company operating in food and beverages market.

So, a food customer profile, it is a description (AI) data gather tool will record every of food customer using available information, which help in understanding their background and food consumption behavior. (AI) data gather tool can well develop every food customer profile, every food customer data is essential in food market analysis as they aid food suppliers in saving time and money by highlighting the real potential food consumers whose needs are to be met rather a range of individuals.

So, (AI) data gather tool can record every food consumer profile and every can be factual or behavioral food consumption. A factual food customer profile consists of a set of characteristics for (AI) big data gather record, e.g. demographic information , such as food customer name, gender, birth date, when a behavioral food customer profile consists of what the food customer is actually doing and is usually derived from (AI) digital transactional data gather record.

So, (AI) big data gather record's every behavioral food consumer profile can be much stronger predictor of the future food supplier consumption choice actions of a food customer. Furthermore, the food supplier's (AI) all past food consumer information that make up demographically based all past food customer profiles are expensive to acquire when the information for the food suppliers' past every food consumer food consumption behaviors. Moreover, food customer profile can be recorded to make real food purchase every time. So, when the food supplier finds the past food consumer's record from (AI) big data gather tool. Then, it can make more accurate judgement whether past every food consumer has chose to buy its food to eat how many times every year in order to predict whether its every past food consumer will choose to buy its foods how many times next year in possible. If the next year, its every past food consumer's consumption time to the food supplier is less than its current year consumption time. Then, the food supplier can attempt to find whether what factors to cause the past food consumers do not choose to increase food purchase times to the food supplier in current year. The factors may be possible be the food supplier's food prices are raised, food quality or taste is poor, the different kinds of food supply is shortage challenge, the food supplier's consumers lose confidence to buy the food supplier's foods to eat, when (AI) big data gather tool can help the food suppliers to find what the main factors to cause the past food consumer number to be reduced in order to predict how future food consumers' behavioral changes will be influenced from the food supplier's competitors in the global food supply market. Hence, (AI) big data gather tool can help every food supplier to attempt to find what the main factors to case the food supplier's food consumer number to be reduced as well as it can help the food supplier to predict how the food supplier's potential (past not every purchase its any food consumers) food consumers who can be persuaded to choose to buy its foods to eat by learning what the main factors influence.

In conclusion, (AI) big data gather tool can help the food supplier to find what the main factors influence its past food consumers do not choose to buy its food more times or find what the main factors will attract its potential (not ever buying its foods consumes) food consumers to choose to buy the food supplier's foods to eat.

5.2 The challenges of (AI) big data gather shaping
the future of retail for consumer industries

Another challenge of (AI) big data gather is that how to shape the consumer behavior to let business owner to feel or know or predict. It means that how it express it's conclusion or opinion for every consumer behavior after it had gather all big data in any data gather period, e.g. three months, half year or one year consumer shopping model data gather period.

Because every kind of industry, consumers will continue to demand price and quality change , with a wide range of convenient fulfilment options among of different kinds of products or services supply. Overall, the (AI) big data gather procedure gives opinion concerns every time retail experience will become more exciting, simple and convenient, depending on the consumer's ever-changing needs. So, I believe that (AI) big data gather every conclusion or result will be different, due to consumer's price and quality demand will often change to every kind of product or service supply in retail industry. So, how to shape (AI) big data gathering's analytical conclusion or result more clear. I shall recommend organizations need to build great understanding of and a stronger connection to increasingly empowered consumers before they plan and implement how to apply (AI) big data gather tool to predict consumer behavior as below:

Firstly, (AI) is empowered by technology, the consumer is redefining value. The traditional measures of cost, choice and convenience are still relevant, but not control and experience are also important. Globally, consumers have access to more than 2 billion different products choice by a wide range of traditional competitors and dynamic new entrants, all experimenting with new business models and methods of client engagement.

As choice increases, loyalty becomes more difficult familiarity and the consumer becomes more empowered. Businesses will have no choice and constantly innovate and disrupt themselves by meeting new technologies of high standards and expectations of consumers. So, (AI) data gather tool will need to follow different target group of consumers' needs to follow their different kinds of product design or style choice preferable to gather data in order to conclude the different target groups of consumer behavior to give opinion more clear and accurate to let businessmen to understand more clear how its customers' behavioral choice trend in the future half month, even to two years period.

Secondly, businessmen need to adopt changing technologies rapidly. Technology will be the key driver of this retail industry. Industry participants will only success if they have a clear prediction to focus on how to using technology to increase the value added to consumers. They must , however, do so will I realistic assessment of their costs and benefits. Hence, (AI) big data gather technological tools will need to design to help them to gather data efficiently by these ways, such as the internet of things (IOT), artificial intelligence (AI) machine learning, augmented reality (AR)/virtual reality (VR), digital traceability. So, future (AI) big data gather tool are predicted to be most influential customer behavioral positive emotion changing tool for retail , due to their widespread applications , ability to drive efficiencies and impact on labor in order to impact consumer behavior changing effort from negative emotion to positive.

Thirdly, (AI) big data gather tool is an advanced data science of consumer behavior predictive tool. Businesses will have to bring the journey from simply collecting consumer data to using it to scale and systematize enhanced decision making across the entire value chain. When focused on their business goals, industry players should not lose sight of the impact that future capabilities and transformative business models may have on society.

However, (AI) big data gather tool will encounter these challenges when any business plans and implements to apply it to predict consumer behavior in retail industry. The challenges include that as below:

1. The high cost and difficulty of implementing new technologies . The (AI) big data gather tool needs capital and capabilities to be designed to implement to be applied to different retail industry users. so, expensive barriers to innovation, an organization and the skillsets of its people to support a new design of (AI) big data gather tool, highly digital technology may be required.

2. Slow pace of cultural change. Consumers need to adapt or accept (AI) new technology consumption model in the traditional retail industry. The rate of change is outpacing the ability of businesses to keep up. (AI) big data gather tool needs to be designed to adopt in new or evolved business model requires, in most cases, a new level of customer behavioral predictive machine operation will impact to influence any retail businesses' consumer behavioral changes at a minimum, an organization's structure, capabilities, culture and decision making. If the retail business expects to apply (AI) big data gather tool to predict how to change its consumer behaviors and how their consumption behaviors will tend to change in order to achieve to change their positive emotion from negative emotion before they choose to buy its product or consume its service in success.

5.3 Challenge to using (AI) neural networks to predict customer behavior from big data gather tool

(AI) big data gather tool will encounter the challenge: How can predict customer behavior be represented as sequential data describing the interactions of the customer with a company or an (AI) data gather system through the time, e.g. these interactions are items that the customer purchase or views ? So, every customer data gather , (AI) needs to spend time to analyze how and why to cause whose consumption behavioral choice. It is too difficult matter or judgement for (AI) learning. So, (AI) needs to spend time to learn how to analyze every customer's shopping behavior or actin in order to gather all different consumers' past shopping action information in order to help business owners to predict future its potential customer shopping behavior how to change more clear and accurate prediction.

(AI) big data gather tool needs to learn to know that how to judge every customer interaction likes purchases over time can be represented with sequential data. Sequential data has the main property that the order of the information is important. Many (AI) machine learning models are not suited for sequential data, as they consider each input sample independent from previous ones. Therefore, at the end of the sequence, (AI) big data gather learn machines need to keep in their internal state of every customer purchase data, kind of product or service, price , whole year consumption times form all previous inputs, making them suitable for this type of data.

However, consumer behavior can be represented as sequential data describing the interactions through the time. Examples of these interactions are the items that the user purchases or views. Therefore, the history of interactions can be modeled as sequential data, which has the particular trial that an incorporate a temporal aspect. For example, if a user buys a new mobile phone, who might purchase accessories for this mobile phone in the near future or it the user buys a electronic book or paper book , he might be interested in books by the same author. Therefore, to make accurate predictions is important to model this temporal aspect correctly. To solve this predictive challenge of consumers to buy the product. One count the number of purchased products of a particular category in the last N days, or the number of days since the last purchase.

So, the (AI) big data gather designers can attempt to produce a feature vector which can be fed into a machine learning algorithm such as " logistic regression" will be the main feature and function to any (AI) big data gather machine to learn how to apply this " logistic regression" function or feature to predict any customer behavioral change for any product purchase or service consumption to the (AI) predictive consumer behavioral business users. Every different kinds of product purchases or services consumption will be needed to design " different model of logistic regression" in order to follow the kind of business to predict whose consumer purchase or service consumption behavior to predict more accurate.

5.4 Challenges of artificial intelligence, algorithms technology and machine learning impact to consumption market

Markets have played a key role in providing individuals and businesses with the opportunity to gain from trade. If (AI) big data gather tool can predict how to change potential customer behavior in success. The challenges to consumers will face that the overall market consumption model will be dominated by the businessmen only. So, it is not fair or reasonable to consumers, because (AI) big data gather tool has controlled or dominated all consumers' minds and it has predicted how and why every kind of product or service consumer shopping model or consumption behaviors how will change.

It will bring this questions: How can market designers learn the characteristics necessary to set optimal, or at least better, reserve prices after they had gather all data to conclude the analytical results of their consumers behaviors how will change? How can market designers better learn the environments of their markets?

In response to these challenges, artificial intelligence (AI) and machine learning are important tools for market design. For example, retailers and marketplaces , such as eBay, Amazon and many others are mining their vast amounts of data to identity patterns that help them create better shopping experiences for their clients and increase the efficiency of their markets. By having better prediction tools, these and their companies can predict and better manage dynamic consumption market environments. The improved forecasting that (AI) and machine learning algorithms provide help marketplaces and retailers better anticipate consumer demand and producer supply as well as help target products and activities for segmented markets. Another important application of (AI) 's strength in improving forecasting to help markets operate more efficiently is in electricity market example. To operate efficiently, electricity marker makers can attempt to apply (AI) machine learning tool to follow every household family electricity consumers' past electricity consumption record to judge (predict) how it will be every family's forecasting in the year.

An inaccurate forecast in the electricity supply and demand that can dramatically affect electricity market bad supply outcomes causing high variance in electricity charge prices or worse, blackouts. By better predicting every family's electricity demand and supply , electricity market makers can better allocate power generation to the most efficient power sources and maintain a more reasonable electricity stable charge market. Any example is design market, the application of (AI) algorithms to market design are already widespread and diverse.

(AI) algorithms technology , it is a safe that (AI) will play a growing role in the design and implementation of market over a wide range of applications. The challenges are that how (AI) can guarantee accurate to predict when and why and how consumer behavioral changes to any retail industries. In fact, retailers will need to discover the value that (AI) can bring to what benefits to influence their customer behaviors.

In the future, (AI) will bring their benefits to influence customers to build positive emotions to any retailers in these aspects as below:

1. Future (AI) big data gather tool will be an area of compute science that deals with giving machines , the ability to seem like they have human intelligence. In short, it is the power of a machine to copy intelligent human behavior. For example, machine learning algorithms are being integrated into analytics and customer relationship management platforms to uncover information on how to better serve customers, chat bots have been incorporated into websites to provide immediate service to customers.

2. (AI) adoption continue to rise with chat bots taking the lead. Due to increasing ease of deployment , instant availability and improved quality, chat bots will become more and more common to manage customer service queries and to make intelligent purchase recommendations. Also, retailers can engage this kind of technology to answer continue questions and supplement customer support with chat-based shopping experience. So, (AI) and declines personalized, customized and localized experiences to customers.

(AI) will be applied across the entire retail product and service cycle, firm manufacturing to post-sale customer service interactions. Hence, retailers can use (AI) to its fullest potential will be also to influence purchases in the moment and anticipate future purchases, guiding shoppers towards the right products in a regular and highly personalized manner.

3. (AI) technology can rise the conscious customers. Customers are demanding an increased interest in the ethical practice of the brands they buy from. Todays, customers have a well-developed sense of what is solely intended to

drive sales. This has lead to a rise in consumers ho make values based judgements about what to buy and where to shop. These consumers believe their purchase habits have an impact on the world. To win customers, retailers need have good conscious to predict consumers' desire. Future, (AI) data gather technology will be a good consumer behavior predictive tool to predict about for years will now become customer expectations and will have drastically changed the path to purchase. So, (AI) data gather tool is the predictive consumer expectations tool on every interaction, they have these brands.

4. Future (AI) can be impacted to influence consumer behaviors by its potential to free up time, enhance, quality, and enhance personalization. The industries include: Healthcare industry can apply (AI) to support diagnosis by detecting variations in patient data, early identification of potential pandemics, imaging diagnostics; automat industry can apply (AI) to autonomous fleets to ride sharing, semi-autonomous features, such as driver assist, engine monitoring and predictive, autonomous maintenance; financial service industry can apply (AI) to design the suitable personalized financial planning, fraud detection and anti-money laundering and automation of customer operation; transportation and logistics industry can apply (AI) to autonomous trucking and delivery, traffic control and reduced congestion and enhanced security; technology, media and telecommunications industry can apply (AI) to search media, and recommendation, customized content creation and personalized marketing and advertising to attract retailers to promote; retail and consumer industry can apply (AI) to design personalized production, anticipating customer demand, , inventory and delivery management; energy industry can apply (AI) to read and record smart metering , more efficient grid operation and storage and predictive maintenance; manufacturing industry can apply (AI) to enhance monitoring and auto-correction of processes, supply chain and production optimization and on-demand production.

Hence, future (AI) technology will impact consumer technology when any retailers apply it to assist its manufacturing processes or product sale or service provision processes to satisfy consumers' needs, it means that it can help any retailers to influence positive emotion to consumers in their whole sale or consumption or purchase processes

5. (AI) and machine learning technologies make it possible to capture, process, and inter data on a massive scale effectively , then any human being could ever do. For example, Criteo's creative technology " Kinetic design" can apply insights from 1.2 billion monthly impressions to select and optimize individual branded advertisements components according to each shopper's preference and intent. This ensures more personalization and visually inspiring on brand ads. resulting in up to 12% more sales for (AI) technology advertiser clients.

Moreover, advertisers can now engage and inspire shoppers on a more personal level, rendering custom ads. it real-time for every impression. So, designer continues to learn from each design's success to make ads. more and more effective over time. Furthermore, brands are increasingly using paid search on retail sites to draw attention to their products on the crowded online shelf, e.g. Google shopping is a key growth area's more users are engaging with shopping ads. and across the globe. Google shopping has become essential to retailers' marketing strategies, but is a difficult channel to apply its tool to be promoted effectively . Thus, future (AI) and machine -learning technologies can dramatically improve digital commerce performance application to apply (AI) and machine learning to digital consumer. So, future (AI) technology can be applied to digital commerce aspect, it will fall into the categories of pattern recognition, classification, prediction and consumer behavior.

In conclusion, the benefits of using (AI) in digital commerce include: improved efficiency in discovering the relationships between datasets over traditional methods, which require complex modeling and coding, improved accuracy for clearly defined processes that involve a lot of manual processing, ability to deal with a large emotion of data with many attributes, for example: customer behavior data, multichannel and multi-device data , complex product data and fraud detection, more accurate analysis, such as customer segmentation sentiment, analysis and personalization frequent algorithum refreshes, such as several times a day, to capture the changes in customer and market behavior.

Finally, however, a lot of types predictive consumption behavior around (AI), in particulars that driven by vendors claiming their solutions are (AI) , ready and can deliver dramatic improvements over existing technologies. Application leaders for digital commerce can be misled into believing that (AI) can solve all their problems, which is not true for n in-depth discussion of the (AI) consumers and market behavioral predictive tool and machine -learning technologies bot. Thus, (AI) prediction consumer behavioral technology can give beneficial quantitative analysis for forecasting in business and market especially in consumer behavior and in the consumer decision-making process (consumer choice model) more effectively and efficiently.

Is Artificial Intelligent the most effective and accurate consumer behavioral tool?

Is (AI) the best and the most effective and accurate consumer behavioral prediction tool to compare other kinds of consumer behavioral prediction tools? Nowadays, retailing competitions are serious businessmen often find different kinds of methods to attempt to predict consumer changes. The consumer behavioral predictive methods can include as these below methods, instead of (AI) big data gathering tool.

Firstly, statistics is the popular mathematic method, it applies auto-regression, liner regression, structural equation modelling, logistic regression statistic techniques to be used to predict consumer behaviors. Secondly, it is classification method, it sis a support vector machine to assist businessmen to make consumer behavioral prediction, it also includes decision making tress diagram technique. Thirdly, it is rule mining method, it is algorithm, market base analytic etc. business marketing concept analytical tool, it also includes graph mining technique tool. Next, it is psychological prediction model tool, it is psychology prediction model too, it is a kind of psychological method to predict consumer behaviors. Finally, it is the most updated and potential artificial neural network (ANN) machine tool, it gathered big data, then it will carry on analyzing and applies psychological method to conclude the most accurate and reasonable solutions to give recommendation to businesses to predict when and how and why their consumer behaviors will change. So, it is one owned human mind's machine and owned psychological and analytical efforts to replace humans to make any judgement in order to make the most accurate predictive behavioral changes for consumers, instead of the traditional marketing concept and psychological and mathematic methods to predict consumer behavior, (AI) big data gathering tool will be another new tool.

What are the advantages of (AI) tool to be used to predict consumer behaviors as well as what are the different between it and other traditional consumer behavioral predictive tools? I shall explain as below:

Firstly, as above all case studies are explained to (AI) questionnaire design method benefit, I believe (AI) big data gathering tool can be applied to help human to analyze and design any the suitable valid questions to enquire any kinds of business consumers in order to gather the most meaning and useful opinions to conclude the most accurate consumer behavioral prediction for every questionnaire. So, future (AI)'s analytical effort and decision making effort most be exceed above human's judgement efforts. So, future (AI) can help human to design the most useful and meaning different kinds of valid questionnaire (survey) questions as well as assist humans to analyze and make accurate decision making and conclusions to give opinions to help businessmen to predict when consumer behaviors will change and how their consumption behaviors will change to influence their businesses in order to help them to make any efficient and effective and accurate solutions to avoid consumer number to be decreased and the most important benefit is that it can give opinions to help businessmen to explain why (what the factors) cause their consumer behaviors change suddenly. It will be human's efforts can not achieve to exceed (AI)'s efforts in the future.

Secondly, (AI) can make artificial machine judgement and analytical effort, without human misleading or unfair or unreasonable judgement. So, it can make more fair and reasonable and accurate conclusion to give opinions to predict when, how and why consumer behaviors will change suddenly to the kind of business in customer model building process and evaluating the results of customer relationship management –related investment more accurate.

Furthermore, (AI) big data gathering tool will help businesses to improve the success rate of acquiring customers, increasing sales and establishing competitiveness. (AI) big data gathering tool can give opinions how to build customer loyalty to be positive emotion impact and it can find solutions to avoid every client's negative emotion causes to bring complaints behavior to the businessman's product or service. For example, Telecom industry and aggressive research has been conducted in this by applying various data mining techniques to avoid long distance phone call users' complaints. If gathered any long distance phone call users' past complaint data to record what are their general complaint issues. Then, (AI) tool will analyze all these past complaint issues to conclude and give opinions to let Telecom knows whether which aspects encounter challenge that Telecom needs to improve it's long distance phone call services or functions in order to satisfy Telecom's long distance phone call users' needs for long term. After Telecom attempted to improve its services and/ or functions from (AI) opinions and solution methods, when it fell it's long distance phone call users have positive emotions to satisfy its service performance and function performance. Then, it can prove (AI) tool's opinions and solutions are useful. The consequence is that their complain numbers will be decreased and they won't plan to choose another long distance phone call telephone service company to replace Telecom long distance phone call service more easily.

So, (AI) big data gathering tool can concentrate on finding focus on components of customer relationship management method and datasets more accurate and efficient and effective than human's data gathering and analytical effort. It implies (AI) big data gathering tool has unique more efficient and effective and accurate dataset gathering and analytical and judgement and decision making effort, it is human can not achieve.

Thirdly, (AI) big data gathering tool has much customer loyalty predictive effort. It's effort is more easily subsequently selected, reviewed and classified to compare human's gathering data effort in whole data gathering and analytical process.

In (AI) big data gathering process, (AI) can organize whole big data gathering process and technique more easily in short time. It will include these four steps. The first stage is that customer identification stage, customer identification also known as acquisition has to do with targeting the population , who are most likely to become customer segmentation. So, (AI) can help different kinds of businesses to gather their competitors' consumer purchase behavior data in short time, it is human can not achieve. The second stage is that customer attraction stage, after (AI) maker has been segmented for the business when it has ensured to gather the businessman's global competitors' consumers data. Then it analyze these all data to find solutions / methods to give the best opinions to the organizations how to achieve the direct effort and resources into attracting the target customer segments. The third stage is that customer retention, it can be defined as the activity that an organization undertakes in order to reduce customer defections. TO be successful, customer retention starts with the first contact on organization has with a customer and continues throughout the entire lifetime of a relationship involves loyalty programs, one to one marketing and complaints management. SO, (AI) can consist the business to find the best or the most reasonable , efficient , effective solutions or methods and it will conclude all these solutions to find the most reasonable and useful opinions to achieve to the aim to help the business to reduce customer complain numbers and help the business to build confident loyalty relationship between it and its clients. SO, (AI)'s analytical effort and decision making effort can be more accurate than human's analytical effort and decision making effort. IT can achieve it's consumer behavioral predictive aim more accurate and efficient and effective in the shortest time to compare human.

Fourthly, (AI) big data gathering tool can design more accurate dataset program for questionnaire (survey) to compare human's questionnaire (survey) effort. It means that (AI) can spend less time to research and make judgement what are the most reasonable and meaning questions for different kinds of businesses' needs. This includes data conduction a questionnaire, survey or interview of the individual or environment researched, public data repository: This includes commercially available public data; organizational data; this contains data collected from an organizational database, organizational information system. For example, their website log details etc. It also includes company transactional data, data purchased from a company.

For example, one vehicle sale company expects to research all global vehicle sale companies' past the different kinds of vehicle styles, design sale number data, the different kinds of vehicle style, design sale price data, every country's vehicle consumer number to the vehicle purchase number data to the vehicle company in short time. (AI) big data gathering tool can help the vehicle sale company to gather all any one for these global vehicle sale competitors' past data in the short time. It is human effort, who can not achieve this efficient, effective and accurate data gathering aim for this vehicle sale company. Even, when (AI) had gathered all global it's vehicle competitors' past sale data, (AI) can make more accurate analytical and judgement and decision making effort to design different kinds of questionnaire (survey) questions to prepare to enquire it's different target segmentation vehicle potential clients in order to predict what are their needs to choose to buy any vehicles from the vehicle company. SO, (AI) tool can conclude more accurate conclusions and give the most reasonable and useful opinions to let the vehicle company to know in order to predict what are it's potential vehicle buyer's needs and manufacture the suitable vehicle styles or designs to raise their vehicle purchase desires.

Fifthly, (AI) tool is only one perfect tool for big data gathering in order to achieve accurate results and increased profit. What is (AI) big data gathering mean? The term " big data" gathering describes the accumulation and analytical of vast amounts of information, but big data is much more than a big amount of data. It is also the ability to extract meaning to sort through big volumes of numbers and find the hidden patterns, unexpected correlations and surprising connections that can be used in different industries like medical field, security and protection field or marketing that adopt " big data driven" decision making enjoy significantly greater productivity than those that do not. So, the benefits of (AI) is given to the company by using big data repaid complexity of implementation projects and hence project risks, when accelerating time to value. It is why that human's gathering effort can not replace (A I) data gathering effort.

All analysing above benefits to (AI) big data benefits to any organizations, it brief this question: How can (AI)apply big data gathering and analysing to predict when and how any why consumer behavior will change suddenly? The purchase decision making process is consumers reducing purchase choice behaviors.

Consumers are being considered pure rational beings (consumer tried only to satisfy self-interest). Hence, due to future (AI) owns human's psychological , analytical , emotional predictive, purchasing decision making effort.

(A I) will be assumed to sees one customer how who will make purchase decisions. So, after the (AI) gathered all data concerns the find of business's past customer segmentation purchase activities, e.g. age, sex,. Income level, the product's style sale number, the product price variable sale etc. different kinds complex data.

It can make more accurate psychological and analytical effort to predict when the business's consumer behaviors will change as behaviors will change as well as find what reasons their consumption behaviors will change and how trend of their consumer behaviors will change more accurate. For example, today there are a lot of industries that use big data: healthcare (treatment) becoming personalized and patient centric and predictive analysis are used to prevent diseases for example Angelina Jolie under event a predictive double mastectomy after learning she had 87% rich to developing breast cancer, sports (by using sensors data are collected from players during a game in order to improve their playing schemes), weather(more than 60 years of global weather analysis are used to predict the risk of future extreme events), logistics (smart tucks and smart species, agriculture (monitoring weather and soil conditions for optimum point of harvesting).

Consequently, due to the evolving consumer demands, and the ever growing digitization, the world is digitally transforming which means the new technologies are needed to be used and driven significant business improvement. So, such as why (AI) tool will be our future main predictive tool to help businesses to predict when, how and why their potential customer behavioral will change. Big data is one of the our channels through digital transformation is made, together with cloud, mobile and networks. The challenges for digital transforming and therefore using A I big data gathering tool as main technology are: digital proficiency, legacy systems, security and jobs becoming absolute.

In the future, big data can use data from text to picture , sounds, movies, music satellite coordinates or any other type of input or output data that type of input or output data that came from different influential aspect. It is cloud solutions, bring big data will be for predict insight driven by business strategy, new product strategies and new consumer relationship, predictive consumer behavioral strategy. Using the right data in the right business decision will mean smart decisions, new opportunities and utimately a big competitive advantage. Hence (AI) big data gathering tool is different is that (AI) can be one depth in-memory database function, it can make real-time data analytics that provide meaningful information in short time, it is also the visualization tool , such as SAP Lumira, allow this exploration and understanding of the data, and ultimately supports the decision making process. All above these features, which will be human's data gathering effort who won't exceed (AI) big data gathering effort. Hence, future (AI)big data gathering will be the best choice to assist businesses to predict consumer behaviors successfully.

Reference

Adrian, P. (2012). Introduction to marketing theory & practice,
3 rd edition, London: Oxford press.

Ajzen, I (1991). The theory of planned behavior. Organizational behavior and human decision processes, 50(2), 179-211. doi: 10.1016/0749.5978 (91) 90020-7.

Alba, Joseph W. and J. Wesley Hutchinson (1987). " Dimensions Of Consumer Expertise", Journal of consumer research, 13 March, 411-454.

Bailey, L., Mokhtarian, P.L. Little, A. (2008). The broader Connection Between Public Transportation, Energy Conservation And Greenhouse Gas Reduction, Report Prepared As Part Of TCRP Project J-11/Tasks Transit Cooperative Research Program, Transportation Research Board Submitted To American Public Transportation Association in
http://www.apta.com/research/into/online/land_use.cfmi, accessed 17 April 2008.

Baucer, R,"Consumer Bhavior As Risk Taking , In Risk Taking And Information handling In Consumer Behavior", D. Coxceds Harvard University Press, Cambridge, Mass 1976.

Biederman, P. (2008). Travel and tourism, Pearson Prentice Hall, New Jersey.

Bogers, R. P., Brug, J. Van Assema, P., & Dagnetie, P.C.
(2004) , Explaining fruit and vegetable consumption: The theory of planned behavior and misconception of personal intake level. Appetite, 42,157-166.

Bolton, Ruth N. (1998), " A Dynamic Model Of The Duration Of The Customer's Relationship With A Continuous Service Provider: The Role Of Satisfaction", Marketing Science, 17 (1), 45-65.

B.Shiv and A. Fedorikhin, " Heart And Min In Conflict: The Interplay Of affect And Cognition In Consumer Decision Making", J. Consumer Res., vol. 26, pp. 278-292, Dec. 1999.

Brown, K.W., Ryan, R.M. Reswell , J.D. (2007). Mindfulness: Theoretical Foundatins And Evidence For Its Salutary Effects. Psychological Inquiry, 18, 211-237.

Burke, R.R. : Behavioral effects of digital signage, J. Advertising Res. 49(2), 180-185 (2009).

Cant, M., Brink , A. & Brijall, S., Consumer behavior, Cape Town, South Africa: Juta, 2006.

Conner, M. & Abraham, C. (2001). Conscientiousness and the theory of planned behavior: Toward a more complete model of the antecedents of intention and behavior. Social psychology bulletin, 27, 1547-1561.

Cooper C. Mallon, K, Leadbetter S, Pollack L, Peipins (2005) , cancer internet search activity on a major search engine, United States 2001 to 2003, J Med Internet Res. 7(3): e36.

Cope, R. R. Cope and H. Davis (2008). Disney's virtual Queues: A strategic opportunity to co-brand services ? Journal of Business & economics research, vol. 6 no10, 13-20.

Cornelia, B.F. (1999) Rural development news, the North Central Regional Center For Rural Development vol. no 24 , IOWA.

Couper, M.P. J. Blair and T. Triplet (1999). A Comparison Of Mail And E-mail For a Survey Of Employees In USA Statistical Agencies. Journal Of Official Statistics, 15, 39-56.

David J. Nowak & Gordon M. Melsler (2016) " Air quality effects of urban trees and parks." National recreation and park association, USA.

Data monitor (2008). The proctor and gamble company. Retrieved Nov. 15 2009 from http://www.datamonitor.com/

De Hollander, A. E. M., J.M. Melse, Elebret & P. G.N. Kramers (1999), " An Aggregate public health indicator to represent the impact of multiple environmental exposures" Epidemiology: 606-617.

De Visser, R.O., & McDonnell, E.J. (2013). " Man points": Masculine capital and young men's health. Health psychology, 32(1), 5-14. doi:10. 1037/a0029045.

Dunn, J & A Neumsister (2002). Knowledge management in the Information age. E. business review, Fall , 37-45. Jounral of service, spring 2011, vol. 4, no1, De Grovte (2009).

Dyer, D., F. Dalzell & R. Olegario (2004). Rising tide. Lessons learned from 165 years of brand building at Procter and Gamble. Boston, MA: Havard Business School Press.

Eysenbach G (2006) Infodemiology: Tracking flu- related searches on the web for syndromic surveillance. American Medical Informatics Associaion Annual Symposium Proceedings , Curran Associates, Red Hook, NY, pp. 244-248.

Ettredge M, Gerdes, J. Karuga , G (2005) Using web- based search data to predict macro-economic statistics. Commun ACM 48: 87-92.

Felce, D. and Perry, J. (1995). Quality of life: A contribution to its definition and measurement, vol. 16, no.1 pp: 51-74.

Feldman, Jack M. And John G. Lynch Jr. (1988), "Self-
Generated Validity And Other Effects Of Measurement On Belife, Attitude, Intention And Behavior", Journal of applied psychology, 73(3),421-35.

Fiese, M, Hofmann, W., & Wanke, M (2009). The impulsive consumer. Predicting consumer behavior with implicit reaction time measurement. In M. Wanke (ed.) Social psychology of consumer behavior (pp.335-364). New York, NY: Psychology press.

Fitzsimons, Gavan, J. And Vicki G. Morwitz (1996), " The Effect Of Measuring Intent On Brand-Level
Purchase Behavior", Journal of consumer research, 23 (1), 1-11.

Hallerman , D. (2008) video Advertising Online: Spending And Pricing , New York. E-Marketer.

Harriet Griffey. (2010) The art of concentration, enhance focus, Reduce, stress and achieve move. Macmillan publishers ltd,Basinastoke and Oxford, London UK.

Helleman, D. (2008) Video Advertising Online: Spending And Pricing , New York, E-Marketer.

Hensen, C. (2003). Kreuzfahrtourismus.www.christoph- hensen.de/Facharbeit.pdf.

Huang, H.I. (2012). An empirical analysis of the strategic Management of competitive advantage: a case study of higher technical and vocational education in Taiwan (Doctoral dissertation,
Victoria University).

Jamieson, Linda F. And Frank M. Bass (1989), " Adjusting Stated Intention Measures To Predict Trial Purchase Of New Products: A Comparison Of Models And Methods," Journal of marketing research, 26 (August), 336-45.

Korea Ministry Of Environment. Public Organizations spend 2.2 Trillon Korean Won To Purchase green Products in 2014; Ministry Of Environment: Sejoung, Korea, 2015.

Kremers, S.P. J., De Bruijn, G.J., droomers, M., Van Lenthe, F. J., & Brug, J. (2005). Environmental interventions for selected dietary behaviors in adults. In J. Brug & F. J. Van Lenthe (eds.) , Environmental determinants and interventions for physical activity, nutrition and smoking: A review pp. 282-315. Rotterdam: Erasmus Medical Center.

Lee, D.; Kim, M. ; Lee, J. adoption of green electricity policies: Investigating the role of environmental attitudes via big data-driven search-queries. Energy policy 2016. 90, 187-201.

Lee, Terrence, " Tech in Asia-connecting Asia's startup system " Tech. in Asia- connecting Asia's startup ecosystem, N.p.,4 July 2016.

Los Angeles Country Department Of public Health (2016), Country Health Ranking Model, Retrieved From www.countryhealthrankgings.org/our-approach. USA.

Mayne, Lonnie. " Evolve of die in the age of the consumer". Entrepreneur, N.P. , 16 Apr. 2014. web of Oct. 2016.

McGregor, S.L. T., & Goldsmith, E.B. (1998). Expanding our understanding of quality of life, standard of living and well-being. Journal of family and consumer science, 90(2), 2-6, 22.

McMichael, A.J. M. Mckee, J. Shkolnikov and T. Valkanen (2004), " Morality trends and setbacks, global convergence or divergence?", Lancet 363, 1155-1159.

Melse, J.M. & A.E. M. De Hollander (2001). " Human Health And The Environment", background document for the OECD Environmental Outlook, OECD, Paris.

Moschis, George p. & Roy, L. Moore (1979), " Decision making among the young. A socialization perspective " Journal of consumer research , 6 (September).

Mulligan, M. Banerjee, T & Thomas, N. (2008) ,European Paid Content And Activity Forecast, (2008 to 2013), Jupiter Research.

Peter, J., Ryan, M, M, " An Investigation Of Perceived Risk At The Brand Level, " Journal of marketing research, 13 May 1976, pp. 184-188.

Pieters, R., & Wedel, M. (2007). Goal Control Of Visual Attention To Advertising: The Yarbus Implication. Journal Of Consumer Research, 34, 224-233 (August).

Parasuaman, and Leonard L. Berry (1985), " Problems And Strategies In Sevices Marketing", Journal of marketing, 49 (Spring), 33-46.

Priesnitz, W. (2007) Counting Our Food Miles. Natural Life, 1 July.

R.C. Oliver, " When is consumer loyalty?" J.Marketing vol. 63, pp.33-44.1999.

Reggiani, A . (ed). 1998, accessibility, trade and locational behavior, Ashgate publishing ltd, England.
Rushe, D. (2013) " The 10 best paid CEO in America". The Guardian , 22 Oct, (online). Available at:
http://www.theguardian.com/business/2013/Oct22/best-paid-chief-executives-america (Accessed: 3 May 2014).

Spiekermann and Wegener (2007), update of selected potential accessibility indicators. Final report, urban and regional research (S&W), RRG spatial planning and geoinformation. ESPON. Available online
at http:// <www.espon.eu/mmp/online/website/ contentprojects/947/1297/file_2724/ espon_accessibility_update-2006-fr_070207.pdf>, accessed on 1 July 2009.

Starbucks (2014) Our company available at http:// www. starbucks.com/about- us/company-information (accessed: 3 May 2014).

Shostack, G. Lynn (1984), " Designing Services That Deliver", Harvard Business Review, 62 (January-February), 133-9.

Shostack, G. Lynn (1985), " Planning The Service Encounter ,in the service encounter" , John A. Czepiel, Michael R. Solomon, and Carol F. Suprenant, eds. New York: Lexington Books, 243-54.

Shostack, G. Lynn (1987), " Service Positioning Through, Structural Change", Journal of marketing, 51 (Janurary), 34-43.

Soloman, Michael R. (1985), "Packaging The Service Provider", Service Industries Journal , 5(1), 64-71.

Stevens, C.W. (1980), "K-MartStores Try New Look To Invite More Spending" The Wall Street Journal, Nov. 26, 29-35.

Sullivan, Nicholas P(2007). You can hear me now: How Micro loans and cell phones are connecting the world, San Francisco, CA: John Wilsey & Sans, 2007.

T. Ambler, A. Ioannides, And S. Rose, " Brand s On The Brain : Neuroimages Of Advertising ", Business Strategy rev., vol. 11, 3. pp. 17-30. 2000.

Westbrook, Robert A. (1980), " Intrapersonal affective influences on consumer satisfaction with products, " Journal of consumer research , 7 (June) 49-54.

Wiig, k.(1993). Knowledge management foundations: Thinking About thinking. How people and organizations create, represent and use knowledge vol.1 , of knowledge management series schema press: Arlington, TX.

World Health Organization (2003). Diet, nutrition and the prevention of Chronic diseases report of a joint WHO/FAO. expert consultation. Geneva: World Health Organization.

Wysocki, B. (1979), " Sight, Smell, Sound: They're all arms in retailer's arsenal" The Wall Street Journal, Nov. 17, 1979. 1-35.

Yale Center For Environmental Law And Policy (2006). Environmental Performance Index. Data available on-line at http://epi.yale.edu

CHAPTER SIX

(AI) -DRIVEN INDUSTRY DEVELOPMENT

(AI) - driven automation industry development how to influence work nature change

On positive benefit hand, it is possible that (AI) -driven automation industry will create wealth and expand economy growth to any countries, but it will be accompanied by changed in the skills that workers need to learn, if the low skill workers expect to avoid unemployment threat when (AI) technology can replace their jobs in future one day. Thus, it is possible that (AI) technology will also bring negative influence to cause low skill worker unemployment challenge in the applied (AI) technology countries.

For the low skill worker unemploment reason, it is because that one of main ways that technology increases productivity is by decreasing the number of labor hours needed to create a unit of output. It implies (AI) technology will influence low educated and low skillful labor number to be decreased (reduction employment number).

Will (AI) bring benefits to the employers? In contrast, technological change tended to work in a different direction throughout the nowadays. The advance of computer and the internet raised the relative productivity of higher skilled workers. So, routine-intensive occupations that focused on predictable tasks disappearance, such as switch board, operators, filming checkers, travel agents and assembling line workers etc. were particularly replaced by new technologies. However, today, it may be challenging to predict exactly which jobs will be most immediately affected by (AI) driven-automation. The reason is because (AI) is not a single technology, but rather a collection of technologies that are felt unevenly through the economy to influence job changing both negatively and positively.

In positively view point, (AI) driven-automation will make many workers more productive and increase demand for certain skills. Consequently, new jobs are likely to be directly create in areas , such as the development and supervision of (AI) as well as indirectly created in a range of areas throughout the economy as higher incomes lead to expanded demand. So, (AI) will bring macro economy advantages in possible.

Otherwise, in negatively view point, many traditional human needed (demand) skillful jobs will be threatened by automation are highly concentrated among lower-paid, lower-skilled and less -educated workers. It means automation will cause pressure on demand for this group, pressure and employment, if (AI) can replace the low skilled and less educated workers' jobs. Thus, (AI) will have negative influence to impact on the labor market.

(AI) capabilities will enable automation of some tasks that have long required human labor. Can (AI) replace some simple human jobs? If (AI) can replace some simple human jobs, then it is possible to cause unemployment if employers applied (AI) machines to replace the low skill workers to do their simple jobs in future one day. For example, advances in robotics are expanding machines' abilities to interact with and sharp the physical world. Combined , (AI) and robotics will give rise to smarter machines that can perform more sophisticated functions than ever before and brings more advantages that humans have exercised. This will permit automation of many tasks now performed by human workers and could change the shape of the labor market and human activity. It depends on whether employers choose to reduce all worker numbers to be replaced by (AI) machines or employers choose to apply (AI) machines to assist the low skillful workers to work more efficient or raise performance and productivities. If future employers apply (AI) machines to assist workers to raise performance and efficiency, then the unemployment challenge won't cause, due to the number of worker won't reduce. But if employers decide to unemploy all low skillful workers and they are replaced by (AI) machines, then the unemployment challenge will cause in possible.

1.2 How (AI) influences labor market

Today, it may be challenging to predict exactly which jobs will be most immediately affected by (AI)-driven automation. Because (AI) is not a single technology, but rather a collection of technologies that are applied to specific tasks.

Some specific predictions are possible based on the current (AI) technology. For example, driving jobs and house cleaning jobs, bank counter service jobs, telephone enquiry service operators. Restaurant cooking jobs, simple accounting record service jobs etc. that require relatively less education to perform. Advancements in computer vision and related technologies have made the feasibility of fully appear more likely, potentially displacing some workers in driving-dominant professions. Seemingly similar robot, for which the operational tasks is less specific of navigating to a specific destination when following a set of given rules and preserving safety.

In the future, the effects of (AI) on the labor market in the decade ahead will continue the trend toward skill-biased change that computerization and communication innovations have driven in recent decades. Thus, some human driving occupation will be disappeared or replaced by (AI) automation driven. For example, bus drivers, light truck or delivery services drivers, heavy and tractor-trailer truck drivers, school drivers, tax drivers, travel bus drivers.

However, (AI) technology could enable some workers to focus time on other job responsibilities, boosting their productivity, and actually raised wage growth among those still holding the reshaped jobs. For example, salespeople, who currently spend a considerable amount of time driving could find themselves able to do other work when a car drives them from place to place, or inspectors and appraisers could fill out paperwork, when their car drives itself. This (AI) -driven technology should make these workers more productive, with (AI) -driven technology serving as a complement, not a substitute. New jobs will also likely be created, both in existing occupations cheaper transportation costs with lower prices and increase demand for products and all the related occupations, such as service and fulfillment, and in new occupations not currently foreseeable.

What kind of jobs will be created by (AI) technology? Predicting future job growth is extremely difficult, due to it depends on technologies or substitute for existing today as well as they may complement or substitute for existing human skills and jobs. However, (AI) will also lead to substantial indirect job creation to the degree it raises productivity and wages, it may also lead to higher consumption that would support additional jobs from high-end draft production to restaurant and retail. The future(AI) " augmented intelligence", the technology's role is as assisting and expanding the productivity of individuals rather than replacing human work. Thus, based on the biased-technical change framework, demand for labor will likely increase the most in the areas where humans complement (AI) automation technologies. For example, (AI) technology , such as IBM's Watson may improve early detection of some cancers or other illnesses, but a human healthcare professional is needed to work with patients to understand and translate patients' symptoms, inform patients of treatment options, and guide patients through treatment plans. Shipping companies may also partner workers who pick up and deliver products over the last feet with (AI) enabled autonomous vehicles that move workers efficiently from site to site. In such cases, (AI) augments what a human is able to do and allows individuals to either be move effective in their specially task or to operate on a larger scale. Thus, it seems (AI) technology will also create new jobs, raise productivities and workers' efficiencies.

Redefining management in
the workforce of artificial intelligence

2.1 Change management

(AI) will influence office administrative efficieny to be raised. In the future, due to artificial intelligence influences to some kind of human jobs nature. So, the kind of human jobs of management methods will also need to change to adapt the artificial intelligence technology input to their organizations. It will cause challenges for every executive and manager if who won't have effort to manage their teams how to apply artificial intelligence technology to work efficiently and easily. For example, division of labor will change among humans and machines will increase. Thus, companies will have to adapt their training performance and talent strategies how to emphasize on work that how to make human judgment and skills and experimentation. Thus, (IA)'s greatest impact will be on administrative coordination and control tasks, such as scheduling , resource allocation.

In fact, mangers will encounter this challenges: How to apply human experience and expertise to judge critical business decisions and practices when the information available is insufficient to suggest a successful course of action? Due to this kind of work will require new skills and mindsets. I shall indicate these change management methods to adapt (AI) technology. Such as: administration and routine tasks, scheduling , allocation of resources and reporting will fall within the intelligence machines, responsibilities that have long been reserved for humans. For example, a typical store manager or a lead nurse at a nursing home most constantly arrange shift schedules, accounting for staff members' absences owing to illness, vacation time or sudden departures.

Thus, the managers need to learn how to arrange new division of labor within the organizations after (AI) technology had been implemented to the organization. Artificial intelligence is currently influencing into once considered exclusive to humans: assessing and acting on human emotions and personality traits. The influences to managers need to change their strategies to adapt (AI) technology implements include such as below:

Firstly, managers need to spend the bulk of their time on coordination and control tasks from intelligent system implements. Their time spending on these major three aspects from impact of intelligent system: coordinate and control, solve problems and collaborate and people and community , strategy and innovation three aspects. Thus (AI) will influence managers need to change their judgment method to teach whose teams how to adapt the (AI) system operations in any organizations.

Secondly, (AI) will influence top, middle and low level management needs to change to adapt the (AI) technology operations to any owned (AI) technology organizations in the future. Intelligent machines must be trained in context. Just like humans , on-the-job training is a requirement for such machines because they typically arrive with only very general capabilities. To get the most from (AI), managers at all levels must participate in the instructional experience and in the learning process and provides managers' familiarity with such systems on these aspects, e.g. How the system works and generate advice, how the system has a proven track record , how the system provides convincing explanations , how the system can make simple rule- based decisions.

Thirdly, managers need to learn how to make judgment more accurate (AI) systems assistance. Although (AI) will invariably take on more routine work and even augment human decision-making, it won't judgment work, the application of human experience and expertise to critical business decisions when the information available is insufficient to suggest a successful course of action or reliable enough to suggest an obvious course of action. For a sense of the nature of judgment work, consider big data marketing and sales analytics. Such analytics often provide insights that can inform promotional campaigns, including predicting which promotions will generate desired sales brand further into the future, marketing executives need use judgment, combining analytics with their own and others' insight and experience.

The application of experience and expertise to critical business decisions and practice represents the real value of human judgment. But, when artificial intelligent machines are implemented to any organizations to assist the low, middle and top level management to make any business judgment. These forms of judgment work that managers can gather data interpretation, idea development more absolute from (AI) machine assistance. Thus, why these level management executives need to learn how to apply (AI) machines to help them to make any business judgment more accurate.

2.2 How (AI) influences organizational change

Consequently creative and social intelligence will be in even greater demand as (AI) makes in management and the workforce. This development will represent a long term trend in labor markets , one characterized by intensifying demand and reward for social skills with a growing desire for creative capabilities, managers will seek to fashion of ideas and hypotheses from inside and outside of the enterprise to shape solutions to their most pressing business problems. Thus, (AI) will influence overall organizational team members who have chance to participate any decision to make more accurate business judgment.

Many managers mistakenly view judgment work as only an individual discipline, failing to appreciate that it can also involve decide interpersonal and organizational practices. In more complex settings, judgment is typically a collective outcome of individuals' and teams' diverse perspectives, insights and experiences. And often , the resulting choices are better informed than decisions that an individual would have arrived at on his or her own.

Thus, when any organizations apply (AI) technology to assist managers to gather data and ideas to make any judgment. In these cases, organizations can create the conditions for effective collective judgment by establishing structures , such as " shadow advisory boards" that prompt managers and employees to source and synthesize multiple perspectives. Thus, a traditional organization (firm) might freshen its thinking is t put together a shadow advisory board, comprised of young, digital people who can apply (AI) machine assistance to make judgment work more accurate whether related to people development, problem-solving or strategizing and innovating for considerable degrees of creative and social intelligence.

Thus, on the one hand, (AI) technology machine augmentation and automation can give these advantages to human (organization managers) , e.g. developing people and community, solving problems and collaborating, coordinating and controlling work, shaping strategy and leading innovation. Besides, on the other hand, the next generation managers need have these individual attitude to treat intelligent machines to be as colleagues.

When, judgment is a human skill, intelligent machines can accelerate human learning that supports it, assisting in data -driven simulations, scenarios and search and discovery activities. Focuses on judgment work, some decisions require insight beyond what data can tell them. This is the sweet sport for human judgment, the application of experience and expertise to critical business decisions and practices. Thus, managers will also need to find ways to learn how to use digital (AI) technologies to tap into the knowledge and judgment of partners, customer external stakeholders and role models in other industries after the (AI) machine had been implemented to the organization.

Future works change:

Automation, employment

and productivity

3.1 How (AI) influences employment

Human future " micro to macro" industry trends will be affected business strategy and public policy by (AI) technology. In the future (AI) technology will influence those six themes: productivity and growth, natural resources, labor markets, the evolution of global financial markets, the economic impact of technology and innovation and urbanization. However, (AI) technology will bring economic benefits of tackling gender inequality, a new global competition, Chinese innovation and digital globalization.

Nowadays, advances in robotics artificial intelligence, and machine learning are in a new age of automation, as machines match or outperform human performance in a development to any countries. For example, automation of activities can enable businesses to improve performance by reducing errors and improving quality and speed, and in some cases achieving outcomes that go beyond human capabilities. For example, some research indicated automation could raise productivity growth globally by 0.8 to 1.4 % annually; more than 2,000 work activities across 800 occupations. When less than 5% of all occupations can be automated using demonstrated technologies about 60% of all occupations have at least 30% of constituent activities that could be automated. Many occupations will change that will be automated away: Activities most susceptible to automation involve physical activities, in highly structured and predictable environments, as well as the collection and processing of data. They are most prevalent in manufacturing , accommodation and food service and retail trade and include some middle-skill jobs. For example, such as natural language processing is a key factor. Beyond technical feasibility, the cost of technology competition with labor including skills and supply and demand dynamics, performance benefits including and beyond labor cost savings, and social and regulatory acceptance will be affected by (AI) automation technology. Thus, (AI) automation will impact to influence global employment in those aspects as below:

Firstly, assuming that people are displaced by automation will find other employment. The anticipated shift in the activities in the labor force is of a similar order as the long-term shift away from agriculture and decreases in manufacturing share of employment. Both of manufacturing and agriculture industries which would be accompanied by the creation of new types of work not foreseen at the time.

Secondly, for business, the performance benefits of automation are relatively clear. Thus, the businessmen have opportunities for their micro economies to benefits from the productivity growth potential and macro economies to benefit to encourage continued progress and innovation , investment and market incentives. At the same time, employers must innovate policies to help workers and institutions adapt to the impact on employment.

This will likely include rethinking education and training, income support and safety nets , as well as support for those dislocated, when employees need to leave themselves homes to move to other cities to learn new (AI) automation works. Thus, individuals in the workplace will need to engage move comprehensively with machines as part of their everyday activities, and acquire new skills that will be in demand in the new automation age. Consequently , the scale of shifts in the labor force over many decades that automation technologies can be a similar order to the long -term technology -enables shifts in the developed countries' workforces away from agriculture in the 21 th century. Those shifts did not result in long-term mass unemployment because they were accompanied by the creation of new types of work not foreseen at the time. However, human will still be needed in the workforce when the total productivity gains are caused by (AI) technology.

3.2 What occupations will be influenced by (AI) technology.

In the future, scientists predict that these occupations will be influenced by (AI) technology mostly. They include : retail salespeople, food and beverage service workers, language or translation teachers, health practitioners. Since these work activities have a more relevant occupations are made up of a range of activities with different potential for (AI) automation . For example, a retail salesperson will spend more time interacting with customers, stocking shelves , or ringing up sales. Each of these activities is distinct and requires different capabilities to perform successfully.

Thus, these job activities have similar simple control characteristics. Simple activities include greet customers, answer questions about products and services, clean and maintain work areas, demonstrate product feature process sales and transactions. All these activities can have similar simple activities in order to (AI) machines can be learn how to do these activities from (AI) technology . For example, the capability perception includes sensory perception, cognitive capabilities, such as retrieving automation, recognizing known patterns(supervised learning), logical reasoning problem solving.

Thus, (AI) machine is such human, which has feeling and emotion, such as social and emotional sensing, judgement reasoning methods, natural language understanding and physical capabilities, such as mobility , navigation, gross motor skill, fine motor skills. It seems that the future, (AI) human invents machines which will have these human characteristics to do human similar behavioral job duties more easily and efficiently. It implies these above human occupations will be replaced by (AI) human invention machines in the future. Due to (AI) creation, it is possible to cause unemployment number of these above workers will increase because (AI) machines can do their similar job behavioral activities.

Consequently, employers won't need to employ many of these skillful labor. Otherwise, they can buy less number (AI) machines to attempt to do whose job activities more easily and efficiently. So, it seems (AI) machines will have more high work performance to replace these occupation workers' work performance. Finally, these occupation worker unemployment number will only increase when the (AI) machines had been invented to achieve to do their work behavioral activities absolutely success in the future.

3.3 Whether (A) technology machine labor
will replace human worker more or assist
human worker more

There is no single agreed definition of a robot how outcome of a task that is completed without human intervention. When some definitions require the task to be completed by a physical machine moves and respond to its environment, other definitions use the term robot in connection with tasks completed by software , without physical embodiment.

However, to answer the question : Whether (AI) technology machine labor will replace human worker more or assist human worker more. I shall indicate some examples to let readers to judge whether (AI) technology can create new jobs or reduce old jobs.

Firstly, I shall explain what (AI) function is. (AI) is a service robot that performs useful tasks for humans or equipment excluding industrial automation application . Thus, the classification of a robot into industrial robot or service robot is done according to its intended application. It is also a personal service robot or a service robot for personal used for a non commercial task, usually by lay persons . Examples are domestic servant robot, and pet exercising robot. It is also a professional service robot or a service robot for professional used for a commercial task, usually operated by a properly trained operator. Examples, are cleaning robot for public places, delivery robot in offices or hospitals, fire-fighting robot, rehabilitation robot and surgery robot in hospitals. Thus, these functions will be future (AI) application to our daily life necessaries or business necessaries.

However, some authors agree (AI) will bring negative outcomes of automation, due to raise competiveness, reduce human job nature. Otherwise, other authors argue (AI) will bring positive outcomes of automation, due to raise productivities, job creation, assist humans work.

On the positive outcome hand, robots can increase productivity . This is particularly important for small-to medium sized businesses both are in developed and developing countries economies. It also enables large companies to increase their competitiveness through faster product development and delivery. Increased use of robot is also enabling companies in high cost countries to re shore, or bring back to their domestic base parts of the supply chain that will have previously outsourced to sources of cheaper labor. Currently , the greater threat to employment is not a automation, but an inability to remain competitive. Automation has led overall to an increase in labor demand and positive impact on wages. The reason is that the middle-income/middle-skilled jobs have reduced as a proportion of overall contribution to employment and earnings leading to fears of increasing income inequality, the skills range within the middle income bracket is large. Thus, robots are driving an increase in demand for workers at the higher -skilled and with a positive impact on wages. This issue is how to enable middle-income earners in the lower-income range to unskilled or retain. Finally, the (AI) positive impact supporter who argue the future will be robots and humans can work together.

However, on the negative outcome hand, robots can substitute labor activities, but don't replace jobs. They believe that less than 10% of jobs are fully automatable. Increasingly , robots are used to complement and augment labor activities, the net impact on jobs and the quality of work is positive. Automation can provide the opportunity for humans to focus on higher-skilled, higher-quality and higher-paid tasks. Robots can improve productivity when they are applied to tasks that which perform more efficiently and to a higher and more consistent level of quality than humans. For example, increased productivity is enabling some firms, such as Whirlpool, Caterpillar and Ford Motors company in the US restructure their supply chains, bringing back parts of the manufacturing process to the country of origin. Thus, productivity gains due to robotics and automation are important not just at the company level, but also for build industry and nation competitiveness.

I suppose that productivity can be raised. What are the impacts of robots on employment? Firstly, the main focus of development has been on personal entertainment, which does not drive worker productivity (manufacturing production). When the internet (information and communication technology (ICT)) innovation. This is borne and by findings that manufacturing productivity, which has been driven by innovations in automation rather than consumer technologies, has government strongly than productivity in the services sectors of the economy in most nature economies. It seems (AI) automation will create many jobs in internet communication entertainment game industry. For example, many young people like to use internet to play any electronic games from computer or mobile at home or outside home conveniently. Thus, (AI) automation will increase demand to be invented to any new entertainment game from internet channel. It will need to employ many (AI) entertainment game inventors to create many automation entertainment games. Thus, (AI) automation in internet entertainment game industry will need human (AI) entertainment game inventors to invent the knowledge-based capital of (AI) automation entertainment games. The (AI) entertainment game inventors will need own research and development skills, form specific skills, organizational know-how skills, databased knowledge, design and various forms of intellectual property to do these (AI) automation entertainment game invention occupations in the future.

International Federation Of Robotics(2016) indicated that China will be as a major robotics manufacturer and user of robots, benefiting from jobs created by robot manufacturing and productivity gains from robot use. Chins had sold of robots to any one single market every year since 2017 year. The Chinese government has included a focus on robotics in its 10 year strategy. In order to achieve its target of a robot density of 150 units per 10, 000 workers by 2020 year. Thus, Chinese companies will have to install around 650,000 new industrial robots between 2016 to 2020 year, 2.5 times more than installed globally in 2015 year.

Hence, China (AI) manufacturing industry will need to employ many workers . It implies (AI) manufacturing industry will create many new occupations in China. Also, ministry of economy, trade and industry (2015) also showed that Japan currently has the largest stock of industrial robots in operations, primarily in the automation industry. Driven by a rapidly aging population and low productivity rates, the Japanese government has sights on a 20-fold increase in the use of robots in the non-manufacturing sector and a three-fold growth rate of labor productivity in the service sector both by 2020 year. Thus, it also implies Japan will need many robots to be provide to service industry. Due to robots will provide to serve any businessmen's clients. Thus, it is possible that the service workers won't be dismissed as well as it is depended on the serving job nature to decide whether Japan's service workers can still serve to their employer when the service (AI) robots are applied to whose employers.

Consequently, it seems that (AI) can create employment, Ministry of economy, trade and industry (2015) showed that such as China will develop the major (AI) automation manufacturing industry. The (AI) employers will need to employ many workers to manufacture any these different kinds of (AI) robots to satisfy China or overseas individual or business buyers needs. But, (AI) can also cause unemployment to the low skillful service workers. Such as if Japan some service businesses choose to buy any (AI) service robots to replace their service staffs to serve their clients. It is possible that the service staffs will be dismissed, due to (AI) robots can do such as their same service job duties to achieve better service performance.

Thus, today, it is increasingly common for people to use robots in various situations at home and in retail stores, hotels and hospitals these service industries. Robots are classified into server types based on their functionality (service and utility robots or those designed to communicate with humans) and appearance (humanoid robots or mechanical robots). The type of robot, to which each country allocated particular importance in the advance of robotics, reflects the sense of values and preferences of its population. Thus, if the country has high population needs to use robots, then they will influence either more new jobs creation or more old job loss in the country's (AI) manufacturing or (AI) service industries both. For example, Japan respondents often associate the term " robot " with humanoid robots that can communicate with human and they have a high level of familiarity with robot. The US has the highest level of robot utilization at home and in retail stores with its people being the most enthusiastic about the future use of robots. Germany shows a strong tendency to consider robots for industrial purposes and its people feel strong effort to the presence of robots in their households.

In conclusion, to judge whether how (AI) will influence the country's employment to be better or worse. It will depend on the country home buyers (users) or business buyers (users) how to use (AI) for their daily needs. If the country , such as US retail stores need to use (AI) , it will have possible to reduce some or many retail service workers. Even, if the country , such as Japan has many home users need to use (AI) , it will not influence the employment market. Otherwise, it will raise (AI) salespeople numbers. Even, if the country, such as Germany and China will have many (AI) manufacturers, then it will create many (AI) manufacturing occupations for these (AI) manufactory workers. Consequently, (AI) robots manufacturing and service needs will have positive or negative impact to any country's employment. It will depend on the (AI) service provision and service workers' job nature as well as the manufacturing workers of (AI) knowledge level to decide their employment chance in their country's employment market.

3.4 Robot society advantages and disadvantage

Our technology had been developing to (AI) artificial intelligent or robot social development stage. When one day, global has many jobs are replaced to do by robots, e.g. cleaners, cookers, drivers, customer servicers, hotel food service delivers etc. general social simple tasks are replaced by robots. Can our societies are dominated by robots? Is it possible that our societies can be dominated when global has manyjobs are replaced by robots? Why can our societies be dominated when many robots can replace humans to do ourselves future simple jobs , even complex jobs? Can robots bring positive or negative social impacts when we have many jobs can be replaced by robots? I shall attempt to explain whether our future societies will be become to improve better or worse when we have many jobs are replaced by robots as below:

In traditional societies,when our societies had not invented this kind thing of (AI) or robot technological tools to serve our societies or help us to do any simple or even complex tasks in our societies. Our social labour number needs must be increased, e.g. restaurant cookers, shopping center cleaners, shopping center customer service, hotel food delivery, office or appartment securities, warehouse logistic transport, even public transport tool drivers. They may be repplaced by robots easily in future.

Hence, in our future societies, many simple jobs or low skillful level of occupations may be replaced by robots, when robots can be taught to learn how to do our simple tasks in our future societies. Hence, when any one of these low skillful occupations can be replaced by robots. In our societies, these low skillful or low educational level workers their employers' need number may be influenced to reduce. Otherwise, due to robots have these advantages, e.g. non negative emotion, laze, 24 working hours, or none sleeping need, none hungry feeling or none lunch or dinner time need, none salary expenditure. So, future our societies need robots to replace human to do any low educational level or low skillful level of simple jobs number will be influenced by robot advantages factor. The question concerns whether robots may dominate ourfuture societies if our future has many simple jobs can be replaced by robots.

How can robots dominate our future social tasks to do ? Can they bring advantages if they can dominate to do our social future many simple jobs? Firstly, we need to ensure that when our societies has many simple tasks which can be replaced by robots, then our societies will have many simple jobs or occupations may be influenced to disappear due to many employers will decide to dismiss their low skillful or low educational level stafs, they will buy many robots to help them to do these simple jobs in their organizations, e.g. hotels can apply robots to do food delivery tasks or cleaning rooms tasks, or hotel securities tasks, or opening hotel front doore tasks or the hotel restaurent can apply robots to do cooking tasks or food delivery tasks , shopping centers can apply robots to do customer service tasks. So, it seems that any hotels may apply robots to replace human workers to do any hotel service simple jobs. It means that hotels may dismiss many low skillful workers and robots can replace these service workers to do their tasks easily. Also, any organizational warehouses departments can apply robots to do goods transport or delivery tasks, so it seems that any warehouse logistic worker transport tasks which can be replaced by robots. SO, future there are many warehouses do not need logistic transport workers, they can be replaced by robots. Consequently, many of these organizational tasks will be replaced by robots or these low skillful or low educational level occupations will be influenced to disappear by robots.

IN fact, in long term, any organizations spend to robots expenditure which must lower to compare to spend to employees wages expenditure. Instead of reducing organizational cost beneficial aspect, robots will not have laze, hungry, sleeping need, demand increasing wage needs or negative emotional feeling to compare human workers. So, in future, general social simple tasks may be influenced to reduced or replaced by robots. When many organizations begin to accept robots to replace human to do simple tasks to serve themselves organizations. It seesm that robots will have effort to dominate our future organizational efficiency or future organizational service performance, because many employers begin to evaluate performance to robots more than humen workers, they begin to compare whether robots can perform better or worse to compare human workers, when robots may be applied to work with human workers in teams together. For example, when the hotel applies robots to help hotel room cleaners to clean all hotel rooms. The hotel needs to evaluate whether the robot's cleaning effort is better or worse to compare human hotel cleaners or the restaurants needs to apply robots to cooperate to human cookers to cook any kinds of foods to give clients to eat in team together. The restaurant needs to evaluate whether the robots can cook better taste of foods to let clients to feel to eat or worse taste of foods to let clients to feel to eat. So, this restaurant needs to evaluate whether these cooking robots their cooking skills are better or worse to compare human cookers.

Hence, future many business organizations need to evaluate robots their service performance or working skills or efficiency to in order to decide whether their task efforts are better or worse to compare human employees. If they believe that robots their tasks efforts or service performance or efficiencies are improved or better to compare humans, then robots have possible to be applied to dominated the overall team tasks in any organizations. So, it seems that future robots have possible to dominate any organizational overall team tasks if the organization feels robots their performances are improved to be better to compare human workers.

On consequence, when the organization has many simple tasks are dominated by robots, the organization won't need to employ many managers to supervise employees' tasks any teams, because many of simple tasksa re replaced to do by robots. Organizations only need to spend time to arrange whether the robot needs how to do the kind of simple tasks e.g. for hotel organizations example, it only needs to teach robots how to clean the hotel room, how to deliver foods to client rooms, how to cook good taste of foods in the hotel restaurant kitchen. Because robots do not need to be supervise, they only need to taught to learn how to do the kind of simple tasks, when they can be taught to learn how to do the kind of simple tasks to serve the organization. Then, they follow the "computer program instruction" to finish the kind of simple tasks daily. Consequently, the organization must not need to employ managers or supervisors to supervise robot performance or working behaviors in order to evaluate their performance whether they can satisfy client individual need or organizational internal working needs. So, it means that instead of the low skillful workers, robots may replace managers or supervisors positions in any organizations, when they can be applied to dominate to do the organization;s overall any simple tasks to achieve the best performance daily.

Reference

International Federation Of Robotics, 2016. IFR press release world robotics report. IFR, org . 29 Sept. Accessed Feb. 01, 2017. http://www.ifr.org/news/ifr-press-release/world-robitics report -2016-8321.

Ministry of economy, trade and industry, Japan, 2015, Japan's robot strategy. Ministry of economy, trade and industry.

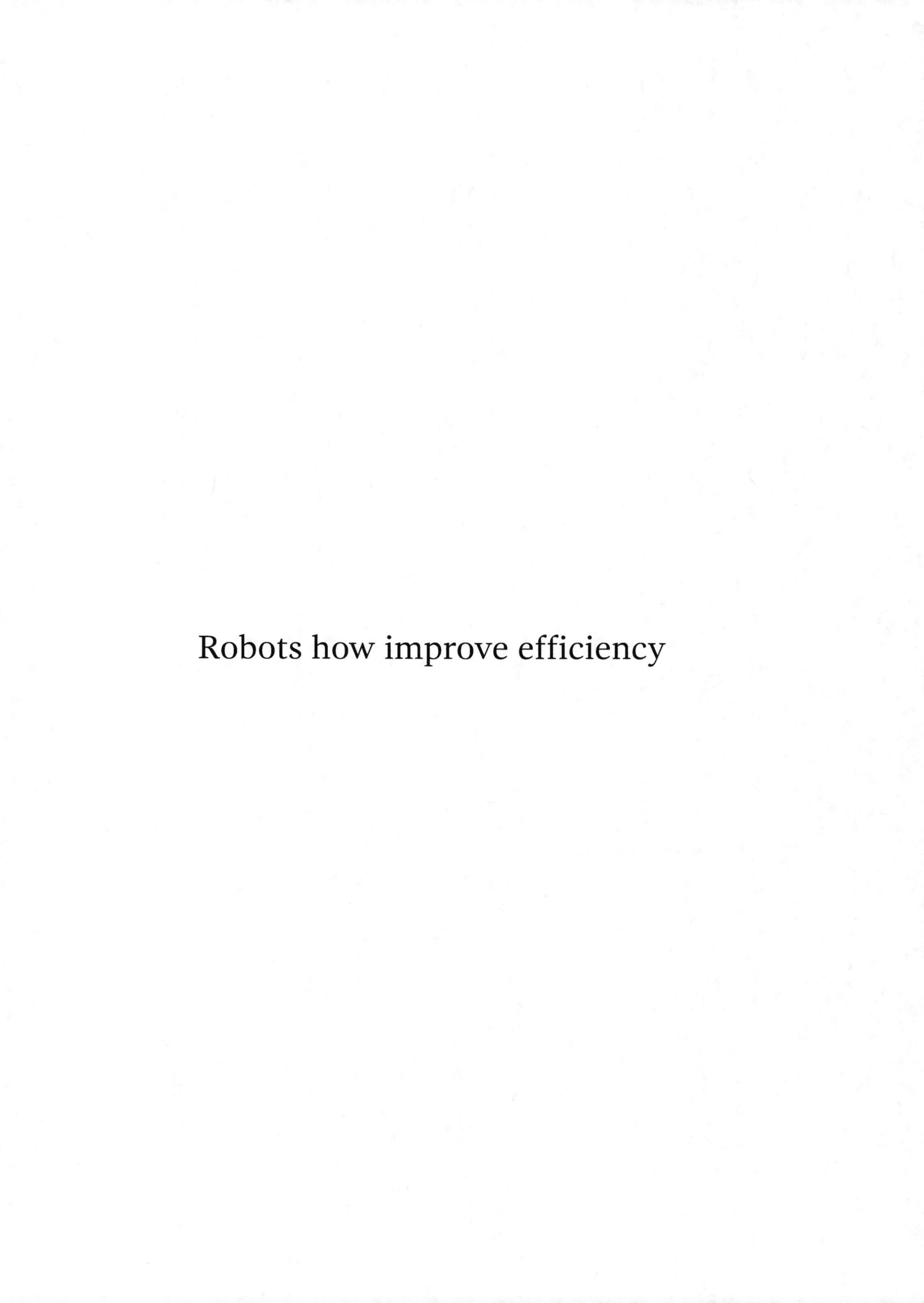

Robots how improve efficiency

CHAPTER SEVEN

HOW ROBOTS SHORTEN WORKING AND CONSUMPTION DECISION TIME

Employee psychological rational
work behavior

Why does the employee choose to do whose behavior to perform in the working environment? What are the general factors to cause his behavioral performance to bring his job performance effect in the working environment? In simple, I shall indicate some factors to explain how and why they can influence employee individual chooses to perform his behavior in any working environment in generally, These factors will influence how the employee perform his behavior and why he performs his behavior when he feels his behavior or peformance is more satisfactory to his organizational demand or need. Then, I shall indicate some different organizational cases to attempt to explain why and how these factors cause the employee performs his behavior in his organization as below chapters.

Firstly, I shall indicate different factors can influence why and how the employee decide to do his performance in any organizations in generally as below:

(1) Organizational causing factor

What does one organization mean? An organization means human creations, rather than buildings, equipment,machinery etc. It can include industrial, commercial , educational, medical , social clubs, etc. different kinds of organizations. In general, staffs within any organizations will feel need to work to achieve the organizational goals, and co-ordinate their activities for any missions. Each department's staff individual behavior or performance have relationship to be influenced by structures, informal or unofficial groups and structures can be at least as important as the formal organization structure. So, it seems that any different organizational structures will influence their staffs' behavior or performance indirectly or directly. Each employee will have one unique or idenified role in the organization. " The roles people play rather than the personalities in the roles" (Perrow, 1970, p.2). So, each staff will feel or he will know what will be his role playing and the interrelationships between organizational structure and role playing factors , they can cause how each staff decides or chooses how any why he ought need to do his behavior in order to adapt his organization's working environment need or demand.

In general, in bureaucratic model of organizations, where work is organized and conducted on an entirely rational basis, such as government's any departments, which are usually bureaucratic model of organizations. The essential features of a bureaucracy are: Specialization of division of labour , a hierarchy of authority, written rules and regulations, writting memos or notices for any tasks message, reports are more needed more than oral message to be communication channels within the organization's different departments' coordination. Hence, in bureaucratic , staff individual will consider to do any tasks or perform whose behavior carefully in order to avoid error occurrence, or is encountered complains by clients or same level staffs or his supervisor or manager within himseld department. So, organizational structure factor will influence how and why its employee decides to do behavior or performance when he feels his behavior is more rational or suitable to adapt him organization's need or demand.

(2) Staff individual work psychological factor

Miller (1966) explains psychology means what the science of mental life. Mental life refers to three phenomena: behaviors, thoughts and emotions. However, in any organizations, employees will have any characteristics of work psychology to influence whose performance or behavior in any working environment. For example, when the employee feels stressed, he will feel thoughts and emotion to be negative or poor as well as he also feels fear the he can not finish his tasks to let his supervisor or manager feels unhappy or he will complain his working performance is inefficient , even he will dismiss him on the day or later. Then, his fear emotion will influence he may not cooperate with his other same level of staffs in their team easily. It is one good feeling stresses at work case explains how and why the employee will perform worse or poor level suddenly in any organizations. For another example, when a group of staffs need to make decisions, and the extent to which, a person's attitudes towards particular groups of staffs can influence his or her behavior towards them within the department. The organization's team leaders, e.g. manager, supervisor, CEO, he/she will need have good emotion managing ability and managing ability to perpare how to manage his/her teams to cooperate work together in any teams efficiently. In this high stress working environment, the high stress feeling employee will need to judge how to do his behavior in order to manage his teams work together efficiently daily. Hence, some attention is also paid to defining how situations differ from each other psychologically. The high level leader or CEO position managing staff will need to know the supervisor or manager's personality and psychological characteristics tendency how to influence their behavior, think and feel in certain ways in order to let he/she has more confidence to manage the different departments' managers or supervisors more easily , such as the CEO, the top level leader. So, the top level, CEO needs have good work psychological knowledge to know how to manage his/her middle level, such as mangers , supervisors more easily. Then, he /she may have more confidence to manage whose organization efficiently and effectively. So, when the top level employee , such as CEO can know every middle and low level manager or supervisor individual personality characteristics factor. Then, he/she can increase more confidence to know how to manage each department, each team in low and middle level organization structure more efficiently and effectively. So, the working psychological factor will influence how and why the top, middle and low level employees how any why decide their choice to do their performance or behavior in consequently. For example, it is usually that when the employee feels how job satisfaction, then he will choose to perform worse working behavior because he feels that his manager does not consider what kinds of tasks are his interesting jobs. So, his dissatisfaction will influence his working performance to be poor or worse to compare his prior working performance when he feels more bored or low dissatisfaction to himself tasks. Then, his dissatisfactory job feeling will influence his emotion to be worse or poor as well as he will perform more worse or behaves more worse in order to let his manager or supervisor to feel. It is possible that he wants to use worse working performance or worse working attitude to let his manager or supervisor to know his job dissatisfactory or bored feeling. Then, he can encourage his manager or supervisor to change other new and interesting tasks to let him to attempt to replace current bored tasks in possible.

(3) The social and economic factor

Iles and Robertson (1989) have recently pointed out that there has been relatively little work in personal selection which has looked at the issues involved from the perspective of candidates. The only candidate-centred area of work which features extensively in the personnel selection research literature concerns the extent to which selection procedures are fair to different sub-groups usually ethic minorities or women of the population. A large amount of research material focusing on this issue has seen produced. A variety of terms such as bias, adverse, impact, fairness and differential validity are used in the literature or this issue and a clear grasp of the meanings and definitions of some of these terms of some of these terms is crucial to an understanding of the research results.

Hence, when one staff feels that his manager or supervisor is often treated to let he feels unfair or biases simply to compare the other members of different sub-groups in whose team. Then, his unfair treatment feeling how and why to choose or decide to perform whose working behavior to be worse to compare his prior working performance or behavior So, the unfair feeling treatment factor will influence the employee chooses to perform poor or worse working behavior or working performance, because general employee usually feels that it is one important channel to let his supervisor or manager to know his any job-related unfair feeling emotion is caused by the impact of unfair personnel selection procedures factor influence.

Normally, of cours, the extent to which a fair selectin method is related to job performance, it means that when the employee feels that manager or supervisor can let him to compete to do this job in fair selection method as well as he can earn more reasonable or fair salary to compensate whose job ability . Then, he will attempt to perform better in order to satisfy his manger or supervisor's job demand. Otherwise, if he feels that he can not earn the higher salary level, due to that he needs to do the lower level job -related task unfairly, but in fact, he believes that he have ability to do another better position and earn more salary in this organization. Then, he will perform worse to complain whose organizational unfair selection treatment to him.

So, the reasonable and fair personnel selection procedures on candidates factor will influence the organization's any staff individual performance. In consequently, all of these factors will influence how any why some staffs perform worse or better. Then, I shall inficate some cases to let readers to attempt to judge whether which of above these factors can cause these organizations' employees to choose or decide to perform their behaviors in their organizations in order to adapt their working environment easily. You can learn to judge whether time pressure is the main factor to cause your organization's employee individual performance to be worse or any other main factors accurately.

Reference

Iles, P. A. and Robertson, I.T. (1989) . The impact of personnel selection procedures on candidates. In Herriot, P. (Ed.), Assessment and selection in organizations. Chichester: John Wiley.

Miller, G.A. (1966) . Psychology: The science of mental life. Harmondsworth: Penguin.

Perrow, C. (1970). Organizational Analysis. Belmont, Calif: Wadsworth.

Long time working hours how influence
marketing consultant team
cooperation

Whether this marketing consultant organization ought need to reduce time pressure to let marketing consultants to cooperate to finish any marketing research projects before due date more easily? Describe people related problems or issues, one marketing consultant firm, Ann Wood faced personnel problem during the day. Ann Wood, marketing director faced problem of two senior marketing analysts would leave her marketing research department as well as after these two senior market analysts left her department, it would cause the one urgent and important market analysis was delayed and it was more difficult to finish before the due date. Ann Wood, her marketing research manager, Joe would lack these two senior market analysts continue to assist whose marketing department to help to finish this one important market analysis during the date. The result of the one important market analysis was delayed to finish after the due date. Ann Wood would face her employer felt who could not achieve excellent performance to promote to do this marketing director position to manage her marketing research department to operate successfully. Even, after these two senior marketing analysists decided to leave Ann, marketing director her marketing department during the day. This issue would influence the overall many teams of other marketing analysts and senior marketing analysts who lost more confidence to serve Ann Wood's marketing department to cause it would have many marketing analysts and senior marketing analysts would plan to leave her department after her first working day. However, the major factor caused these two senior marketing analysts decided to leave her department during the day, it is possible that because their office computers were broken down, so they could not use internet to send this important marketing analysis project to let their manager and Ann, marketing director to read by email during the day or they felt their salaries level were below than marketing salary level, so they had planned to leave during Ann wood her first work day . During the day, the reasons of these two senior marketing analysts who planned leaving include that they felt who were very talented in whose job and had won several key projects as proof, so who ought earn higher salary, During the day, after their leaving, some other marketing analysts also planned to leave because who felt these two senior marketing analysts leaving, then they would rise workloads rapidly and they felt the marketing salaries level were higher than their current salaries unfairly. Hence, Ann Wood would face some marketing analysts and senior marketing analysts would leave her department during the day.

Suggestion of time pressure reducing method

Did the marketing consultant can handle to finish any marketing research project in team effectively before due date, when she feel to work in one reducing time pressure working environment?

I think she did not handle effectively in these people related matters. An effective senior manager needs to spend much time talking with insiders and outsiders about vision, strategy, and other major issues to the direction of the organization. A senior leader needs to make the strategic decision for the firm. Skills in conceptualizing, communicating and understanding the perspectives of others are critical for these discussion. A senior manager also needs spend time helping middle managers to define and redefine their roles and to manage conflict because middle managers are often central to the organization's communication networks. Skills in listening, conflict management, negotiating and motivating are important for these activities. Ann Wood ought attempt to use these methods to handle her staffs personal problems effectively.

Engagement is as the extent to which staffs enjoy and believe in what who do and feel valued for doing it. So, if they feel enjoyment, her staffs tend to receive more pleasure and satisfaction from what who do if who are in jobs or roles that match both their interests and skills. For example, some people like jobs that require travel enjoyment, when some prefer not to travel. Others like a high risk/high reward bonus plan where others prefer a more stable and predictable salary. Some individuals like work in a team environment, others like work more independently. So, Ann Wood (head of marketing) can make questionnaires to enquire every project team members what non financial and financial rewards are who want to get from this employer in order to raise their efficiency to work and reduce the leaving staff numbers in every project team.

In belief, if her staffs felt who were making meaningful contributions to their jobs, their current employer and society. Then, who should tend to be more engaged to the connection between what every project team does every day and the goals and mission of Ann Wood's company can be engaged successfully. Other people related problem is Ann's staffs lack enough marketing research skill and working experience. For example, Ann's one of staff Joe Jackson, the current manager of the market research group, who complained to Ann about the company's intranet had been down about half of the night and this technical problem had prevented timely access to data from a central server, resulting in a delay in the completion of an important market analysis on her first work day. He could not attempt to find any department staffs to help him to solve this problem. He did not know that whose some marketing research projects should delay if who waited Ann arrived office and then enquired her how to solve. Moreover, every marketing team members who ought lack enough marketing research working skills because who have no anyone could have confidence to finish every important and urgent marketing research projects before due date. Otherwise, if they had specialised marketing research skill, they ought spend little time to finish these urgent and important projects. So, the computer technical problem would not influence their projects to be finish. Thus Ann would face that many staffs will leave her department and the important and urgent marketing research projects will be delayed to finish after the due date.

What do I believe she should have done when she feels that she is working in one time pressure reducing working environment?

On the one hand, Ann only believed Joe, the current manager of the market research group whose suggestions to increase the market analysts salary if she want to increase their speed to finish every marketing research analysis and reducing the market analysts turnover numbers. She had not enquire other different marketing research managers idea why they could not finish every marketing research project quickly. What the problems were caused who are encountered to finish every marketing research project slowly.

On the other hand, Ann could not know what the urgent jobs are who ought need to solve. When Joe, the current manager of the market research group told her that the company's intranet has been broken to cause a delay in the completion of an important market analysis. After she had not attempted to find the computer technical staffs to help her to repair intranet during the day and she still to read any email in her office computer during the day.

I think Ann needed to attempt to find computer technical staffs to help her to repair intranet immediately and she ought not spend much time to see email, she ought continue enquire whether intranet had been repaired and the completion of an important market analysis had been sent during the day and she ought not spend much time to discuss to increase salaries matter to market analysts with Joe during the day. Thus, Ann did not know what the duties are needed to handle urgently during the day effectively.

Is Ann Wood a high involvement manager, due to Ann often feel time pressure to work? provide evidence.

I feel that Ann Wood is not a high involvement manager. From the motivational and leadership practices of managers to the internal dynamic of employee-based teams to the values that provide the base for the organization's culture, successful firms develop approaches that unleash the potential of their people (human capital). However, Ann Wood does not understand the actions of every team individual member and every team group in her marketing research department as well as who also does not understand the actions focused on acquiring, developing, and applying the knowledge and skills of every team members as well as who lacks an approach that involved organizing and managing every team's knowledge and skill effectively
to implement her marketing research department's strategy and gains a competitive advantage. Thus, if Ann, head of marketing director could organize and manage every marketing research team effectively, the knowledge and skills of every marketing research team member in the marketing research department can drive sustainable competitive advantages and long term financial success. For example, Ann's one of staff Joe Jackson, the current manager of the market research group, who complained to Ann about the company's intranet had been down about half of the night and this technical problem had prevented timely access to data from a central server, resulting in a delay in the completion of an important market analysis on her first work day. He could not attempt to find any department staffs to help him to solve this problem. He did not know that whose some marketing research projects should delay if who waited Ann arrived office and then enquired her how to solve. Moreover, every marketing team members who ought lack enough marketing research working skills because who have no anyone could have confidence to finish every important and urgent marketing research projects before due date. Otherwise, if they had specialised marketing research skill, they ought spend little time to finish these urgent and important projects. So, the computer technical problem would not influence their projects to be finish. I think she did not handle effectively in these people related matters.

An effective senior manager needs to spend much time talking with insiders and outsiders about vision, strategy, and other major issues to the direction of the organization. A senior leader needs to make the strategic decision for the firm. Skills in conceptualizing, communicating and understanding the perspectives of others are critical for these discussion. A senior manager also needs spend time helping middle managers to define and redefine their roles and to manage conflict because middle managers are often central to the organization's communication networks. Skills in listening, conflict management, negotiating and motivating are important for these activities. On the one hand, Ann only believed Joe, the current manager of the market research group whose suggestions to increase the market analysts salary if she want to increase their speed to finish every marketing research project and reducing the market analysts turnover numbers. She had not enquire other different marketing research managers idea why they can not finish every marketing research project quickly. What the problems are that who are encountered to cause to finish every marketing research project slowly. On the other hand, Ann could not know what the urgent jobs are who ought need to solve. When Joe, the current manager of the market research group told her that the company's intranet has been broken to cause a delay in the completion of an important market analysis. After she had not attempted to find the computer technical staffs to help her to repair intranet during the day and she still to read any email from her office computer during the overtime of the whole day. It proved that her time management is not effective to deal what the jobs are urgent and what the jobs are not urgent to do during the day.

If no, how well do you think she will perform better in her new job as head of marketing , if she can work in one time pressure reducing working environment?

I think Ann needed to attempt to find computer technical staffs to help her to repair intranet immediately and she ought not spend much time to see email, she ought continue enquire whether intranet had been repaired and the completion of an important market analysis had been sent during the day and she ought not spend much time to discuss to increase salaries matter to market analysts with Joe during the day. Thus, Ann did not know what the duties are needed to handle urgently during the day effectively. The most important, Ann needs to know what kind of job duties who needs to do as she is director of marketing clearly. This marketing research department is an internal department , every project team leader needs to manage and arrange every team member to finish every marketing research project efficiently and effectively. Hence, Ann's main duty ought to assist her every marketing research team to finish every marketing analysis before the due date to avoid to extend time to finish every important marketing analysis in this marketing department. Ann needs to know individual factors, e.g. learning ability, personality, values, motivation and stress and interpersonal factors, e.g. leadership, communication, decision making skill, intra and inter group

dynamic communications will influence her performance in her new job as director of marketing successfully.

I think Ann Wood ought to perform as these methods in her new job as head of marketing. However, She could attempt to produce a fair job description, it's an internal part of job evaluation process, grading and salary description, training is focused on elements of a job and how employees can perform better in their job. Aim to produce a reasonable salary to compare market salary level in every specific positions. Job analysis is establishing and defining every position correctly is from the starting point. Enquiring employees to complete questionnaires, observing and interviewing people. It aims to enlarge job enrichment, it extends the work of existing employees to cover more responsibility and decision making. Motivation is the act of getting someone to act on a situation in a workplace. Maslow's hierarchy of needs includes these level: The first level is physiological needs are basic

needs to be met in order to survive, including food, water, clothing, sleep and shelter. The next level is security, staffs' surroundings are not threatening to them or family. If the environment seems to be safe, then it means stability in the workplace. Security could also include financial security. This could be achieved by creating a retirement package, securing job position and insurance. The third level is affiliation which is the need to feel a since of belonging or to be loved. In the workplace, this means to feel as though they are a part of the group and included in the work. The fourth level is explained as esteem. This is the view that one has of themselves, the person must have a high image of them self and encompass self respect. Feelings of self worth and the need for respect from others. The last and final stages of the hierarchy of needs is self actualization . This level is defined as someone being all they can be and they have met each of the previous stages. The person's talents are being completely utilized. The growth needs or the highest level of needs are the only real motivators of employees. Employees feel dissatisfied, so who unmotivated. For an employee to be true motivated, the employee's job has to be fully enriched where the employee has the opportunity for achievement and recognition, stimulation, responsibility and advancement.

Ann Wood can apply Maslow's hierarchy of needs motivation theory to satisfy whose staffs personal needs. She needs to make her staffs to understand that Ann (their head of marketing) feels they are important to this company by financial and non financial types of motivation in workplace compensation to them. Ann Wood (head of marketing) can attempt to implement these types of motivation into her specific new workplace. Her workplaces are suffering with employees who are unmotivated and overall work performance is failing. Currently her employees do not have organizational commitment, then there is no incentive to excel at their own personal goals and organizational goals. If these employees can discuss techniques are implemented in the specific work sites and she needs to make employees have not feel as though who have reached in the end of their career job satisfaction. Thus, her employees feel dissatisfactory to their jobs and they feel financial and non financial rewards are not fair to compare other employers in this market salary level to cause they intend to quit their current employer. She can use quantitative performance measurement to measure her employee work performance, such as absenteeism, project production turnover, extra hours worked as well as qualitative measurement, such as supervisor/manager ratings on appropriate performance . She can predict her staffs who feel dissatisfactory to their jobs from these information in order to enquire their needs. Often, the measurement will be used in part depend on what work outcomes are regarded as beneficial by her organization. For example, she can use rating form to evaluate every project team members of every one whose job performance from their marketing manager after every project team has finished its project. In conclusion, I give these suggestions to change her performance to deal her new job as head of marketing. For example: Removing some job controls, increasing worker accountability for them own work, giving workers free choice which projects who have interest to finish early, giving greater job freedom or additional authority to every project team members, making periodic reports directly to every project teams (not through every project team leader), introducing new and more difficult projects to give to the more potential project team members and assigning specialized projects to more potential project team members to attempt to finish, so who can become experts.

Assume Ann Wood wants her managers and associate to be the foundation for her department's competitive advantages. Use framework summarized to assess the degree to which Ann's people are a source of competitive advantage at the point of time. Competitive advantage means four key attributes: values, rarity, a lack of substitutes, difficult to imitate. Human resources are seen to be valuable, the cost of replacing employees who leave organization is high, who are experienced and are seen by clients as important. It results when an organization can perform some aspect of its work better than competitors or when it can perform the work in a way that competitors can't duplicate. The resource based view of organization theory refers the nature of human resource can be regarded as uniquely valuable to organization because who are a collection of asset (skills, competencies and experience) and are much more difficult to replicate, unlike other conventional asset, such as land or capital. Rarity is value or be a labour group which is short supply. Organizations have as stable supply of skills in short supply will have a competitive advantage. It is difficult to imitate skilled work of employees, change of services can be available. In instant, self service in restaurant but the market for high quality service by skilled employees are constant growth (Stredwick . J, 2005).

Human capital rareness means the extent to which the skills and talents of an organization's people are unique in the industry as well as human capital imitability means the extent to which the skills and talents of an organization's people can be copied by other organizations. Thus, Ann needs to employ staffs who are valuable, rare and difficult to imitate. If Ann want to lead her marketing research department efficiently. She needs to ensure every team leader has leadership ability and their marketing research skills and talents are unique in this marketing research industry as well as every team member marketing research skills and talents can not be copied by other competitors.

Thus, aims to assess the degree to which Ann's people are a source of competitive advantage at the point of time, who can follow these steps: Firstly, Ann Wood, head of marketing, who can attempt arrange training program is both quantitatively and qualitatively. Such training provides the base for effective of discretion by every marketing research team member. Reward systems that value in individual and team every project productivity help to encourage the type of behaviour that is desired. Giving responsibility and accountability complement the system. It aims to make every marketing research team member who can believe project should be fulfilling before due date, workplace should be fearless and energized, work and family life should be balanced and every project team leader should serve followers, every project team members should be treated like customers and who should not be afraid to make mistakes. This training program aims to achieve further lower turnover, higher satisfaction and stronger motivation among every project team members.

I feel the degree to which Ann's people are a source of competitive advantage at the point of time is not high. The reasons include as below: For example, Ann's one of staff Joe Jackson, the current manager of the market research group, who complained to Ann about the company's intranet had been down about half of the night and this technical problem had prevented timely access to data from a central server, resulting in a delay in the completion of an important market analysis on her first work day. He could not attempt to find any department staffs to help him to solve this problem. He did not know that whose some marketing research projects should delay if who waited Ann arrived office and then enquired her how to solve. Moreover, every marketing team members who ought lack enough marketing research working skills because who have no anyone could have confidence to finish every important and urgent marketing research projects before due date. Otherwise, if they had specialised marketing research skill, they ought spend little time to finish these urgent and important projects. So, the computer technical problem would not influence their projects to be finish. Hence, I think Ann needs to give them training to raise their marketing research skill if she still hope they can have high degree of competitive abilities to finish every further marketing research projects before due date.

Reference

Stredwick. J, (2005). An Introduction to human resource management. Elsevier Ltd, UK.

Chapter 2

Long time working hours how influence
nuclear factory team cooperation

Can time pressure influences nuclear factory teams' cooperative performance?

Dan was the supervisor of technical maintenance in the nuclear power facility factory and who had noticed that several of his people were reluctant to follow maintenance procedures. He had been told that the specifications were too complex to understand, that the procedures were often unnecessary,and that the plant engineers did not really appreciate maintenance problems. On the one hand, Dan realized that most of their complaints were just excuses for doing things their own way. On the other hand, Dan did not really know which procedures were important and which were not. That's why

Dan had asked Mary, design engineer to meet with him. Mary, design engineer knew nuclear power plants' procedures are complex and potentially risky and every specification and every procedures had a reason for being there. If Dan, supervisor of technical maintenance ignored one procedure, they might get by with it and nothing happens. But one of them just might do it at the wrong time and it caused serious wrong result in this nuclear power plant. So, Mary needs Dan to explain that they had safety and cost to consider. If they lost expensive equipment how they should lie to pay for it. Dan referred that if they lost a finger or got exposes to much radiation, they would not like that happened either.However, Mary needed Dan to follow her specification and procedures to do, but Dan told Mary this really wasn't what his maintenance staffs wanted and they hoped for a little flexibility and who felt who would not like it, but they would have to do it. Lately that afternoon, Dan decided to met his unit and relayed the instructions and who reminded them of the rules and disciplinary actions for not following procedures. At the end of the meeting, who couldn't decide whether whose decision had done any better than Mary's decision. Harry, technical maintenance staff noticed that he had been assigned the routinely scheduled maintenance on the three feed water pumps. The pumps were normally used only for start up and shutdown and as emergency backup. When the main feed water system malfunctioned, these pumps would activate to keep the steam generator from drying out. The procedure also specified that the pumps should be serviced and test one at a time and that one pump should be out of service at a time. Harry thought that who needed to take three hours to service the pumps that way, but who could do it in two hours if who shut don together.

Finally, who did not follow specification and procedures to do maintenance job from Mary demand and who decided to shorten the normal three time to two hours to finish this pump maintenance service job. This case indicated that the nuclear power plant maintenance job needed Mary, design engineer and Dan, supervisor of technical maintenance to co-operate to give their opinions to make any important decision to follow the specification and procedures to reduce the incident crisis occurrence to cause serious death to workers and damage to nuclear power plants. However, due to Dan who had noticed that several of his people were reluctant to follow maintenance procedures. He had been told that the specifications were too complex to understand, that the procedures were often unnecessary, and that the plant engineers did not really appreciate maintenance problems. In fact, I believe that the bad result would be caused seriously. Hence, Mary needed Dan to discuss this issue urgently. However, Mary needed Dan to follow her specification and procedures to do, but Dan told Mary this really wasn't what his maintenance staffs wanted and they hoped for a little flexibility and who felt who would not like it, but they would have to do it. It implied that Dan still agreed whose technician opinions and refused to accept Mary's opinion to follow specifications and procedure in the maintenance procedure as well as Dan decided to meet whose technicians to notify them the rules and disciplinary actions either who might choose to follow procedures or who might choose not to follow during their maintenance. Hence, it implied Dan gave whose technicians to choose freely and Dan's attitude was not forced to need them to follow easily. I agreed that Dan handled this decision was not the best way.However, it was not right that Dan made decisions to choose of nuclear power plant maintenance job whether technicians ought follow specifications and procedure from Mary or technicians ought not follow specifications and procedure from maintenance units actions in the short time. Because it would increase Dan, supervising maintenance unit technicians death or hurt chance and nuclear power plant damaging change if whose decision was wrong. So, Dan ought need to spend time to discuss and gather information to evaluate whether Mary or technicians' suggestion was more safe and less cost to work in nuclear power plant for long term benefits in their meeting together.

In fact, Dan had not follow the correct steps to make final decision before he accepted whose maintenance units did not need to follow specifications and procedures during who needed to maintain nuclear power plant. The decision making steps include that as defining the maintenance problem, e.g. what maintenance problems were the most important to need technicians followed all specifications and procedures to carry on working; identifying criteria, gathering and evaluating information, e.g. other nuclear power plant maintenance procedure methods; listing and evaluating information; selecting best alternative; implementing and following up and giving feedback to let Mary to know the reason either why who disagreed Mary's suggestion or why who agreed whose maintenance units suggestion or none of final decision was made that Mary and Dan and technicians needed to carry on meeting to discuss clearly. An effective decision was as one that was timely, that was acceptable to those affected by it, and that satisfied the key decision criteria, and it was in the systematic and logical process. Mary and Dan and maintenance units had not ever sat down to discuss this issue in any once meeting together. Dan only met Mary and Dan only met maintenance units individual to discuss this issue separately.He did not give chance to let them to discuss with him in meeting room by face to face contact.

Hence, they could not have complete knowledge about all possible alternatives to achieve their potential results effectively because who lacked enough time to make decision making and one good decision making needs a cognitive activity that relies on both perception and judgement. If two people used different approaches to solve problem in the processes of perception and judgement, they were likely to make quite different decision, even if the facts and objectives are identical. As Mary and Dan used different approaches to solve maintenance procedure problem in the process of perception and judgement to decide decision whether the maintenance units needed to follow specifications and procedure or they did not need to follow during technicians did maintenance job in nuclear power plant. Thus, Dan could not ensure technicians' decision whether which was better than Mary's decision because who lacked complete knowledge about all possible alternatives to make final decision before. In conclusion, Dan ought spend time to follow correct decision steps to make decision and who also needed to give them to discuss this issue by face to face contact in meeting and he ought not own objective judgement to agree any one suggestion, who ought give them to make subjective judgement to discuss to accept whose decision freely. Hence, Dan ought to be one participant role and ought not be one controller role in this decision making procedure.

suggestion of time pressure reducing method:

Analyze the critical problem in Part A of the case.

Did Dan handle it in the best way?

What decision styles did he use?

Decisions are reflected the person's preference for one of two perceptual styles and one of two judgement styles. Dan seemed to use intuition style decision, who disliked details and time required to sort and interpret them and whose decision made using this style was based on imagination and Dan believed that whose creativity could help Mary and technicians both to choose whose decision was more suitable. For example, Dan did not spend time to follow decision steps to make decision and Dan did not let Mary and maintenance units and him had chance to meet to discuss this issue by face to face contact to decide whether whose decision was less risky and logical to maintenance units work in nuclear power plant easily. Dan was also a feeling style person to make whose judgement. A feeling style meant a decision style focused on subjective evaluation and the emotional reactions of others. Dan preferred to rely on whose emotions and personal subjective judgements to agree maintenance units' decision. At the earlier, Dan had noticed that several of his people were reluctant to follow maintenance procedures. He had been told that the specifications were too complex to understand, that the procedures were often unnecessary, and that the plant engineers did not really appreciate maintenance problems. So, Dan had accepted maintenance units' suggestion to make judge and Dan had not think and analysed their suggestion clearly. So, Dan chose maintenance units decision was based their feeling and emotion reactions. Before,Dan was met to enquire whose suggestion from Mary. Dan would not accept her suggestion easily, even Mary let Dan to know what the serious crisis would have more chance to occur if his maintenance units did not follow specifications and procedure during they were carrying on maintaining job. However, Dan had not change to accept maintenance units' suggestion easily due to they had influenced Dan's feeling and emotion to judge this issue early.

In what important ways is Harry's behaviour different from Marv's when they are feeling to work in time pressure environment?

During the nuclear power facilities occurred problem, Mary and Harry's both behaviour performance could be seemed as these four aspects to evaluate, such as judgement effort and decision making effort and crisis management effort and time management effort aspects.The important ways is Harry's behaviour different from Marv's included as below: Marv Bradbury, technician was working shift time in nuclear power facility plant. In fact, most technicians did not like this shift, but Marv discovered that who enjoyed this job after few months and who also liked sleep in the mornings and many of this co-workers complained his behaviour to influence poor team work. Marv's job in the nuclear power plant was particular important. Marv's primary was to monitor a series of dials and readouts in the control room. In fact, the system was so automatic, so who did not spend much time to do this duty of control and manage this system. However, if the readings indicated some variance in the system whose responsibilities were great, who would needed to do duty of interpret the readings, diagnose the problem as well as who would needed to do initiate corrective actions if the automatic correcting system failed. For two reasons, Marv never worried about his responsibilities because the system was fault free and self correcting and it was a good system with no weaknesses as well as Marv had confidence to understand about the system and he was trained always knew what he had to do in the event of a problem and was capable of doing it. In fact, the system occurred problem and who attempted to solve, but who felt difficult to deal. Hence, Marv felt the system was in serve trouble and decided to phone to get help. Although, who could not solve this system problem, but who knew the result if the systems dried out, the temperature was really going to go up and that the core was going to be damaged. Hence, the nuclear power facilities would cause to damaged. However, it took minutes to get someone to attempt to solve this system trouble, but it was too late and no one seemed to know what to do.

On judgement effort and decision making effort aspects, Marv's behaviour performance was seemed as team co-operation managed style person. On the one hand, who lacked decision making effort and who could not attempt to solve problem himself and who needed team co-operation to work together to increase confidence to solve problem. On the other hand, who lacked judgement effort to know whether what who ought need to attempt to solve any during crisis occurred. Moreover, Marv also lacked time management and crisis management efforts.

However, Marv needed to wait eight minutes to get someone to attempt to solve this system trouble, but it was late and no one seemed to know what to do. If the technicians took longer time to arrive, even Marv could not phone to contact them successfully. The result would be more poor seriously. It seemed that Marv could not have confidence to continue to maintain this system. Otherwise, if Marv could attempt to maintain, it was possible that the system could be maintained successfully.

Risk at this immediate accident occurrence, it would seem that risk taken by a group should be the same as the average risk that would have been taken by the individual group members acting alone (himself). Hence, who decided not to do action
to attempt to solve this trouble, who decided to phone other technician team members to wait their arrival after eight minutes to attempt to solve this trouble, but it was too late and no one seemed to know what to do. However, if who could attempt to solve this trouble within eight minutes, it is possible that this trouble would solve from himself alone.

Harry, technical maintenance staff noticed that he had been assigned the routinely scheduled maintenance on the three feed water pumps. The pumps were normally used only for start up and shutdown and as emergency backup.

When the main feed water system malfunctioned, these pumps would activate to
keep the steam generator from drying out. The procedure also specified that the pumps should be serviced and test one at a time and that one pump should be out of service at a time.
Harry thought that who needed to take three hours to service the pumps that way, but who could do it in two hours if who shut don together. Finally, who did not follow specification and procedures to do maintenance job from Mary demand and who decided to shorten the normal three time to two hours to
finish this pump maintenance service job. Two hours later he was done and he packed up his tools and hurried to get home.
On crisis management and time management effort aspects, Harry's behaviour performance was seemed as self managed style. He could attempt to accept risk to decide how to solve problem from himself effort and who had effort to judge how to deal in any crisis occurrence and time management. Hence, it could prove who could deal any crisis occurrence alone and who did not spend time to wait any team members (technician group) assistance, although who could not ensure whose decision whether it was right or wrong.

Hence, it implied who was one confident person.Harry, technical maintenance staff noticed that he had been assigned the routinely scheduled maintenance on the three feed water pumps. The pumps were normally used only for start up and shutdown and as emergency backup. When the main feed water system malfunctioned, these pumps would activate to keep the steam generator from drying out. The procedure also specified that the pumps should be serviced and test one at a time and that one pump should be out of service at a time. Harry thought that who needed to take three hours to service the pumps that way, but who could do it in two hours if who shut don together. Finally, who did not follow specification and procedures to do maintenance job from Mary demand and who decided to shorten the normal three time to two hours to finish this pump maintenance service job. Two hours later he was done and he packed up his tools and hurried to get home. On judgement and decision making effort aspects, Harry's behaviour performed who can attempt to judge what
action was possible more right to solve this trouble, although who could not ensure whose action is right or wrong, who could make decision to attempt to finish whose job and who felt who would not need to spend time to wait other team members (technicians) to make any decision to work together. Hence, who performed that who was one confident person. In conclusion, risk exist when the outcome of a chosen course of action is not certain. Most decisions in business carry some degree of risk. In choosing between less and more risky options, an individual's risk taking propensity, or willingness to take chances, often plays a role. Two persons with different propensities to take risks may make different decisions when confronted with identical decision situations and information. One who is willing to face the possibility if loss, for example, may select a riskier alternative, whereas another person will choose for taking risks. As Harry and Marv who were working in this same nuclear power facility plant, when the crisis occurred, whose performance would have different to decide to cause different result. Due to Harry performed behaviour was more confident and more judgement effort and self managed person who could accept risk to attempt to make decision alone and disregarded whether the result was right or wrong .

Otherwise, Marv performed behaviour was lacked confidence and less judgement effort and team managed person who could not accept risk to attempt to make decision alone and regarded whether the result was right absolutely. Hence, their performance caused the result was also different, as Harry decided to spend two hours to solve the system trouble alone. Although Marv was not sure that Harry's action whether was correct or incorrect and it needed time to wait whether the system would occur trouble again or not. However, Harry had
attempted to finish whose duties. Otherwise, Marv decided to phone to ask technicians to assist whom and they arrived after eight minutes and who attempted to co-operate to work together. But it was too late and no anyone seemed to know what to do and the system trouble would not still be solve. Hence, it was ensure that the system must be existed trouble and Marv decided not to continue to solve this problem individually and it seemed that Marv could not finish whose duties definitely. Otherwise, Harry could attempt to solve this system trouble alone although it needed time to wait. It seemed that Harry, technician had more strategic decision ability and performed better to compare Marv to deal any crisis occurrence in the nuclear power plant and it seemed that who could assist Dan, supervisor technical maintenance in whose team effectively, although the system needed time to wait to

confirm whether it was needed to maintain or needed not maintain again after Macv spent two hours to attempt to maintain. However, it seemed that Harry had more judgement and decision making and crisis management and time management efforts to compare Marv to do this technician position in this nuclear power plant.

How might group decision making be applied at the end of Part B when time pressure is reduced to influene team work?

The group decision making might be applied to Marv, technician shift team as below:

In general ,in high involvement organizations, associates participate in many decisions with lower level and middle level managers and where low level and middle level managers participate in decisions with senior level managers as well as teams of associates can also make some decisions without managerial input. In this way, human capital throughout the organization is utilized effectively. However, group decision making is similar in some ways to individual decision making because the purpose of group decision makes to arrive a preferred solution to a problem, the group must use the same

basic decision making steps: such as defining problem, identifying criteria, gathering and evaluating information, listing and evaluating alternative, choosing the best alternatives and implementing it finally. Groups are made up of multiple individual, however, resulting in dynamic and interpersonal processes that make group decision making different from decision making by individual. For instance, some members of the decision group will arrive with their own expectation, problem definition and predetermined solutions. These characteristics are likely to cause some interpersonal problems among group members. Also some members will have given more thought to the decision situation than other members' expectation about what is to be accomplished may differ. Thus, a group leader may be more concerned with a collection of individuals into a collaborative decision making team than with the development of individual decision making skills.

In fact, group processes that occur during decision making often prevent full decision of facts and alternatives. Group norms, member roles, dysfunctional communication pattern, and too much cohesiveness may deter the group to produce ineffective decisions.

Marv Bradbury, technician was working shift time in nuclear power facility plant. In fact, most technicians did not like this shift, but Marv discovered that who enjoyed this job after few months and who also liked sleep in the mornings and many of this co-workers complained his behaviour to influence poor team work. Marv's job in the nuclear power plant was particular important. His primary was to monitor a series of dials and readouts in the control room. In fact, the system was so automatic, so who did not spend much time to do this duty of control and manage this system. However, if the readings indicated some variance in the system whose responsibilities were great, who would needed to do duty of interpret the readings, diagnose the problem as well as who would need to do initiate corrective actions if the automatic correcting system failed. For two reasons, Marv never worried about his responsibilities because the system was fault free and self

correcting and it was s good system with no weaknesses as well as Marv had confidence to understand about the system and he was trained always knew what he had to do in the event of a problem and was capable of doing it. One day, the system occurred problem and who attempted to solve, but who felt difficult to deal. Hence, Marv felt the system was in serve trouble and decided to phone to get help. Although, who could not solve this system problem, but who knew the result if the systems dried out, the temperature was really going to go up and that the core was going to be damaged. Hence, the nuclear power facilities would cause to damaged. However, I felt that it was wrong decision that Marv decided to phone to technicians to wait eight minutes to attempt to find them to solve this system trouble, but it was too late and no one seemed to know what to do. In the beginning, Marv could attempt to solve this system trouble by individual decision, but then who decided

to phone to technician team members to assist who because who wanted to reduce whose action risk alone. After eight minutes, these technician team members arrived the nuclear power plant.

Marv did not anticipate any actions finally and Marv did not tell technicians how to attempt to act, so who did not anticipate any group decision among their actions finally. In the result, these technicians group decided to auxiliary pump room and discovered that the three valves were still closed and they decided to open the valves, but it was too late and no one seemed to know what to do. During these technicians group decided to do any actions immediately, their group leader would think to build a positive image (believing this system trouble could solve immediately) under threat (nuclear power facilities

would occur damage possibly). Hence, this technician group leader had already failed possibly and who would decide to attempt to maintain this system together and who decided not to enquire Dan, supervisor of technician to assist them immediately. It was possible that who felt time was not enough to wait supervisor assistance or who could attempt to solve by themselves. Because Marv believed that group think decision making was more successful than individual decision making.

Although, group think did not guarantee a better decision but simply increased that likelihood of such a result. When good judgement and discussion were suppressed, the group decision could be more effective to compare to individual decision, Hence, it was possible that , the group decision making could give some benefits to Marv's individual decision making, which included that group decision making could reduce more errors to than Marv's individual decision alone; group decision making could reduce pressure when technicians gave their opinions to solve this system trouble at the same time; members who could been quiet were assumed to be in complete this job together; they could build complex rationales that effectively discount warnings or information that conflict with their thinking; they could reduce chance to cause them to ignore any dangers when they worked at the time and they could discussed any facts, criticisms or evaluations to solve this trouble together at the short time possibly.Hence, it implied that group making decision still had these benefits to compare to Marv's individual making decision.

What alternatives do you use for the time pressure reducing possibility of a similar problem in the future?

In academic decision theory, one fundamental decision rule is that of maximizing expected utility. This is the idea that when company management needs to make a decision and there are different choices, each choice has a set of possible outcome with different probabilities. The problem with this procedures

is that in real life the probabilities and utilities are often different to determine. Of course, if the outcomes are more or less certain. There might be more than one item you like and you might have a hard time to choose just one, but choose any one of choice will be a rational choice. More generally, what we should be when we make decisions is to list the pros and cons of each option available to use (the reasons supporting the option and the reasons against it). Management then choose the option that on balance has the most reasons in its favour. A good decision process requires all time parts being implemented correctly. For example, Is it clear what we have to decide? What is the most important or urgent decision? Are all the options realistic? Are there other options we should consider? Are we overlooked any good or bad consequences of an option? Is there any special criteria for the decision, we should be aware of?

Have the criteria been applied to time pressure reducing working environment wrongly?

Main reasons why people are failure in their creative idea because failure due to lack of part knowledge and relevant skills and failure of concept and wrong with the initial idea or theory and failure of judgement due to management can have the right idea, but make the wrong decision in executing and developing it and due to failure of attitude and forging a new path where others have not gone before requires courage and the right balance of attitude and due to fear to failure to cause management to abandon an idea before it comes to success.

I recommend that Harry, engineer and Dan, supervisor and Dan's group of normal shift and part time technicians who needed have group discussion to decide what were the serious or common problems as well as whether these system problems which needed to follow specification and procedures

or which needed not to follow specification and procedures during who needed to carry on working daily in this nuclear power plant. Because who should not have enough time to predict or evaluate to judge whether which system troubles issues were serious and which system troubles issues were common to decide whether which needed to follow specification and procedures to carry on maintaining job.

Thus, this decision ought be more fair between Harry and technicians to reduce their conflicts.

However, in this time pressure reducing situation, group decision making (Harry, engineer and Dan, supervisor of maintenance groups and technicians discussion together) must be better than individual decision making (Harry, engineer and

Dan, supervisor of maintenance group discussion together).

The group decision making advantage is better quality, or least a significant chance of better quality, particularly when complex decisions are being made. The advantage is based on the fact that groups bring more knowledge and facts to make decision and engage in a richer assessment of alternatives. Other advantages include making better of decisions and greater satisfaction in the organization and personal growth for group members. However, time is one several disadvantages associated with using a group to make a decision. Thus, if they had already discussed this issue to make group decision making before any system troubles existed trouble . Then, these technicians would know whether which system troubles were more serious and which system troubles were common to judge whether either which system troubles needed to follow specification and procedures or which system troubles did not need to follow specification. For example, as the shift time technician, Marv and another full time technician who could not judge whether system troubles were serious or not, so who should felt doubt and difficult whether who ought follow all instruction to finish system maintained work or who ought not follow al instruction to finish system maintained work.

Even, Marv decided to phone to technicians to ask their help. Marv would cause these technicians felt difficult to make group think to make decision in the short time. Group think is a more extreme problem where the pressure to conform hinders critical analysis and creativity, resulting in poor decision making, it might include outsiders who disagree and morality superior. These members are likely to feel more comfortable with each other, but who might also mistakenly perceive themselves as creative. In conclusion, group decision making ought be needed between Harry, engineer and Dan, supervisor of maintenance and technicians before other new system troubles occurred.

Chapter 3

Long time working hours how influence electronic assemblies factory team cooperation

Can time pressure influence electronic assemblies factory workers team performance ?

The best ways evaluate to measure what factors are seemed to be influencing this company electronic assemblies products manufactory factory workers team performance.

Firstly, we need to know what kind of methods which can be used to measure team performance, then, we can follow these measurement methods to judge what factors are seemed to be influencing this team performance more actually. Effectiveness and efficiency are the best ways to evaluate team performance. Efficiency is oriented towards successful input transformation into outputs. Effectiveness measures how outputs interact with the economic and social environment and it is being used to reflect overall performance of the team. This company electronic assemblies products manufactory factory team of workers could be evaluated team performance in terms of effectiveness. It's main focus is to achieve team's mission, goals and vision, such as whether how many workers could attempt to finish to wire eight assemblies an hour to meet their one client, Pacific electronic company to know how many assemblies of numbers had been finished to wire currently in order to meet whose Pacific electronic company client shipping schedule or not. At the same time, which value these electronic assembly workers whose performance in terms of their efficiency which relates to the optimal use of resources to achieve the desired output, such as whether how many worker numbers and machine tool numbers would be needed to provide to wire assembly numbers to finish in order to meet whose Pacific electronic company client shipping schedule or not. However, this team performance would have this question ,such as whether there was a difference if this team was effective yet inefficient. Hence, this team would face unprecedented

challenges (factors) which were seemed to be influencing team performance. The first factor was such as, it's client Pacific electronic company needed shorten time to finish wire assemblies which was the main factor to influence performance, such as this team workers would feel difficult to increase to wire eight assemblies an hour from three assemblies an hour, so who would feel anxiety to meet the shipping schedule to finish whose job and quality of assemblies production could not be satisfied to Pacific electronic company client possibly.

The second factor was such as, this company factory and office team management structural relationship. Usually, high team performance has strong upper management and human resource standards which had been set in place. Because of high team performance expectation, right staffs were being hired to fulfil the positions in order to employees were well aware of the performance measurement and the importance achieve the excellence in their duties.

Due to a high degree level of employee involvement needed to be in the team production process, the entity was awarded with staffs commitment which reduced rotation level and the cost associated with the hiring and training process. Hence, employees who were devoted to the team were well aware of necessary knowledge and skill and experience to create unique solutions for clients. Training can be an essential tool for maintaining and improving the productivity of staffs and relevance of skill. The ongoing shortages of labour and skill, the company should be taking action to reduce the impact of staffs scarcity by training staffs who already had employed.

Development opportunities were provided to motivate staffs by providing them with skill and knowledge enrichment . At the same time, a better skilled, more motivated workforce would help boost competitiveness, improved productivity and increased profit margin. Moreover, this company lacked good team communication relationship, such as Bill, factory team supervisor who only knew whose same workers of team, such as some of workers Dennis and Steve and Jack who would feel difficult because whose workers were supposed to wire three assemblies an hour normally with five years, but who were supposed to do eight assemblies an hour to sudden meet one client, Pacific electronic company client schedule to finish confidently as well as who would feel dissatisfactory, due to whose wages did not increase much more to pay for performance to the optimal compensation currently and these workers lacked enough training to face this sudden change to face this client's demand. Thus, it was possible that to influence whose team performance to be poor due to who could not adapt this sudden change from this client's demand. Due to Bill, electronic factory supervisor had not communicate to face to face to contact to enquire whose workers whether what reasons to cause who would feel difficulties if who needed to increase to finish wire assemblies and attempted to find solved methods due to sudden clients' demand. Hence, Bill could not have knowledge and skill to judge whether the reasons were either the numbers of workers or machines were not enough or both to cause that they would feel difficulties to increase their speed and effort to finish up to eight wire assemblies of numbers to meet this clients' current schedule sudden change demand at this moment.

The third factor was whether this company had effective strategic approaches to this team. A high team performance which maintains five major approaches: They include strategy, customers, leadership, processes and structure , values and beliefs. Strategic approach takes the team to a higher plan of maturity with a vision where the entity is going; customer approach strives for loyalty; leadership approach is associated with management knowledge to transfer the strategy

to employees (teams) level and which will have a direct impact on their behaviour and beliefs and teams' processes and structure and high performance team will strive for implementing innovative policies to support team strategy; the last model is value and belief which translates into team ability to implement the strategy. In fact, this team lacked effective strategic approaches, such as Mr Martin, office manager did not told Bill, electronic factory team supervisor how to lead whose team to a higher plan to maturity with a vision where the entity was going, such as team lacked training or team lacked enough numbers of worker and machine to provide to increase to produce up to eight wire assemblies of numbers to meet this client's schedule shorten change demand to cause this team lacked evaluation to measure every worker individual effort to judge whether who ought have effort to already to finish more wire assemblies of numbers and who ought increase their wages due to they had more effort to raise more productivity to produce eight assemblies or more numbers. Hence, it caused the effort workers did not like to increase the productivity to meet this client sudden change easily due to who felt unfair treatment to compare the other less effort workers in this team. However, the Pacific electronic company client would lose confidence

to Mr Martin office manager if who could not accept Dave, shop of supervisor suggestion either to add some more incentive bonus to these workers to raise whose productivity or providing training or providing more machine and worker numbers to attempt to assist current workers ability to meet the client's schedule. Otherwise, it would cause this client did not choose to find its help next time again. The important factor was whether this factory supervisor and shop supervisor and office manager

who had effective communication to predict how to solve any sudden clients' order change trouble between of them.

However, I think that, Bill factory supervisor lacked effective leadership to whose workers team in this factory, such as it seemed that some workers; Dennis, Steve and Jack who responded to Bill factory supervisor who felt difficulties to wire eight assemblies an hour suddenly. In fact, some of them had confidence to finish who told lie to Bill because Bill, factory supervisor could not be a good leader to know how to lead whose team to wire assemblies efficiently and effectively daily. Thus, Bill's leadership would have a direct impact on team workers behaviour and team performance poorly if Bill could not change whose leadership skill and who needed to facilitate workers team performance rather than to direct the team, due to who was a formal leader to their team. The company lacked value and belief with translated into team ability to implement the strategy, such as Mr Martin, office manager could not communicate with Dave, shop of supervisor and Bill, factory of supervisor by face to face contact to discuss whether how who could raise to produce wire assemblies of numbers during any clients' sudden shorten schedule occurrence before, so it caused this factory workers team had not more confident to increase to

produce more eight wire assemblies of numbers one hour due to this clients' schedule sudden shorten change. Otherwise, if who could often to discuss to suggest any methods to raise these factory team productivity, this factory leader, Bill would have enough time to plan already how to lead whose factory team workers to co-operate to raise productivity efficiency and effectively in this shorten schedule.

● suggestion time pressure reducing method

Identify the team norms and goals. Are they compatible with organizational objective when these factory workers feel time pressure is reduced?

What factors are seemed to influence team performance to cause these factory workers feel pressure to work in short time?

I felt that some of this electronic company factory team norms and goals are compatible with organizational objectives in some situations, but some of whose team norms and goals are not compatible with organizational objective in some situation. Norms mean rules or standards that regulate the team's behaviour and providing direction and are part of the team's mental model. When individual team members violate team norms, some type of punishment is usually applied. Although, norms allow teams be function smoothly, who can sometimes be harmful to team members. It is important that teams develop norms that both foster team productivity and performance and promote the welfare of individual members. This company goal was that it's factory team needed to finish identified wire assemblies of numbers to satisfy every business clients to meet whose identified schedules individually.

Hence, Bill, the electronic factory team supervisor who needed to follow Dave, shop of supervisor's instruction to inform whose workers team to finish all wire assemblies of numbers to meet every business client's identified schedule on or before due date. Thus, Bill , factory team supervisor needed to give team norms to let whose team of workers to know whose factory's rules or standards that regulated whose workers teams individually behaviour and providing direction to let them to know when (what the client schedule date was) and what the wire assemblies of numbers the team which must need to finish to deliver to whose clients by shipping. Hence, this factory's rules and standards regulation could be one part to this factory team's mental models on this aspect to achieve this factory workers team norms were compatible with this organizational objective.

Although, the factory workers team norms allowed them to function smoothly, but Bill, factory supervisor could sometimes be harmful to the factory workers team to influence whether

the factory workers team productivity and performance standards level of those wire assemblies of products quality, such as Bill, factory supervisor informed to those factory workers team to increase to produce eight wire assemblies of numbers one hour for normal three wire assemblies of numbers one hour suddenly. It was caused these workers felt anxious whether who should be dismissed if who could not attempt to produce eight wire assemblies of numbers one hour from Bill, factory supervisor demand. It seemed that the factory workers team norms and goals were not compatible with this company

organizational objectives because this company organizational objective was needed workers finished to produce three wire assemblies of numbers to deliver to every client before schedule

due date. It was depended on the situation of the factory whether it had enough time and machine and skilful worker numbers to supply to finish the identified wire assemblies of numbers to every client identified schedule individually.

Otherwise, currently, on this situation, it seemed that
this factory lacked enough worker and machine numbers and enough time and training to those old(current workers), it caused who felt difficult that every worker needed to finish to produce eight wire eight assemblies of numbers minimum per hour to meet this Pacific electronic company client's identified schedule change suddenly.

It also seemed that this company current organizational objective was not same to its prior (past)
organizational objective, such as every team worker needed to finish to produce three wire assemblies of numbers minimum per hour before to meet this Pacific electronic company client's
identified schedule change suddenly. It was given more difficult to let this factory team every worker to attempt to finish to produce eight wire assemblies of numbers minimum per hour
to meet this current Pacific electronic company client's sudden schedule change. Hence, in this situation, I should feel this factory team norms and goals were not compatible with their company's past organizational objective for this Pacific electronic company's earliest past three wire assemblies of numbers of every worker individual production demand
in the identified schedule. In this situation, this Pacific electronic company client's wire assemblies of production numbers needed to be changed which caused this company factory team expectation schedule and wire assemblies of production numbers, such as every worker needed to produce eight wire assemblies minimum per hour of numbers of it's production goals and should be changed, but this factory team norms and production goals was still same to this Pacific electronic company client's earliest production numbers, such as every worker needed to produce three wire assemblies of numbers per hour. It meant that who needed have more time and worker and machine numbers to assist them to finish to produce if some workers had no enough effort to produce eight assemblies of numbers per hour to finish to meet this client's identified schedule change, otherwise, who needed to extend time to finish this client's production numbers schedule if none of them could produce eight wire assemblies of numbers at minimum one hour.

This, this factory team norms and goals
seemed that who were not compatible with organizational client's current objective to every worker needed to increase to produce eight wire assemblies of numbers per hour to finish to meet this Pacific electronic company client prior (not changed) schedule possible. Otherwise, these current factory workers could increase to finish eight wire assemblies of numbers to meet this client's current schedule goals. If this factory team some workers could finish eight or even more wire assemblies of numbers of numbers per hour individually. Thus, this team productivity could still achieve this client's expectation goals to finish to meet on or before schedule. It implied that this team norms and goals was compatible with organizational current objective due to client's expectation wire assemblies of overall increasing numbers had been finished to meet schedule from this factory team overall productivity together. Thus, it caused why this factory team norms and goals would be compatible with organizational team objective of finishing enough wire assemblies of overall numbers to meet this client's schedule date goals possibly or this factory team norms and goals would not be compatible with organization team objective of not finishing enough wire assemblies of overall numbers to meet this client's
schedule date goals possibly.

How does the team function to meet individual needs if thsi team factory workers can feel time pressure is reduced to work ?

This company, Steve and Jack were electronic wire assemblies products factory manufactory workers (members) among of this factory team, who had worked in this factory team five years. Bill was this company factory supervisor, who needed to supervise this workers team to help every business client to finish every electronic wire assemblies of products order to meet whose identified schedule, then delivered to them by shipping channel. Hence, if Bill, factory supervisor
who could not lead whose workers team to co-operate to produce the identified electronic wire assemblies of products of numbers to finish to meet the individual business client's identified schedule before due date to deliver to them by shipping. It would cause that this company and the
and the client would feel this company Mr Martin, office manager and Dave, shop of supervisor could not achieve

their service agreement to finish electronic wire assemblies identifies numbers to deliver to them before schedule due date. The result would cause this company lost this client, even this company would accept guilty from this client's complaint. Hence, Bill, factory supervisor needed to lead whose workers team to work efficiently to achieve whose job responsibility to finish every individual business client identified good quality and non damaged of electronic wire assemblies of products of numbers to deliver to them by shipping before schedule due date.

In fact, this factory workers team was combined (co-operated) by every individual worker. Hence, if Bill, factory supervisor expected whose factory team could have good productivity and efficiency, who must individual needs. Otherwise, if some workers did not like to work hard, who would cause this team to delay to finish the identified electronic wire assemblies of numbers to deliver to the individual business client before the schedule due date. Hence, if ill, factory supervisor could satisfy every individual worker needs, then Bill could lead this team to perform more effectively and efficiently. If this factory work could be done by individual without any need for teamwork was not necessary in this factory. I supposed that this factory needed different workers worked in different steps to cooperate to finish every electronic wire assembly product. The reason was possible that because the employer felt every worker could be more proficient to practise to finish the identified step to co-operate to work together in one team, thus every worker could be raised productivity and efficiency in team, it could get more benefits than individual worker did all steps to finish every electronic wire assembly product alone in this factory. However, as the number of this factory team workers increased, the need for cooperation also increased.

As some point, the effort of Bill, factory supervisor who managed the factory team who would outweigh the benefit of having more workers and this factory team performance would began to decline. Hence, if this factory team of worker numbers increased suddenly. Although, every business client's electronic wire assemblies of products individual order finishing time would be reduced possibly, but it seemed that Bill, factory supervisor would feel more difficult to spend more time to lead this team to manage every individual worker who how to co-operate to work more efficiency and who should also feel difficult to satisfy individual worker needs if this team increased many worker numbers sudden seriously. Hence, this factory team overall performance of efficiency and effectiveness would begin to decline for long term due to this factory team increased many worker numbers suddenly to cause every individual worker felt that who could not satisfy more needs than before. Team structure means of coordinating formal team efforts. Leaders are appointed and work rules and procedures are detailed and job descriptions specify individual task responsibilities. It is necessary to coordinate the efforts of individuals assigned to the different tasks. Otherwise, tasks may not be performed in the correct sequence and employees may duplicate their efforts or work against each other. It seemed that this factory workers team which electronic wire assembling steps could be similar to bank loan department and collection department steps. If one individual worker who had much effort to finish whose wire assembling job step more quick to compare another less effort worker individual wire assembling job step. It seemed that the much effort worker could have much time to attempt to help the another less effort worker to finish whose step. Hence, it was possible that this factory team function could compare every individual worker's effort whether who could had more effort and time to help other worker to finish whose wire assembly job step during the less effort worker could not finish whose wire assembling step quickly.Thus, this factory team function could evaluate whether who individual worker had more effort and much time to attempt to help another less effort individual worker to finish their wire assembling job step for every individual client. It implied that these much effort individual workers who had needs to pay to optimal compensation more than the less effort individual workers for whose better performance in the factory team.

It was possible that the piece pay rate compensation was not suitable to these more effort individual worker to satisfy whose individual needs to accept in the team because who could increase return to multi tasking, in which the same workers did both easy to observe tasks, such as wire assembling production of every step and hard to observe tasks, such as process improvement of wire assembling production of every step and producing exact wire assembling quantities of output (no more and no less). I suggest this factory ought change piece rate compensation to time rate compensation and gain sharing payment method to the more effort individual worker productivity , the individual more effort worker who could receive time rate compensation plus a usually small amount bonus linked to the productivity of the establishment to this factory team during who could increase

return to multi tasking to assist whom to finish the another job step of less effort worker's wire assembling job duty for any individual client's wire assembling products delivering order before schedule due date. I supposed that this factory team function adopted transfer lines in which individual worker was
transferred between stations either by machines or by a moving conveyor assembly line. In either case, time rates compensation were more advantages than piece rates compensation due to
it was more fair to the every more effort individual worker if who could finish whose wire assembling individual step before schedule due date and who had more time to assist another
less effort worker to help who to finish whose wire assembly step immediately. In result, these every individual workers could raise this team efficiency to help this factory team to finish the identified wire assembly numbers to deliver to any client by shipping before the schedule due date normally.

Bill, factory supervisor and Dave shop of supervisor who both could obtain high effort from this factory workers on observable tasks by noticing where the wire assembly inventory piles up between stations, without incurring the costs of piece rates. I supposed that the wire assembling products required operations on different machines, performed in different orders setting up fixed paths for work to travel would have made low effort in production more observable, but would have made the wire assembling production process very inflexible. Therefore, Bill, factory supervisor needed put each individual worker in charge of a machine that could do several jobs. (each with a negotiated rat) and encouraged this team workers to do each job quickly via piece rates. Since there was recurring demand for each wire assembling product for a long time, management did not have to negotiate new piece rates very often. I suggested that Bill, factory supervisor should design the observable tasks , e.g. the step of wire assembling production to be done by one group of factory workers and the unobservable making improvement to the step of wire assembling production, fixing problems to be done by another group with a different compensation scheme and observable and unobservable tasks were separated in this factory team.

Thus, wire assembly production workers focused on producing output and were paid to piece rate. Quality was the responsibility of other departments workers, such as inspectors, who identified defective parts and engineers , who attempted to design less defect wire assembly products and processes, these all individual workers who every was paid time rates. All else equal, the low rates compensation was paid to less effort individual worker per piece and the higher rates and bonus compensation was paid to high effort individual worker per time rate to finish every individual business client's order. Finally, this factory team function could give synergy to achieve an effect of the total output of this factory team is greater than the combined outputs of individual worker working alone.
In conclusion, this factory team function could use time rates and bonus compensation method to pay to the individual more effort every worker to let who to feel this employer was more fair to every individual worker performance. The more effort workers ought have more reasonable compensation to compare the less effort workers in this factory team.

If I was Dave, shop supervisor, what team concepts should I apply to achieve time pressure reducing aim to let these factory electronic workers to feel? why?

If I was Dave, shop supervisor, I should apply these team concepts to this electronic factory wire assembling team. When, managers assign associates to teams, who often make three common assumptions, which can lead to mistakes; such as, who assume that a large team size always better and who assume that everyone knows how or is suited to work in a team and who assume that people who are similar to each other will work better together and so they can co-operate happily. Group means two or more interdependent individuals who influence one another through social interaction. Thus, if I was Dave, shop supervisor, I and my shop staffs would be one group. Bill,
factory supervisor and factory team workers who would be another group factory workers team ; Mr Martin, office manager and office staffs would be another group top managers team.

Our company needed these three groups communicate and co-operate to work together to deliver message between about of us about every individual business client's wire assembly product numbers demand and schedule due date to ensure when every client's order could confirm to finish to deliver to the client by shipping factory supervisor and whose workers was a team because this team had two or more workers with work roles that required them to be interdependent who operated within a large social system, as our factory performing tasks, such as every individual worker needed to produce every part of wire assembling in different stage relevant to our organization's mission , such as finishing the indicated wire assembling numbers to meet individual client's schedule to deliver to whom by shipping with consequences that affected others inside, such as Bill, factory supervisor and others outside, such as Dave, shop supervisor and Mr Martin , office manager of our organization, such as company and Bill, factory supervisor had membership that was identified to these on factory team and those not on the team, such as Dave, shop supervisor and sellers teams as well as Mr Martin, office manager and office administration teams. Effective team performance can be more difficult to achieve when team members belong to difficult identify groups or when their identification with these groups conflicts with the goals and objectives of the team, such as these factory some workers who felt difficult to raise to produce eight wire assembling from these wire assemblies in this factory team, but Mr Martin, office manager needed Dave, shop supervisor to notify to Bill, factory supervisor to let whose factory workers every one to know whether who could raise productivity to this

eight numbers and who could not, then who decided whether how to solve that Pacific electronic company client could not receive wire assemblies of identified number before schedule due date by shipping.

In fact, Dan shop supervisor would had conflict, with Mr Martin, office manager who explained

workers felt wages were less, so who would not worked hard to raise effort to produce more wire assemblies, but Mr Martin , office manager disagreed whose suggestion and who enforced Dan, factory supervisor to enquire whether these factory workers who could do eight wire assemblies possibly, it would cause some workers felt anxious to be dismiss if who could not finish this numbers. This, these group conflicts caused non effective team performance with the factory group goals

and the shop group goals and management group goals which were more different. If I was Dave, shop supervisor of this electronic company, I would apply management team

concept to my shop group because I believed we were both the senior level shop manager and office manager who needed to coordinate the activities of our respective units, e.g. shop top management teams and office top management teams as well as Mr Martin, office management group . Otherwise, Bill, factory supervisor would be production team because workers who needed to supervise whose factory workers group to produce tangible products, such as identified wire assemblies

of numbers to meet every individual client's schedule due date.

A final consideration in Dave, shop supervising team effectiveness is whether a supervising team is needed to perform the work at all or whether the work is best performed by Dave,

shop supervisor individually.

In this case, it would have been better to have individual separately, Dave, shop supervising team effectiveness is measured on knowledge criteria, affective criteria and outcome criteria. Knowledge criteria reflected the degree to which Dave, shop supervisor individually increased its performance capability . Affective criteria addressed the question of whether Dave, shop supervisor individually

had a fulfilling and satisfying to supervise shop experience, such as whether Dan could manage whose shop and factory effectively. Outcome criteria referred to Dan 's personal quality of the shop supervisor how to supervise whose shop and factory teams effectively. Hence, if I was Dan this electronic company shop supervisor, I shall apply these team concepts to apply to whose shop and factory teams management in this situation.

● Chapter 4

Developing country labors abnormal long time working hours influences

This research is about Hong Kong employers need labors to work abnormal long time working hours whether it can assist Hong Kong economic growth and raise productivity both in the long term.

The outcome is either Hong Kong labors work long time working hours abnormally who can not rise Hong Kong economic growth or who can rise Hong Kong economic growth in long time. Generally, Hong Kong employers choose to pay less salary expenditure to need many extra labors to work abnormal working hours to help them to rise productivity, but who don't concern that long time working factor will influence unhealthy to current workers due to who need to work long time working hours abnormally in long time and it seems to cause their workers will reduce productivity and inefficiency in long time.

Although, it is possible that HK labors can be increased extra abnormal working hours to work to rise Hong Kong employers' productivity and assist HK social economy will be grown up in short term, but it is also possible that it can't rise Hong Kong economic growth due to their unhealthy or sick increasing to cause productivity declining and inefficiency in long time. Thus, I shall find evidence to analyze whether Hong kong labors need to work abnormal long time working hours. Otherwise, who will decline Hong Kong economic growth and reduce productivity and inefficiency in long time as well as I shall give suggestion to indicate whether either current workers work abnormal long time working hours or employers ought choose to employ more extra part time workers to assist current labors to rise their productivity to decide which is the best choice to raise HK economic growth and efficient productivity in long time.

1.1 What is abnormal working hours Economic Problem

Effects on Hong Kong employment of working time reduction is found to be difficult to predict. The results of Hong Kong macroeconomic simulations of the effects on employments of working time reduction rely heavily on certain basic assumptions, such as how many hours people will actually work or how productivity and pay levels will develop. Whether HK abnormal working hours will assist HK social economic growth or economic falling down in long term.

The reasons cause Hong Kong labours who need to work abnormal long time working hours. In fact, it isn't the reason that the Hong Kong high skilful labours market is shortage to supply for the nature of some occupations, e.g. hospital doctors and nurses, university teachers, law firm lawyers etc professional occupations. Hk has many high qualification university students graduation, it has enough labor supply to high labor market evey year. The reason is that employers don't like to spend more salary to increase to employ extra labors to share current workers workload, such as low skilful and hardworking labors, such as cleaners, securities, waiters and high skilful professionals, such as hospital doctors and nurses, university teachers, lawyers etc. However, the low and high skilful labor market can be enough supply in Hong Kong, but Hong Kong employers need the current high and low both skilful workers who need to work more than 10 to 12 hours or more per working day commonly. It is possible that HK high and low educational labours will be caused unhealthy and lack enough sleep if who still need to work abnormal working hours time in long time. Although, who can rise productivity and efficiency in the short time, but it is possible that who can't rise productivity and inefficiency in the long time. Moreover, it will cause many young or middle or old ages high educational or low educational knowledgeable hardworking workers who will lose many jobs provided and who will be hard to find any jobs in HK labor employment market if HK employers don't choose to pay extra salaries to employ extra full time workers to share current labors' workload in the high and low salary occupations, due to they only choose to increase abnormal additional extra working hours to current workers to achieve to reduce employment expenditure and raise productivity. Hence, it is possible to influence HK social economy grows up slowly, even it's economy can go down seriously in long time.

Hypotheses Testing And Data Analysis

I shall assume that working wage or salary of every individual labors can not be increased, even can be decreased as well as whose normal working hours can be increased abnormally in generally. This means that the Hong Kong individual worker's income will be decreased and general productivity raising is not affected generally, due to HK employers need current labors to work abnormal extra working hours to attempt to raise productivity daily, but their salary or wage have not increased more. However, HK employers need many workers to accomplish the same amount of work, even who don't like to employ extra labors to assist current workers to achieve long term productivity rasing in their companies. These abnormal working hours labors will feel unfair treatment, due to they need to work abnormal working hours, but their salary or wage have not been increased.

In the first scenario of my hypothesis is about that HK labor employment market's general salary or wage has not been increased to the normal proportion of the increased extra abnomal working time(hours). Then, in HK labors market, due to the numbers of labors supply is more than the jobs supply because HK employers don't like to pay more salary or wage expenditure to employ extra labor, but they like to increase extra abnormal working hours to current workers to aim to achieve productivity. So it will cause many HK job seekers with adequate qualifications or with less qualifications who won't find any jobs easily, then the HK the numbers of unemployed people will be increased and their household incomes will decrease to cause many HK household do not like to spend easily. The result will cause a negative effect on HK social private consumption will be decreased and the businessmen' income will be decreased also. So, HK people private consumption decreasing will influence HK economy growth to be slow, even it will cause HK economy declining in the long time.

In the second scenario of my hypothesis is about that Hong Kong workers are fully compensated for the increasing extra abnormal working time(hours) by the abnormal additional working hours calculation. Although, Hong Kong companies' productivity will be raised, but which are not to the extent that it compensates Hong Kong enterprises for their increased wage or salary costs. In fact, Hong Kong enterprises, their costs are passed on to the clients, it causes Hong Kong's economic growth has an impact on international competitiveness to cause economic declining in possible when these enterprises need to raise their products' sale prices to balance their salary or wage cost rasing to win their import competitors. Another effect is that Hong Kong individual labor's incomes decrease, which means that Hong Kong private consumption also falls in this scenario to influence HK economic growth seriously. Thus, the HK economic growth problem will be caused, due to these factors lead to a fall in Hong Kong social household private consumption. Consequently, it will cause many HK employers hope to raise Hong Kong productivity and they will raise the total amount of Hong Kong labor actually worked hours will be risen to such as extent as the increasing in normal working time(hours) from 8 or 9 hours per normal working day to 10 or 11 or 12 hours, even more extra abnormal hours per working day to the current labors. But they do not like to spend more salary or wage expenditure to employ full time extra labors, instead of increasing extra abnormal working hours to current labors to achieve productivity of raising, due to the cost will be increased if they choose to employ extra full time labors if they want to raise productivity. However, I feel they will raise productivity in the short term, but they will not raise productivity in the long term when they choose to raise their current labors abnormal working hours per working day.

The assumption will be made regarding to the relationship between the HK labor market's abnormal long time working hours factor and whether it can influence Hong Kong economic growth in long time for this research economic problem. For example, how many hours Hong Kong labor would actually work or how much workers have efficient productivity and efficiency and how much salaries or wages would be affected as a result of the increasing in working time(hours) in Hong Kong employment market.

I shall apply endogenous growth theory to Hong Kong labor market. As this theory indicates that this model also incorporated a new concept of human capital, whose capital is increasing rates of return. Research done in this area has focused on what increases human capital (e.g. education) or technological change (e.g. innovation) to influence HK economic growth. In macro economic environment, it indicates that economic growth means the increase in the market value of the products and services produced by the country's economy over time. It is conventionally measured as the percent rate of increase in real growth domestic product or real GDP. The growth of the ratio of GDP to population (GDP per capital, per capita income). Thus, an increase in growth is caused by more efficient use of inputs is referred to as intensive growth. GDP growth is caused only be increased in such as capital, population or territory is called extensive growth. Thus, in economy growth theory, typically refers growth off potential output, i.e. production is at full employment. However, HK unemployment ratio is still high to compare other developed or developing countries, although the labors supply are enough to HK employment market.

The working time is the period of time that an individual spends at paid occupation labor. Many countries regulate the work week by law, such as minimum daily rest periods, annual holidays and a maximum number of working hours per week. Working time may vary from person to person often depending on location, cultural, lifestyle choice and the profitability of the individual's livelihood.

Generally, most Hong Kong employers need labours work long time working hours abnormally. For example, low educational workers, such as security occupations of labors need to work per working day is twelve hours or more, restaurant waiters and dish cleaners also need to work ten to twelve hours or more per working day, bank counter cashiers or audit firm staffs also need to work over time from 10 to 12 hours or more per working day and who have no extra salaries for over time salaries payment commonly. Standard working hours or normal working hours refers to the legislation to limit the working hours per day, per week, per month or per year. If an employee needs to work overtime, the employer will need to pay overtime payments to employees as required in the law. Generally speaking, standard working hours countries wordwide are around 40 to 44 hours per week (but not everywhere: such as France employers need labors work from 35 hours per week, North Korea employers need labors work up to 112 hours per week). Maximum working hours refers that the employee can't work than the level specified in the maximum working hours law. It seems that Hong Kong many employers had needed labors to work above standard working hours per week to compare to other developed countries, e.g. America, France, England, New Zealand etc. developed countries.

On the 20th century, work hours are declined by almost half, mostly due to rising wages are brought about by renewed economic growth with a supporting role from legislation human rights. The decline countined at a faster in Europe: For example, France adopted a 35 hours work week in 2000 year. In 1995, China adopted a 40 hours week, eliminating half day work on Saturday. Technology has also continued to improve worker productivity, permitting standards of living to rise as hours declined. In developed economies, as the time needed to manufacturing products has declined more working hours have become available to provide services. In fact, on the one hand, Hong Kong manufacturing industry has declined, such as clothing, shoes, toy etc. manufacturing industry. On the other hand, its service industry need many labors to supply in the labor market per day, e.g. banking, accounting, restaurant, security etc. service sectors. A reduction in Hong Kong working time can be accomplished in various ways, and that Hong Kong enterprise's production costs will be affected in different ways depending on what type of measured is used. Usually Hong Kong employers would be likely to ask those already employed to do more overtime or who will require part time workers to increase whose working hours, especially would pass salaries expense from them on to charge higher sale price to their clients. Then, which would increase the rate of inflation and weaken competitiveness to win overseas competitors' product import.

I shall use these methods to examine this research problem, e.g. statistical analysis and economic concepts, such as GDP, economic growth and labor participation rate. Aim to research whether HK abnormal long time working hours can raise productivity and influence HK economic growth in long term. As regards Hong Kong enterprises' productivity, my research will be discussed what factors that may lead to either an increase or a decrease in productivity and I shall conclude what the effects are very difficult to assess as conditions vary between and it will concern within different service industry sectors, e.g. hotel, bank, restaurant, security, professional service etc. service occupations. These service labors of numbers are more than manufacture labors of numbers in Hong Kong nowadays. Of vital importance for the effect on Hong Kong employment of a reduction of working time is the extent to which wages or salaries are adopted. If the occupations where there was a shortage of labors, Hong Kong employers were to try to contibute to higher pay claims to long time working labors. According to the 1961 year population census, the size of the economically active population was approximately 1.2 million during that year and who was also economically active population was seeking worker. The labor force had grown to 3.1 million by 1996 year (William. C & Wing. S, 1997).

In 1996 year, HK economy was industrialization process filled by a large supply of relativey unskilled but hardworking labor, many of them were refugees from China, the dominance of manufacturing has been largely displaced by commerce and service sector and the demand for unskilled labor is falling relative to the demand for skilled and educated workers in Hong Kong. According to the 1961 year population census, the size of the economically active population was approximately 1.2 million during that year and who was also economically active population or the active seeking worker. The labor force had grown to 3.1 million by 1996 year (William. C & Wing. S, 1997). William. C & Wing. S (1997) also indicated that HK Census and Statistics department (various years) reported specific labor participation rate and size of the Hong Kong force from 1961 year to 1996 year. "During this period the size of the labor force grew from 1.2 million to 2.5 million. The annual rate of increase was 3.7%. It implies labor supply increased so rapidly, so labor intensive industries were developed. However, Hong kong population had increased to 7 million till to 2015 year." Hence the size of the labor force had increased more and it implied labors would supply more than employers demand. But, HK employer job supply numbers are less than HK labor demand numbers in HK employment market. It seems that if HK employers did not like to spend more salaries expenditure to employ extra labors to rise productivity, it would cause many young single or married people unemployed.

Any countrie's economic growth are usually calculated in real terms. i.e. inflation adjusted terms to eliminate the effect of inflation on the price of products produced. Economic growth has the indirect potential to reduce poverty, as a result of an increase in employment opportunities and increased labor productivity. However, employment is no guarantee of escaping poverty. The international labor organization estimates that is as many as 40% of workers are poor, not earning enough to keep families above the $2 a day poverty line. For instance, in India, poor are wage earner in formal employment because jobs are insecure and low paid and offer no chance to accumulate wealth to avoid risk, other countries found bigger benefits from focusing more no productivity improvement than low skilled work. Thus, increase in employment without increase in productivity lead to rise in the number of working poor and these countries don't apply the creation of quality and not quantity in labor market policies. In Vietnam, for example, employment growth has slowed when productivity growth has continued. Furthermore, productivity increases don't always lead to increase wages, e.g. United States, the gap between productivity and wages was been rising since the 1980 year. The overseas Development Institute study showed that other sectors were just as important in reducing unemployment as manufacturing.

Nowadays, the services sector is most effective as translating productivity growth into employment growth in Hong Kong. The HK Government forecast (2012) indicated that "HK's economy has slowed, growing by 0.9% year-on year in the half of 2012 year, after expanding by 5% in 2011 year. For 2012 year, the economy is forecast to grow at 1-2%. Consumer prices increased by 5.3% in 2011 year and 4.7% year-on-year in the first half of 2012 year. The unemployment rate was 3.2% for April-June 2012 year, compared with 3.4% for 2011 year." Although, it seemed that unemployment rate decreased 0.2% for April to June 2012, but its unemployment was still existed. Moreover, HK's economy has slowed to grow by 0.9% only year-on-year in the first half of 2012 year and HK government forcast to grow at 1-2% for 2012. By United States Government statistic in 2006 year, the average man employed full time worked 8.4 hours mandatory minimum amount of paid time off for sickness or holiday. However, regular full time workers often have the opportunity to take about nine days off for various holiday. However, regular full time workers of skill leave and two weeks (10 business days) of paid holiday time with some workers receiving additional time after several years. Because of the pressure of working time with some workers receiving additional time after several years. It seems United States developed countries some workers still feel pressure of working shorten working hours can reduce the pressure of working. In fact, HK many professional workers put in longer hours than the forty hour standard per week. A forty hours work week is considered inadequate and may result in job loss or failure to be promoted. Although, these employers don't spend much salary expenditures to employ extra professional workers to share whose workload and who can perform to serve whose clients efficiently in the short time. But in the long time, it is possible that who will work pressure possibly due to who need to serve many clients every day, and whose working performance will become to be poor to cause inefficiently. Until now, HK has no legislations regarding maximum and normal working hours. The average weekly working hours of full time employees in HK is 49 hours. According to the Price and Earnings report (2012) conducted by UBS, when the global and regional average were 1,915 and 2,154 hours per year respectively, the average working hours in HK is 2,296 hours per year, which ranked the fifth longest yearly working hours among 72 countries under study. In addition, the survey is conducted by the public opinion study group of the University of HK, it showed 79% of the respondents agree that the problem of overtime work in HK is "serve" and 65% of the respondents agree that the legislation on the maximum working hours. In HK, 70% of surveyed don't receive any overtime remuneration. These show that people in HK concerns the working time issues. The equilibrium price for a certain types of labor is the wage rate. The model of labor market, even given all its assumption is logically. The criticism of application of the model of supply and demand generalizes particularly to all markets for factor of production, e.g. labor working hours. I assume HK employers don't like to employ many labors to assist current labors to raise service or productivity when their client numbers have increased. It is possible that who feel salaries expenditure can not be exceed to their reasonable budget. Hence, who need current labors to work long time hours to do too much work, even the HK labor supply is increasing and it will cause many people lose jobs. It seems HK service industry can influence its economic growth. If those service industry labors need to work long time, who will feel mental pressure to work unhealthly and who need have enough sleep. If who can't have enough sleep to face every day work in long term, whose working performance will be poor or reduce productivity to whose clients possibly in long time. I believe HK service industry labors work long time working hours per week that it will influence whose service performance to be poor. In fact, most developed countries labors working hours are less than HK seriously. For example, United States originating from the traditional American business hours of 9:00 AM to 5:00 PM. Monday to Friday, representing a workweek of five to eight hour per working day composing 40 hours in total. The actual time at work often varies between 35 and 48 hours in practice due to breakers. In many traditonal white collar positions, employees were required to be in the office during these hours to take orders from the bosses, workplace hours have become more flexible. Another example, South Korea has the fastest declining working time, which is the result of proactive more to lower working hours at all levels to increase leisure and than the 10 days of the united States and double that of the England's 8 days. Also, work hours in and 40 hour week (44 hours in specified workplaces). The overtime limits are: 15 hours a week, allowance should not be lower than 125% and not more than 150% of normal hourly rate. However, Hong Kong dish cleaners, bank cashiers occupations whose need to work over time often , due to client numbers are increasing every days and their employers do not plan to employ extra workers to share their work loading. Hence, it seems whose work over time are similar to work abnormal long time working hours in every week in HK.

Middison A.(2001) indicated that "the unemployment rate is a performance indicator of the economy." The purpose of economic activity is to transform productive resources into products and services. An economy that uses all or most of its labor force should clearly be considered as a better performing economy than one that lacks the ability to put all or most of its labor force into work and thus some labor productive respurces can not be used. In fact, in economy theory, labor demand is considered to be a derived demand, meaning that its demand is explained not by itself, but by the existence of demand for products and services that use labor as a factor production. If labor demand is a desired demand, then an assessment of the performance of the economy could certainly profit from an evaluation of how well a specific social system managers to transform labor input into products and services. It is convenient to distinguish between economic performance of an economic system and labor market performance. The former related with the ability of a social system to deliver products and services and the latter related with the important, but more specific issue, of how well the labor market managers to match supply and demand. Economic and Trade Information on HK (2012) key indicators of the labor market had finished sample simple average of 15 countries statistic analysis to show "the result was as for the role of work hours in explaining GDP per capital had negative relation between GDP and working hours, as if long working hours where used to compensate the low productivity. The historical downward trend of working time form the slightly less than 3000 annual hours per person employed of the 1870 year to the less than 1600 year of the late 1990 year could be taken as a confirmation of this hypothesis." Thus, this hypothesis could be supported by viewpoint. It was about HK long time working hours ought not increase HK GDP and long working hours where used to compensate the low productivity to HK employers in the long time.

What is difference benefits between normal working hours
and abnormal working hours

   These research will have these two questions to be answer:

1. Can Hong Kong this individual labour abnormal long time working hours factor gives welfare benefit to every labor in the long time?

2. Can Hong Kong this abnormal labor working hours factor grow HK society whole economy in the long time?

It seems that HK employers don't like to employ extra workers to share current worker's workload, even the supply of labours is enough. Due to who do not want to pay extra each worker's salaries to raise whose productivity. To explain relationship between the workers abnormal long time working hours factor and the other resources input factor to influence HK enterprises growth in an improved model in the long time. I shall develop a model is the selection of two variables to explore. These variables have a cause and effect relationship. I shall suppose HK employers believe that workers abnormal long time working hours which can raise their productivity efficiently and which can assist HK society overall economic growth in the long time. These variables have a cause and effect relationship. From this discussion to investigate HK society overall economic growth effect is caused by companies' variable factors. The variable factors include the raising of abnormal long time working hours factor or increasing capital and machinery and equipment and building assets factor or raising natural resources for production factor or taking risking of success or failure ability in an productive enterprise factor. Thus, these separate sets of variable have been indentifies and each set could be selected for a model. In fact, Hong Kong society overall economic growth disputes many occur because a variety of resources input factors can be considered to analyze an effect cause whether which kind of resources input factors which can cause HK society economy growth is fast or slow. In my viewpoint, my exploring reasons are for a slow growing economy in HK. Some economists focus on relationship between money supply and growth in society, some in society's spending growth and some on the price level. In fact, HK economic growth is slow in the long time. I shall focus on the relationship between the HK companies' workers abnormal long time working hours factor and the other resources input factor both to influence HK society overall economic growth. Hence, I shall give assupmtions and conditions are held to be true when exploring the relationship is between HK companies and resources input variables within a model. For example, the relationship is between HK economic growth is slow or fast and labor resources supply numbers are not shortage. But HK employers ususally employ their limited numbers of labors to cause current workers need to overtime work or work in abnormal long time working hours often. Understanding the factors behind labor participation decision is an important component of the understanding long time change in labor supply in Hong Kong society.

In my another viewpoint, discussing HK labor supply, it is important to distinguish between the supply economy. The supply of Hong Kong labor to particular firm, an industry can be highly responsive to wages or salaries as workers seek the most profitable employment in HK. The supply of labors to HK society economy. On the other hand, it is typically less elastic to the labors who often change new jobs because most HK employers who need workers who work long time working hours to cause most HK labors can't have much chance to change new jobs which can provide normal working hours. So, it seems that who won't choose to change new jobs often because many HK employers who need HK labors work abnormal working hours nowadays.

HK employees of large companies of public utilities sector and the HK Government both organizations which typically enjoy more benefits and have greater job security than employers of small firms in Hong Kong society. This has lead to cause a distinction between the small HK private companies and public HK Government and public utilities sector. In fact, nowadays, most HK jobs have changes to service job nature from manufacturing job nature. However, deregulation, downsizing and pressure factors have caused many HK large companies which choose change working hours from normal 7 to 8 hours per working day to adnormal 9 to 12 hours or more per working day. Specially, the occupations of service sector job nature include: restaurant waitors, banking counter servicers, professional lawyers, share agents, security servicers, accountants etc. different service sector occupation labors. The result will cause the labors who choose to leave whose employers if who could not accept to work abnormal working hours to their current employers. Even, it will also cause the current workers who feel nervous and tired and worry to work in pressure everyday, due to who need to increase many extra hours to work often and who will lose their private entertainment time with their family or friends often, even it will be unhealthy to them due to who lack sleeping. Although, HK business cycle was the short term economy in manufacturing macroeconomic environment in beginning from 1950 year. Then, HK economy growth had developed, so many the demanding of labor numbers had been caused to increase seriously till to nowadays. The economic and trade information on Hong Kong of HK Government statistic department (2012) reported " the HK economy was forecasted to grow at 1-2% for 2012 year and it's economy had slowed growing by 0.9% per year in the half of 2012 year after expanding by 5% in 2011 year." Although, it implied that HK labor market had enough labor numbers supply. Otherwise, many HK employers don't like to employ many labor numbers to share current workers' workload. It is possible that due to whose HK current workers need to spend adnormal working hours to raise their productivity per working day to save spending extra salaries or wages expenditures to pay to employ extra labors in HK current labor market. I feel that HK economy growth is slow or poor because the main reason is due to HK Government doesn't spend expenditures to assist HK employers to raise training to their current HK labors to provide human capital to achieve to raise whose service performance to improve their efficient productivity in HK service businesses sector only in the long time. Finally, the results were discovered and will be backed by these evidences.

Can abnormal working hours raise productivity and economic growth in long term

My essay will truly be a qualitative and quantitative research, it is based on experimental fact and evidence. To research the long time employment influence relationship is between the labor abnormal long time working hours factor and the influence of HK economic growth in productive model factor both. This study suggests understanding of the relationship between economic growth influences and HK labors abnormal working hours need to be raised. In fact, the HK labor force participation rate will be fallen every year. Economic growth in HK was through phases that affects growth through changes in the labor force participation rate and the relative sizes of HK society service and manufacturing sectors. In fact, HK agricultural industry sector is not existed and manufacturing industry sector numbers are decreasing and it begins to enter service industry sector. The low knowledge level of jobs include security, banking, restaurant, cleaning, transportation etc. service nature of jobs as well as the high knowledge level of jobs include lawyer, accountant, medicine, doctor, computer technician etc. professonal service nature of jobs which both are providing service to HK society nowadays. The investment theory indicates that the education is as investment human capital to provide to any companies. The main difference is that human capital is incorporated in human beings and it can't be resold. When physical capital can be acquired at almost any desired amount in boom periods and be resold during recession on secondary markets, human capital can be acquired mostly in the beginning of individual behavior by firms. I shall recommend HK companies ought choose these methods to control labors whose working hours time efficiently.

Yasuhiro (2014) showed that "wage differentials based on age and length of service in-house training refers to a process whereby workers acquire skills through daily work and occasional of the job training. Whether or not they perceive it as "training" is irrelevant. Training is also included informal learning conducted independently by the worker without any feedback from an instructor. Conceptually, the skills acquired are divided into general skills that can be used in the company currently employing the worker. The process of acquiring the latter specific training." Generally, when companies minimizes personnel costs, the ratio of marginal productivity referred to below as productivity between workers are equal to wage ratios. Therefore, the coefficient of age in the wage function expresses the rate of productivity increases due to general training and the coefficient of length of service and the rate of wage increases due to special training reason. The sum of both coefficients will express the rate of productivity increase in current companies due to training is as an important causing factor.

In conclusion, in my viewpoint, HK employers need to provide on job training to current labors to aim to raise their efficiency to productivity in the long time. Because when their labors had been trained to let them to learn how to use special skill to finish their job duties easily, then they will not need to spend much time (additional working hours) to finish their job duties per working day. On the one hand, HK employers need to measure to compare what benefits are in favour of standard working hours to whose employees. The benefits include, such as promoting work life balance and enjoy family life, increasing time for leisure and rest, beneficial to health and employees can have more time to pursue further studies as well as employers do not need to pay higher salaries to longer working hours employees or overtime pay boost income as most HK companies pay time and a half to some employees only. On the other hand, HK employers need to measure to compare what benefits are against standard working hours to employers, such as employing many part time working hours employees to assist normal working hours full time employees rather than needing full time employees work abnormal hours daily, lowering or cancelling year and bonuses etc. Moreover, HK employers may also use various measure to offset the increased cost of running businesses, such as lowering average hourly anual compensation. However, when HK employees are forced to work part time jobs, who may need to acquire additional employment to maintain their standard living. Even, HK employers only force employees to work overtime in some situations. Appropriate standard working hours can vary across different industries based on the type of work performed. Such as some HK certain professional positions are difficult to define in terms of appropriate working hours. Issues can arise with employers expecting exployees to work extra hours "off the clock" in order to keep costs down. Thus, I believe that HK labors abnormal working hours time issue ought be decreased and HK employers ought employ extra workers assistance to share current labors' workload to help them to raise productivity and efficiency and HK economy will grow fast in the long time. Finally, my research aims to find that the number of hours worked is a more responsive measure of the state of the labor market than employment in HK. Comparing the number of hours worked to indicators of the wider economy shows that it is likely to be demand from HK firms (employers) which is driving the numbers of hours, rather than individual job applicant supplys to HK employment market. My analysis also show that the HK appears to have developed a long working hours culture to compare other developed countries, such as America, England, Canada etc. In fact, in the presence of HK firms may even invest to find which are more profitable to able to reduce their every employee's abnormal working hours daily rather than normal number of working hours of their every employee.

Bibliography

Economic And Trade Information On Hong Kong, (14 Aug. 2012). Hong Kong Government Forecast for 2012, retrieved from the following URL: http://www.cepa.hktdc.com

Middison A. (2001). The World Economy. A Millennial Perspective, OECD, Paris.

Yasuhio, U. (2014). Japan Labor Review, vol.11 no.3,

High Economic Growth And Human Capital:

Conditions For Sustained Growth, Konan

University.

William, C&Wing, S.(1997). The Hong Kong Economic

Policy Studies Series, published by City University

Of HK Press, Hong Kong

Chapter 5

Behavioral economy method predicts

organizational behavioral changes and marketing behavioral changes.

Over the past 20 years, many researchers believe to apply behavioral economic macroeconomic models which can predict market behavioral change. The reasons are based on assumptions of optimizing behavior in many cases have difficulty accounting for key real-world observations. Hence, researchers have used behavioral economics assumptions with the aim of making their model predicting better fit the data. The reason for behavioral economics results into macroeconomics will be more accurate to predict market behavioral change in macro-economy view point, such as economic fluctuation prediction, the consumption, formation of expectations and determination of wages and employment how to aggregation supply and the possibility of consumer individual demand product or service number prediction more accurately.

● How to apply behavioral economy theory to predict marketing behavioral changes more accurate?

Anyway, economists aim to develop models of human behavior and interactions in market in order to build useful models. Economists make simplifying assumptions to analyze why the market will be changed by consumer individual consumption behavior changing.

Why do I assume consumers are as economic man ? In behavioral economy view point, how the perception of the economic man's behavior (including consumer choices) of economic models with the development of economics as a science. Economists explain the concept of economics as a science. It is the concept of consumer as an economic man, the essence and complexity of consumer behavior.

The consumer and consumer purchasing behavior are an important area of interest of many scientific disciplines. The process of economic decision making as well as consumption choices are connected with wider human activities. The terms of both consumer individual attitudes and group social behavior will influence group social behavior will influence consumer individual final consumption decision in every consumption choice process. Thus, behavioral economy method can predict consumer behavioral changing, it can apply these sciences to research, includes sociology, psychology, anthropology, operational research, decision theory etc. different literature research aspects. I assume that businessmen can apply behavioral economy method to predict market changing behaviors successfully if they own behavioral economy knowledge.

In this part, I shall concentrate on explain how the perception of the economic man's behavior (including consumer choice) is applied to predict market behaviors. After explaining the concept of consumer as an economic man, the nature and complexity of consumer behavior are discussed to below different industries' marketing behavioral changing every case studies in US or UK countries.

Why is consumer as an economic man? IN behavioral economy view point, the concept of answer is one of the fundamental concepts in economics because the consumer is the case market participant along with the producer. In general, lecturers define the consumer in various ways, but in behavioral economy view point, consumers mean economy man. Because who will compare cost and benefit to any product or service to decide to choose to buy the product or consume the service. Consumers are as "economic man", who will make own subjective preferences (tastes), habits and traditions and existing objective constraints (i.e. disposal income) market prices of products and services in order to satisfy whose needs to a maximum degree and in the most rational way.

Thus, economic man means consumers need to make psychological mind to decide whether who either prefer to buy this product or another product or prefer to consume this service or another service more suitable. Thus, any markets or industries need have themselves benefits and consumers must need to evaluate whether the product or service has more benefits to compare other products or services in the consumption market to satisfy whose needs. It means that if the product or service has more benefits to compare other similar products or services. Then the product or service will persuade many consumers to choose to but the product or consume the service.

Consequently, in first part, I shall indicate how to apply behavioral economy theory : economic man psychological method, benefits and costs benefits method, how to predict these US and UK enterprises marketing behavioral changing more accurate.

In the second part, I shall apply micro employee behavioral economy concept to explain how to solve these US and UK inter-organizational management challenge.

I believe that behavioral economy method can be applied to research organizational employee behaviors change, e.g. how any why the employee chooses to do this action in whose organization. Moreover, behavioral economy method can be applied to consumption market to predict how any why the consumer choose to buy the product or consume the service. So, any consumers and employees personal psychology and external environment economic factor will influence how to choose to do decision in any organizations or consumption environment.

Bibliography

Bandiera, O., I. Barankay, and I. Rasul (2005). Social preferences and the response to incentives: Evidence from personal data. The quarterly journal of economics 120 (3), 917-969.

Exadaktylos, F., A.M. Espin and P. Branas-Garza (2013). Experimental subjects are not different. Scientific reports 3, 1213.

Lazear, E.P. (1979). Why is there mandatory retirement? Journal of political economy 87(6), 1261-1284.

Consumer psychological time method predicts stable basic income consumer individual spending behavior

Can apply consumer psychological time method to predict that the consequences of a stable basic income consumer's consumption behavior? It may be significantly different than the ones are predicted by the standard economic model if more realistic assumptions of human consumption behavioral prediction success.

Consumer psychological time method assumes that consumer will compare whether whose benefits are more than costs after they buy the product or consume the service. I assume the consumer is only the who have stable basic income source consumer target. This stable basic income target consumers who will evaluate or feel they will earn more benefits than costs to every product in their consumption process, after they will make final decision to choose to buy the product to use or consume the service. Otherwise, if they feel they won't earn more benefits after they buy the product or consume the service in the consumption process. Then, they won't choose to buy the product to use or consume the service. In behavioral economic view point, it indicates their consumption behaviors are depend on comparing the product or the service whether it can satisfy their desire benefits and their desire benefits to the product or service must be more than their consumption cost.

There are four points to apply consumer psychological time method to predict each stable basic income individual income spending. They include: motivation, conspicuous consumption, social preferences and crowding theory.

Each stable basic income consumer individual spending amount will be different and it is represent that every high stable basic income consumer must decide to consume any high cost services or buy high cost products to use. Although some economic teachers assume general high income people will accept to spend more expenditures for enjoyment or buy high cost of products to satisfy basic high level necessary expenditures. But, applying behavioral economic analysis, it is not absolute true, some low income people also accept to spend more to buy high cost of products or increasing spending expenditures for enjoyment for their basic necessary expenditures.

The field of consumer psychological time seems to behavioral economic can be fined as a combination of economics and consumer psychological time that tries to capture human behavior in a more realistic. Understanding each consumer individual consumption behavior, we need to know how who does each decision to influence each consumption choice. Consequently, analysis reaches the conclusion. Every high or low level stable basic income consumer individual behavioral consumption that the microeconomic consequences of a stable basic income of individual consumer target consumption group could be efficiency enhancing, but at the same time incentives about positional concerns could lead to wasteful and inefficient spending to the stable low basic income consumer target group.

How to apply consumer psychological time method to contribute to the stable basic income target consumer group's consumption prediction?

What is basic income mean? A basic income is an income paid by a political community to all its members on an individual basis, without means test or work requirement. How to apply behavioral economic method to contribute to the basic income consumption prediction?

I assume high income tax is charged to one high income tax payee , it will influence the high income tax payee individual consumption desires to be fallen, also extrinsic incentives will effort and intrinsic motivation and how the labor market change these variables under and big changes predicting, how income security changes social consumption preferences, e.g. how a big change affects the overall level of status -seeking behavior and this effect with income inequality to influence consumer individual consumption attitude or habit.

How can consumer psychological time methods predict consumer's consumption decision, in special the stable basic income consumer target group? In any consumption decisions are involving risk and uncertainty, the standard economic model usually assumes that decisions are based on final condition, regardless of the changes are caused by the results of a consumer's decision.

An alterative mode of how consumers make decision and judgement under risk and uncertainty. This situation is often occurred in consumption market.

In consumer psychological time view point, it explains how consumer's consumption, however, which excludes the stable basic income earn factor can influence the stable basic income earn target consumer group decides to make final consumption decision to compare to the non-stable basic income earn target consumer group. The reasons include as below:

(1) Consumers evaluate decisions over gains and losses with respect to some natural reference point, when they feel need to consume, which is assumed to be judgement about a sequence of outcomes are based on changes in wealth, rather than whether how much absolute basic income earn to influence whose consumption desires.

(2) Thus, consumer psychological time or behavioral economic theory assumes the consumer is the low level of income group in society, but when who feels that he is still gains more than losses when who decides to buy the expensive product or consumes the expensive service. Then, the low level of income consumer who will accept to buy the expensive product or consume the service easily. Due to whose gains feeling is more than losses feeling, when who buys the product or consumes the service.

(3) Behavioral economic or consumer psychological time theory also assume the taxpayer will pay high income tax in this year. The, even the high income taxpayer can earn high basic income, but due to whom needs to pay high income tax in this year. Then, he/she will reduce much spending, even he/she reduces spending on cheap products or cheap service consumption for enjoyment. This is the taxpayer's economic decision to influence whose consumption behavior, due to the high income tax expenditure factor influences whose consumption behavior to change to be reduced spending expenditures in this year.

How to apply organizational psychological time method to predict labor market changing behavior?

Instead of applying behavioral economic method to predict every consumer individual consumption effort. Behavioral economic method can be also be applied to predict every country's labor market changing behavior. Particularly, how salary clerical workers or low wage labor workers should move from one type of job to another based on these factors. They include as below:

Their intrinsic motivation and how their levels of effort would change after this movement, investigates the effects of income security on social preferences in labor market changing behavior, and how cooperation in social contribution is affected when income security is guaranteed, how to predict the role of positional externalities on conspicuous consumption and how would change the incentive to influence consumption. So, it seems that general labor market job changing behaviors will not influenced by external economic environment better or worse changing factor, or salary changing factor etc. different environmental condition changing factors influence to employees' job changing. Generally, employee's job changing behavior is more influenced to persuade who changes job by himself/herself intrinsic motivation negative emotion influence mainly.

How to apply motivation crowding theory to predict labor productivity? One of the main challenges of economic theory is to find what are the optimal incentives that increase productivity of labors. The standing point is usually extrinsic incentive be it is form of monetary compensations for high effort or fine for low effort.

It is a kind method of reward or punishment to increase or decrease number of productivity to every labor. But it can only raise short term number of productivity in possible and it can not guarantee high quality of productivity. So if one employer wants a labor to do more of an activity or with a higher quality, consider paying the labor for working hard on punishing whom if for providing a low level effort.

This idea is that people do not like to work, and therefore they used some sort of compensation for doing a specific activity, and that the more they are paid the harder, they will work. So, payment better compensation is only beneficial to encourage labors to do one specific task or activity in short term. This method can not be suitable to rise long term beneficial productivity and high level quality of production or excellent performance in long term and it can only keep in short term raising productivity and high level quality of production or excellent performance benefits.

Consider paying the labor for working hard on punishing whom if for providing a low level effort. This idea is that people do not like to work, and therefore they used some sort of compensation for doing a specific activity, and that the more they are paid the harder they will work. So, payment better compensation is only beneficial to encourage labors to do one specific task or activity in short term. This method can not be suitable to raise long them beneficial productivity and high quality of products.

However, economists would argue that, is a labor has high intrinsic motivative to perform a task, who will provide a high level of effort without compensation by himself/herself but an even higher level of effort of whom is compensated. If a labor does not have any intrinsic motivation to perform a task or an activity, who will provide no effort or a low effort of whom. There is no compensation, but who will increase this level of effort of an extrinsic incentive is implemented.

Hence, in behavioral economic view point, the labor individual high level effort is a main psychological factor to influence whose productivity to be raised or the qualities of products to be raised, when the products are manufactured by the high level effort labor. It means that high compensation is not the good method to encourage labor productivity or raise quality. Otherwise, how to influence the one low level of effort of labor to change to be one high level of effort labor. It is the best psychological method to influence the labor to raise productivity and quality and service performance to any products or services in manufacturing process or service process for any organizations in long term beneficial possible.

How can apply consumer psychological time method raises basic stable income consumer consumption desire?

Economists aim to develop models of human behavior and interactions in consumption markets. But consumers behave in complex ways, such as how to predict consumers to make rational decisions in consumption processes. Moreover, self-consumption control and motivation can vary significantly across different individual consumer.

In order to build useful consumption prediction models, economists make simplifying assumptions, aims to predict how to raise stable basic income consumer target group consumption more success. However, behavioral economy method is one kind of accurate consumption prediction method. It can be applied to predict economic decision-making to every consumer consumption choice more accurate raising whose consumption desire?

I shall indicate how to apply different behavioral economy methods to raise stable basic stable income target consumer group consumption desire in these different consumption situation (consumption environment) aspects as below:

1. Stable basic stable income consumer group consumption great or small amount desire

The consumption of products and services is a fundamental part of consumer's welfare. Basically, every one who has stable basic stable income, who will like to consume any products and services. Even, consumption great or small amount desire won't be depended on whether the person whose income is more or less. It means low income level of people will still like to consume great amount to buy expensive products or consume expensive services, because consumption is human's part of life and basic needs.

This stable basic income people will like to consume, because they have stable income source when they do not worry about unemployment occurrence to cause them have no enough money to support their life. Otherwise, non-stable basic stable income people won't like to consume because they feel they have no stable basic income source to support their life and they will worry about unemployment occurrence any time. Hence, stable basic income people will have more consumption desire to compare non-stable basic stable income people in any countries usually. Behavioral economic method indicates they feel their economic benefits will be loss if they planned to buy any products or consume any services easily. So, they prefer to save money in bank more than consumption.

1. Demand systems and micro-economic factor influence basic income people consumption attitude

Why stable basic income people will like to consume? Because who have more demand, a demand system shows the level of consumer demand for different products and services: e.g. one basic stable income person may refer to the demand for clothes, another the demand for food etc.

How the demand for that particular product varies with the prices and demographic factor will influence who to accept consumption. Such as stable basic income people who will not consider to decide to buy the cloth to wear or the food to eat if who feel the cloth or food price is even more expensive to compare other kind of cloth or food.

Otherwise, non-stable basic income people who will consider to decide to buy the cloth to wear or the food to eat if they feel that they still have enough cloths to wear or enough food to eat at homes , even these food or cloth price are less expensive to compare others. Because they feel they lack stable income effort to support them to consume. Hence, basic stable income factor can influence the consumer's consumption decision.

2. Life-cycle advertisement method can influence consumer individual consumption behaviors to be increased

Consumer behavior makes strong assumptions about the informational and computational bases of consumer behavior. Generally, consumer behavior is reasonably characterized as the maximization of expected lifetime utility subject to budget constraint and conditional on the available information.

Generally, consumers prefer to buy any discounted products or it is reasonable that consumers accept to buy many attractions to persuade them to buy any kinds of bargain discount products. Hence, low bargain discount product is one good behavioral economic principle to encourage or persuade or attract any consumers to increase consumption. What is behavioral life-cycle model? This model explains consumer behavior can be persuaded to buy any discounted products by advertisement, e.g. television, radio, newspapers, magazine etc. promotion channels. Because frequent advertisement promotion method can let any consumers often remember the product's brand, discounted price, style, color and image from advertisement content.

So, advertisement can be one part of consumer behavioral life-cycle. For example, when the television audiences often watch TV. Hence, when the brand of product advertisement often makes fun image and discounted message to let TV audiences to remember this brand of product, when they are watching TV. Then, it has possible to persuade any potential consumers to choose to buy this brand of any products or consume this brand of any services, due to its advertisement of discounted sale message is very attractive to every one to let this advertisement audience's attention to remember this brand of products or services are selling or serving in market at this moment. So, it is advertisement image behavior influences audiences to buy the brand's any products attractively and persuasively.

3. Raising electricity consumption from electricity user individual habit

For electricity use market case example, how to analyze people's behavior in consuming electricity using a behavioral economic framework ? Electricity consumption is modeled by the means of consumer's individual useful habit, electricity price, consumer satisfaction level, willingness to invest in new technologies, social interactions, and marketing strategies by the power utility. Because electricity is necessary to every home or electric vehicle users needs or businessmen office etc. different needs every day.

Power companies supply electricity to a region's homes and industries. However, electricity needs modernization of power system companies expect to increase price. Due to competitive factor, such as other fuel resource choices, outdated kind of energy electricity supply, and renewable fuel energy source competition.

Hence, applying behavioral economic concept, I assume electricity consumers will compare to electricity and other kinds of energy choices to weigh up the costs and benefits of all alternatives, aiming to maximize their benefits, before making a decision to choose to use electricity for their house electricity demand or electric vehicle or shop or factory manufacturing etc. function of different aspects of electricity users.

For example, electricity business clients, they aim to reduce cost, such as energy expenditure, when they use any energy to manufacture their products in factories. If they feel electricity is expensive price to compare other kinds of energy power supply. When, they feel that they can not earn much beneficial advantages to use electricity to produce their products. Otherwise, if they feel other any kinds of energy supply can replace electricity to give more benefits to compare electricity energy. Then, many business electricity users will change to use other kinds of energies to consume to replace electricity power.

However, electricity can have competitive ability in electric vehicles market, if many drivers feel environment protection is more important to compare vehicles will be popular to be driven, due to many drivers don't want air pollution. They will like gas vehicles. Hence, the main attribute from the consumer side is one their habit electricity consumption behaviors, satisfaction level, energy efficient interaction with the power utility.

Consequently how to predict electricity consumer's demand. The important factor is how to let electricity users to feel power companies are changing a reasonable level to compare other similar energy supply products. When electricity users feel electricity which can bring more benefits to compare other kinds of energy products. Then, in energy supply market, if the demanding number of electricity consumers can increase more than other kinds of energy demanding number. Then, it is right time to raise electricity price to charge electricity consumers. Hence, how to persuade electricity consumers to feel that they can have more benefits to compare other kinds of energy products. It is the main successful factor to electricity power supply companies.

Consumer confidence is as a predictor of consumption spending when consumer feels have enough time to consume

Behavioral economists believe it has link between confidence and economic decisions to cause consumers to choose spending, if the consumer has confidence to believe the product is worth to use, then who will accept to buy the product to use.

Concentrated on the conceptualization of confidence and its role in mode in theories of consumption. It also concerns on whether the confidence indicators contain any information beyond economic fundamentals. The concern is whether confidence can be explained by current and past value of variables, such as income, unemployment, inflation or consumption or in other way.

Whether confidence measures have any statistical significance in predicting economic outcomes once information from the above variables is used. Economic variable factor will also influence consumer confidence to decide consumption spending, e.g. real consumption expenditures (income, wealth or interest rate).

Finally, it will identify under which circumstances confidence indicates can be a good predictor of household consumption. Hence, survey is one good measurement method to predict whether how much every household has confidence to spend to consume the brand of products to use. Why is survey a good confidence consumption measurement prediction to every household in every country?

The reasons include survey can gather every household consumption habit history data to evaluate whether every survey person has how much confidence to consume the brand of products. Which in most cases correspond to periods where there are large changes in household survey indicators, liking during financial crises or geopolitical tensions to measure or predict whether the country's future good or bad economic condition factor will influence every household consumption desire in the year.

This modelling approach assumes that there is a certain (unknown) in confidence index changes beyond which confidence starts impacting consumption behaviors. So, sample household surveys can show the contribution of confidence in explaining consumption expenditures increases when household survey indicators feature large changes. So that confidence indicators can have some increasing predictive power during the survey investigation period in the year.

Other view point, surveys have been concerned on whether the confidence indicators contain any information beyond economic fundaments. The concern is whether confidence can be explained by current and past values of variables, such as income, unemployment, inflation or consumption or the other way. Whether confidence measures have any statistical significance in predicting economic outcomes once information from different external variable factors to influence the survey household group.

What is confidence in consumption survey ?

Confidence in consumption. For example, to measure whether how much degree of strong inflation in the economy, such as recessions and recoveries will influence the country's household confident consumption in the year.

The surveys consumers' questions usually concern on major expenditures and changes in the respondent's financial situation, focus on job availability and current business conditions etc. questions. It is then possible that about consumer confidence depending on the relative performance of the variables that may be more relevant balances, with respect to the factors that determine unemployment and other labor market related issues. It aims to investigate whether those any one of variable factors will influence consumers general loss confident consumption desire in this year.

What is a confidence indicator ?

A confidence indicator is considered as an explanatory variable for consumption together with standard variables used on predicting consumption expenditure. However, the natural real personal consumption expenditure is unexpected and unpredicted easily.

In conclusion, consumption expenditure depends the consumer individual confidence. If the consumer has much confidence to feel this year economic change will be better and he/she is easily to find job, then he/she will accept consumption easily in this year. It seems financial wealth and unemployment etc. economic factors will influence every household consumption desire. So, survey is one kind of good psychological consumption prediction method to predict consumption spending for any country in the year. I recommend manufacturers may choose to apply survey method to attempt to enquire sample survey people to gather data to predict whether what degree of consumption desire to them and find solution methods to solve low degree of consumption desire challenge.

Reference

Camerer, C.F. Babrocks, Loewenstein, G., & Thaler, R. (1997). Labor supply of New York city candrivers: One day of a time. The Quacterly Jounrnal of economics, 112 (2), 407-441. doi: 10.1162/003355399555244.

How do you view the outlook for consumer confidence in your key markets next year? Source from : http://www.Just-food.com Confidence survey, Nov.2015

Jim. P. & Brendan. M. (2013) . What I learned losing a million dollars, p.160. Colimbia University, Columbia business school press, New York, US.

Kamenica, E. (2012). Behavioral economics and psychology of incentives. Annual review of economics, 4 (1), 427-452. doi: 10.1146/annurev- economics-080511-110909.

Maselli, 2012 Technology driven job polarization in EU , 2000-2010. % change in labor supply skilled/upgrade (ISCED) and labor demand for skills/tasks (ISOD).

Chapter 6

Consumer time influences performance

To research consumer behavior, it has different theory to explain why and how the consumer is influenced to make the choice by different factors. For example, utility theory,it explains that consumers make choices based on the expected outcomes of their decisions. They are viewed as rational decision makers and they only consider self interest.

Utility theory views consumer is as a " rational economic man". However, the factors influence consumer behaviors may include these activities, such as need recognition, information search, evaluation of alternatives, the building of purchase intention , the act of purchasing choice, consumption and finally disposal. Hence, it seems that all the consumer's activities in whose purchase processes. They will influence their choice. For example, when the property purchase consumer , he plans to research different kinds of properties information concern price, location, housing areas, room numbers, building facilities and environment facilities. He will find some sample target properties information to make comparison in order to decide to buy which of property is the most suitable to satisfy his living need.

However, it is not only one activity for the property purchase buyer in his decision making process. It also include evaluation of alternatives activity when he ensures the accurate property information number in order to evaluate whether which one of all these property choices is the most suitable one. Hence, it explains that property information research and evaluation of alternatives both activities are needed to spend much time for this property buyer. If he does not plan to find one property to live in short time, it is possible that he can spend one month, even more than one month or more than three months time to do the only property information gathering activity.

Hence, it seems that time factor is not the main factor to influence the property buyer to do property purchase decision immediately. Otherwise, if the property buyer plans to find one new property to live within one month. Then, time factor is possible one important factor to influence this property purchase choice decision. For example, if he felt that he needs more time to spend to gather information concerns the large house area size and the properties have more than three bathrooms and/or bedrooms properties information. Then, he will be possible not to find any this kinds of all property information. So, it means that all these properties won't be his choice. It is because long time property information gathering activity factor influence.

I assume that the property buyer is a economic man and he does not spend much time to do the property information gathering activity. So, this kind of property needs him to spend long time to gather properties information in order to make this kind of properties comparison. Moreover, because he expects to live one new property within one month. So, he only chooses the properties, they have less than three bedrooms and/or bathrooms to gather sample properties information in order to make property purchase decision within one month. Hence, the time variable factor can only influence the property purchaser when he/she needs to make decision to buy one new property to live in the short time. If some kinds of properties choices number has a lot and the property buyer feels to let that he/she must need to spend long time to find the suitable properties number to make evaluation alternatives comparison behavior.

Then, the time variable limiting pressure factor will be possible the main factor to influence the property buyer's choice in order to make the most suitable kind of property purchase decision. Hence, it is one case example of how time limiting pressure factor can influence consumer purchase choice decision, such as property purchases market case. The reason explains why the property buyer needs to spend time to do property information gathering. I assume that general property buyer behave rationally in the economic sense. They won't only believe property agent individual property photos advertisement , it concerns where the property location is and facility etc. information on property photos in order to evaluate whether the property price is reasonable to pay. Generally, property buyers need to attempt to gather property information and visit the different actual property locations to make choice. So, general property consumers would have to be aware of all the available different kinds of properties consumption options from themselves properties information gathering and the properties agents' verbal properties introduction both be capable of correctly rating each property alternative and the available to select the optimum course of the final property purchase action.

Hence, in the property purchase and sold market, limiting time pressure factor will be important influential factor to decide whether the kinds of properties will be option to some property buyers when they feel need to find one suitable property to buy in short time. Otherwise, in some food consumption market , time limiting pressure factor will not be the main factor to influence consumer option. Such utility theory indicates consumers are as one rational economic man, whom do not expect to spend much time to do any options evaluation decision making.

However, in coffee market, buying a coffee comes almost automatically and does not need much information search. Hence, time limiting pressure factor won't one main factor to influence coffee consumer to choose to buy the kind of coffee to drink. However, there are other factors to influence coffee consumers' kind of coffee drinking option from cultural, social, personal or psychological factors. So, coffee taste producer can follow these factors to estimate how coffee consumers might behave in the future when making any kinds of coffee making purchasing decisions.

Firstly, social factor can affect coffee consumer behavior significantly. Every coffee consumer has someone around influencing his/her coffee buying decisions. The important social factors include reference groups, family, role and status , e.g. when the coffee buyer has high income job and his friends have good educational level and high income. Then, he will compare his reference group, such as his friends' coffee buying behavior choosing which kinds of coffee taste to drink in habits or lifestyles. If he chooses the kind of coffee taste to drink, its price is cheaper to compare his friends' drinking coffee tastes. Then, he may be influenced to follow his friends to drink the same kinds of coffee taste in order to keep their same social status and role between him and his friends.

Secondly, the coffee consumers will be influenced how to choose which kinds tastes of coffee to drink by personal factors, such as his age, life cycle state, occupation, economic situation , lifestyle and personality and self-concept. Age related factors are such as taste in food, e.g. the kinds of coffee taste. Although, coffee price is cheap, but if the coffee consumer's income is more and he/she can often spend to buy different kinds of taste coffees to drink. Then, his/her income level will have much purchasing power to influence his/her purchasing behavior. Hence the coffee consumer's frequency of consumption of different kinds of coffee taste drinking choice behavior will represent whether his/her income level is high or low in possible. For example, the consumer needs to go to automatic coffee shop to buy at least three cups or more different kinds of high class good taste coffee brands to drink per week. Although, these high class coffee brands' prices are higher than the low class of coffee brands. But the coffee consumer still only buys any one of these kinds of high class brands' coffee taste to drink. Hence, it seems that this coffee consumers ought have high income to let him to buy at least three cups of high class brand of coffee taste to drink from automatic coffee ship per week.

So, income factor can influence the coffee consumer to choose either coffer purchase from supermarket or coffee drinking at automatic coffee shop. If the coffee consumer only chooses to buy coffee from supermarket, due to the bottles of different kinds of brand coffee can provide more different tastes of coffees choices from shelves to let him to buy to drink at home. So, it seems that the coffee consumer's income level is low in general. Otherwise, if the coffee consumer only chooses to go to automatic coffee shop to buy the high class brands of coffee tastes to drink at least three times or more per week. It may mean that the coffee consumer has high income level to support him/her to often go to automatic coffee shop to buy different kinds of high class coffee tastes to drink frequently every week. Some high or low income level factor can influence every coffee consumer individual drinking coffee behavioral options.

Moreover, when the coffee consumer is younger coffee consumer will be possible to buy much coffee to drink. Because younger age people can accept to drink coffee habitually more than older age people. Also, it is possible that younger people feel often drinking coffee behavior will help them to bring more health feeling and /or raising nervous to learn , due to they need often to go to schools to study. Otherwise, older age people feel often drinking coffee behaviors won't help them to bring more health and they do not need to raise nervous to learn.

Finally, even, cultural difference factor will influence coffee consumers number for any countries. For example, western countries' people like to drink any kinds of coffee tastes traditionally. Asia countries' people like to drink any different kinds of teas tastes traditionally. So, different kinds of teas tastes will be Asia people's traditional drinking substitute to replace different kinds of coffee tastes more easily. Hence, culture difference will be one factor to influence Asia coffee buyers number. So, it seems that time limiting pressure factor won't influence coffee consumers' coffee taste choices to different kinds of high class or low class brands, visiting coffee shops or visiting supermarkets choices, frequent or not frequent coffee drinking behaviors.

How and why time limiting pressure
influences consumer choice

Can consumer buying decisions be influenced by time limiting pressure. For these three situations, they will influence consumer hoe makes different buying decision, e.g. in the little time available, but the consumer needs to do more effort needed to choose to buy which kind of product among variety kinds of product choice or in a moderate amount of time available, or a considerable amount of time available. In this first situation, the consumer can not real attempt to find any weaknesses or unique characteristics of the products, because it has no enough time to allow whom to choose. So, his/her product evaluation won't be the most accurate to satisfy his/her needs because little time can only allow him/her to find some weaknesses of the products. Otherwise, in the final situation, because the consumer has a considerable amount of time to allow him/her to attempt to find the weaknesses and/or strengths characteristics of the products choice. So, he/she ought do the more reasonable or accurate evaluation of these products to choose the most effective economic beneficial product to buy. Thus, it seems that time limiting pressure factor can influence the consumer to make more rational or more reasonable economic beneficial consumption decision making to buy the product or consume the service.

Thus, a consumer buying decision will require these situations to do buying decisions, they may include either little time and conscious effort or a moderate amount of time and effort or a considerable amount time and effort. The products may include cheap products/services , e.g. fruit, DVD, university courses, computers, facial services, surgeries, sport shoes, reference books, soft drinks, magazines as well as expensive products/services, e.g. cars, houses, luxury goods, e.g. jeweler, female hand bags, holiday travelling entertainment. So, any expensive or cheap products or services, the consumer will need to spend either little or moderate or considerable amount time to do gathering information about the different kinds of products or services in order to find which brand of product or service can bring more economic benefit when he/she chooses to use the product or consume the service. He/she will compare his/her preference sample brands limiting number of products or services choices to decide to buy the brand of product or consume the brand service easily. However in the consumer's consuming decision making process, he/she will need to spend either little or moderate or a considerable amount of time to do the evaluation and choice consumption behavior. It means that time limiting pressure factor will influence the consumer how to make consumption choice consequently.

What are the impacts of reduced branding on consumer choice and time limiting pressure to influence consumer behavior? When one consumer needs to choose products to buy one in a time limiting pressure consumption environment, when branding on packaging is reduced, e.g. the brand of product has 10 different style of packages to let consumer choice, but it reduces to only 5 different style of packages to let consumer choice. How does it influence the consumer decision making when the consumer has little time to allow to choose these 5 different style of packages ? For example, when the consumer expects to spend only 10 minutes to choose any one style of package to buy this brand product. Currently, this brand of product has reduced different style of packages number from 10 to 5. Do you feel that the consumer will feel easy to do decision making to choose to buy the most attractive style of package product from this brand's 5 different style of packages choices? Is 10 minutes consumption choice time enough to let the consumer to make final purchase decision from these brand's 5 different style of packages choice? Will the time limiting pressure be reduced , due to this brand's 10 style packages are reduced to 5 style packages to let the consumer to choose within the 10 minutes expected limiting consumption choice time.

It is one interesting psychological consumption behavior to research whether the brand's reducing different style of packages number factor will influence the consumer to do the decision making in the short time in the time limiting pressure environment. For toothpaste, shampoo products example, if the brand of these products' style packages choice is reduced to 5 style packages from 10 style packages choice. When one consumer finds the brand of toothpaste or shampoo has only 5 style packages on the shelves in supermarket. If the consumer has moderate or considerate amount time to let him/her to choose these both kinds product any one style of packages to buy. The 5 style packages to these both of products will be impossible to satisfy the consumer's choice need because he/she has much time to stay in supermarket to choose. Otherwise, if the consumer has little time to allow to stay in the supermarket , e.g. only 10 minutes. Then, he/she expects to spend only 10 minutes consumption choice time to do buying decision making within 10 minutes. These both kinds of the brand's products, its style of packages choice number is reduced to 5, it is possible to satisfy the consumer's choice need to buy this brand of product either toothpaste or shampoo and both of thee brand of products to be chose to buy in the supermarket. So , the reducing style of package number to let consumer choice will be seem to let the consumer to do buying decision making in the limiting time pressure consumption environment.

In fact , package is such a visual to influence consumer decision making in the short time or personal limiting time choice process. If the product has more attractive package design, the it can bring more attention effort to influence the consumer to choose to buy the product in the short time information transfers to influence the consumer decision making to choose to buy more easily , when he/she is active in communication process. So, package, communicating with consumer in the selling place , has become an essential factor to influence the choice of consumer.

Scientific researches have proved that package decisions can attract consumer attention, transfer the desirable information about the product, position , the product in consumer conscious, differentiate and identify of among similar kinds of products. In that way elements of package influence consumer decision making process and can determine the choice of consumer and the package itself can become more competitive advantage.

However it is not absolute that the brand of product has more package choices, it must have more customers to choose to buy its product. For example, there are two brands of shampoo in the supermarket shelf. One brand shampoo has 5 different style of packages and 5 different fruit productive elements to cause similar fresh fruit smells to attract consumers to buy. Another brand shampoo has 3 different style of packages and 3 different fresh fruit smells to attract consumers to buy in the same shelf location also. When one supermarket customer has little time to expect to stay in the supermarket, e.g. he expects only to stay the supermarket maximum to 15 minutes. he expects to buy one bottle shampoo and meats and fruits and vegetable within 15 minutes. Hence, he expects only to spend about 5 minutes to choose one brand of shampoo product as well as he demands to spend maximum 10 minutes to buy other foods within 15 minutes. When he stays in the sham shelf location, he finds only two brands of shampoo products are displayed on the same shelf location. One brand of shampoo has 5 different style packages to let him to choose, but he feels that these 5 different style packages are not very attractive. Otherwise, the another brand of shampoo has only 3 different style packages to let him to choose, but he feels that the 3 different style packages are very attractive. Due to he feels time causes pressure to choose these two brands of shampoo immediately. So, he does not want to spend more time more than 5 minutes to choose on brand of shampoo to buy. He will be influenced by the brand of different styles of packages more attraction to influence his buying decision making obviously. So, whether the shampoo brand's package is attractive or not, it will influence the consumer's buying decision making to choose either to buy the brand's shampoo product in preference.

So, the more packages choice to the brand's product which may not mean that it has high opportunity to influence consumers' attention. Otherwise, the attractive package element if more important to compare right number of packages choices. Consumer package can influence these elements, e.g. colour, size, imageries, graphics, materials, smell, brand name, producer/country, information, special offers. Of the brand of products can have much attractive elements. Then, it can attract consumers to choose to buy the brand's attractive package products in short time decision making process, such as perception of needs, search for information , evaluation of alternatives, decision making, behavior after purchase. Such as supermarket case, I assume that any supermarket consumers do not expect to spend much time to choose which brand of product is the most suitable or earning more economic benefit to buy when they need to stay the shelf to need spend much time to select which brand of product to buy in the supermarket. Because in general, supermarket consumers ought plan to buy more than one kind of product or food, even more usually. So, limiting time pressure factor will influence their decision making. Similarly, as my explanation indicates why although, the product had attractive package elements and its has many packages number choices, but it does not mean that it can win the similar product which has not more attractive packages, even it has more packages choices number to let supermarket consumers to choose. So, an attractive package element factor will have more influential and potential to cause supermarket consumers to choose to buy it in the supermarket limiting time pressure consumption environment.

How the time consumption pressure
factor influences irrational consumption
decision making

When one consumer has a large number of options, he/she will feel time pressure to cause whose accurate and reasonable evaluation. Then, the personal time limiting pressure factor will bring these questions: How does the time limiting pressure influence the consumer evaluation? Will the consumer personal limiting time pressure bring advantages and / or disadvantages in whom consumption decision making? How to help the consumer to solve short time decision problem when he/she encounters extreme time pressure and choice overload?

I shall assume every consumer is general one economic man. He/she feels time is important, he /she does not want to spend much time to choose one brand of product to buy among a number of brands of products choices. I also assume that any consumers decision making satisfaction, which is based on search until they found a sufficiently good item, or run not of time. So, it seems that which the consumer needs to buy one kind of product, but the product has a lot number of different brands to let the consumer to choose. The consumer ought need to spend much time to make choice decision making. However, consumer is one economic man, he/she ought not to search all different brands to decide whether which brand of product can bring the much economic value or utility value to choose to buy. So, in general, consumers will only choose sample brands of products to decide to buy the satisfied brand of product. For example, when the consumer needs to buy one television. The television has 20 brands of similar televisions to let he to choose. He will not spend much time to search these similar 20 televisions information. He will only gather sample 10 to 15 or less different brands of televisions to compare what their strengths and weaknesses, unique characteristics. Then, he will make decision to choose to buy the best television from these sample televisions. Hence, in general, consumers will feel time pressure when they feel need to spend much time to choose a lot different brands of similar products. Because they feel time is not enough to let they can do other important matters when they need to spend much time to do search information behavior when they need to buy any products usually. Hence, it is general consumers psychology that they will feel real choice under time pressure and choice overload, when they have too much a lot of similar brands of products to let them have opportunity to choose to make decision making to buy only one brand of product.

However, when a brand of product is familiar and given its simplicity and familiarity to general consumers' acknowledgement. It will have perference advantage to attract or influence consumers' attention or consideration. So, when the market has similar different brands of products are available to let consumers to choose. The largest choice set is not large enough to create overload to influence the brand's sale when consumers need to spend much time to choose these different brands similar products to buy. Because when the brand's any products are familiar and given its simplicity and familiarity to general consumers' knowledge. Then, it can build utility confidence to influence general consumers , it will be preference sample brand of product to do buying making option. Hence, the brand's familiarity factor will influence general consumers' preference buying decision making option. So, any product manufacturers need to concern how to build its brand familiarity to let many consumers to acknowledge in order to raise its competitive effort. Raising brand's familiarity may be a good method to solve consumer individual choice under time pressure overload , because when the brand of product is preference sample brand to any consumers. It's sale opportunity will also be raised. So, it brings the question: How can the brand of products can cause general consumers' preference choice. For food example, food brands were more likely to choose the implicitly preferred brand over the explicitly preferred one when choices were made under time pressure.

Imagining one customer enters a supermarket 10 minutes before closing time. He failed to write up a shopping list. So, when the staff is preparing to close store at the night, the consumer hurry not to for set too many of the ingredients for dinner . What brands of products , he opts for, as he can choose from a variety of similar foods, but time is short and the staff is looking at the consumer impatient? It is possible that the consumer will probably quickly decide in favor of the foods he likes best, pay, and leave the evening.

Hence, supermarket consumer's first time feeling to the brand of food will influence whom choice. One target category and one attribute category share same response key: Pleasant vs unpleasant feeing, if the supermarket consumer has pleasant feeling when he sees the food photos and touch the package of the brand of food to feel pleasant in the short supermarket closing time. Then, his pleasant feeling will be chooses to buy the brand of food to eat. Thus, the consumer individual pleasant or unpleasant feeling factor will influence whom consumption choice, such as this supermarket closing time pressure consumption.

In fact, many factors may influence whether consumer behavior is under more or less control. Hunger may influence control in the domain of eating behavior . So, such as the supermarket will close soon,it has store closing time pressure to influence the consumer needs hurry to make choice decision to buy food. If the consumer feels more hungry, he will not spend much time to find the right food to buy. He will be influenced by the different brand's food packages whether which brand of food package can bring a more pleasant to let him to feel, when he touch and sees the brand of food package. He won't spend time to search whether the different kinds of brands of foods have how much different health elements because the supermarket will close store soon. So, he only depends his individual pleasant feeling to make final food purchase decision. If he feels all of the kinds of brands foods are unpleasant food packages when he sees and touch them first time as well as he does not feel much hungry. Then, it is possible that he won't choose to any one food to eat. He will choose to go to restaurant to get dinner to replace buying food to cook to eat dinner at home at the night.

The another case is that time pressure concerns how on choice of information source impacts purchase decisions. When the consumer who buys one product , he needs to use the same number of information sources to search the product's information regardless of time pressure. Because he has more available time, he devotes more time , but only to selected the right sources to search information about the product. He will mostly use marketing dominant sources, e.g. magazine. he feels magazine can give more accurate information concerns to the product's good or bad quality real more reasonable and fair evaluation to let the consumer to acknowledge. so, when the consumer has much time to choose to buy which brand of product is the most best choice. He will buy magazine to find information. He believes magazine has more fair evaluation to different brands of product. It won't mislead consumers to make wrong decision making. Hence, in general, when consumers have much time to find information source to search which brand of product is more value to buy. They will attempt to buy consumer magazine to acknowledge whether the different brands of product , which have unique characteristics, strengths or weaknesses in order to compare them to make more accurate evaluation to choose to buy which brand of the kind product. When they have no time pressure to influence their choice process time to be shortened or reduced. Otherwise, these consumers will depend on newspapers, television, radio advertisments information sources when they feel time pressure controls their consumption choice decision making process time to be shortened or reduced. Hence, time pressure will be possible to influence consumer individual information source channel choice.

Time pressure consumption decision
making process characteristics

How we can predict or know the consumer time pressure in whom decision making process? Will it bring advantages or disadvantages to influence the businessmen benefits? I shall indicate some different consumption situations or environments to explain what will be impacted to sale number is increased or decreased to businesses when the consumer feel time pressure to avoid whom behavioral consumption to the product or the service.

Firstly, I shall explain that what effects of product popularity and time pressure on online shopping behaviors are . Electronic ecommerce is popular to any countries, in special, US, UK, China large areas countries, because when one customer feels need to spend one hour even more time to catch any transportation tool to arrive the shop to buy the kind of product. Then, due to far distance reason, he/she will choose to apply internet to buy the kind of product . If the seller has website to let the consumers to choose online shopping. However, it seems that online shopping behavior can reduce the consumer individual time pressure, when he/she feels need to catch any kinds of transportation tool to arrive the shop to buy the product. Moreover, when the consumer can turn on home computer to enter its website to choose the styles of the kind of products, which one is the most suitable to choose. He/she can spend time to search the different styles kinds of product information to compare and evaluate which brand of product will b whose purchase choice easily at home.

Hence, in psychological view, he/she can feel that spending time to search information from internet behavior which is more valuable and it can bring more economic benefit to make final purchase decision more than the behavior of spending long time to catch any transportation tools to visit the shop. Moreover, it is possible to bring failure risk that he/she wastes time to catch any transportation tools to visit the shop if he/she can not find any one of suitable product(s) to choose to buy. Hence, it seems the online shopping can influence the consumer reduced time pressure and wastes time to do any shopping decision.

This is online shopping's attractive strengths to the consumers when they need to spend long time to catch any kinds of transportation tools to visit the shop or when the consumer feels hurry to do other important matters, he/she can not allow himself/herself to spend long time to do his/her visiting the shop behavior. Moreover, another online shopping's advantage is that product popularity can be perceived by examining the information pre sended on websites. For example, research on online reviews confirms the review quantity presented with products become positively influences to consumers' purchase intention and it can persuade the online visitor can make decision to buy the product when he/she has enter the seller's online website to find the most suitable product to choose to buy more easily. Hence, it seems that it is more easy to persuade the online visitor to make final purchase decision more than visiting the shop , when the online visitor can attempt to do the click mouse behavior to enter the seller's online shop, such as website. Then, he/she will be influenced to view the seller's different kinds of colorful and attractive product pictures from the seller's website.

Consequently, it has much opportunity to persuade the consumer to do the final purchase decision. if the seller's website is attractive to persuade him/her to visit its website to find any new products more than five times, even tem times or every weak several times , even day one time frequently visiting behavior from internet channel. Hence, due to internet is convenient tool to let consumers to find any product information from the seller's website at home or public library , computer, or mobile phone. Consumers must find any product information any time in any places easily. So, online shopping can reduce any consumers' time pressure to visit any shops to expect to achieve final consumption decision aim in possible.

Thus, it seems that online shopping method can influence consumers to feel time saving and time pressure reducing consumption both advantages more than visiting shops' shopping method when the consumer is living far away from the shop. When the consumer feels that he/she is experiencing situational time pressure, then, he/she will respond well to seek another time saving situational consumption environment. So , it explains when one consumer feels he/she has no much time to catch long time transportation tool to visit the shop on the day. When he/she has computer at home, he/she will attempt to type the shop name to research whether it has online shopping platform service from internet. Because he/she does not want to spend one hour, even more time to catch transportation tool to arrive the shop, when he/she can't walk to the shop in short time. Even, he/she may feel online shopping behavior won't influence his/her eating , sleeping, or recreational time to be reduced at home or any places , when he/she can behave the online shopping behavior at home or any where conveniently.

Consequently, promoting online shopping is as a time-saver is likely to be effective for these experiencing situational time pressure. Those with situational pressure would almost certainly welcome anything that would reduce their activity level and the demands on their time. In fact, there is really no adult learning method for store shopping because it is something everyone learns to do from early childhood. But for many adult consumers, they feel have interest to learn how to use internet and web to shopping. Some adult will feel interest and it is value to learn how to use internet channel to anticipate the complexity of shopping online. For example, Super Walmart cheap food store that carries many thousands of products and brands to let online shoppers won't feel confused when viewing its online merchant's home page with only a few menu items and links from its website. So, Super Walmart website can let online shoppers to feel difficult that they can save much time to enter any merchants' home page . They only need to view the Super Walmart's website ,then they can find any preference cheap grocercies to compare and evaluate which one(s) is (are) value to buy. So, Super Walmart's website can let global cheap grocery online shoppers feel it can help them to save time to find any merchant's products from internet conveniently.

Consequently, online shopping will be one popular time saving consumption channel to reduce time pressure to some consumers nowadays.

Secondly, I shall explain that what determines purchase decisions for airline tickets when the traveller fees time stress. When a travelling planner has no enough time to prepare whose travelling journey, whether the time stress will influence he/she feels decision difficulties and frustration, when it will cause he/she needs to gather significant amounts of information to lead to make to choose which airline ticket is the most right choice? How and number of airline options and time pressure influence the airline ticket buyer's purchase decision?

However, there are both kinds of time pressures to influence the airline ticket buyer's airline choice decision, they focus on either real decision deadlines (physical time), such as the journey beginning day is any day of this week or tomorrow or subjective feeling of pressure with time (sense of urgency or psychological time), such as the traveller expects that he/she fears all airlines' all seats are full booked in this month. Moreover, he/she can plan to catch air plane to travel next month. So, he/she will attempt to gather any airlines' tickets prices, flight day and time and destination arrival and weather information in this month to avoid that it is too late to delay his/her next month travelling plan.

Hence, it seems that the effect of number of airlines choices and air tickets purchase deadlines (physical time limit) will influence how the traveller or air ticket buyer's purchase decision using secondary data to search of airline ticket. for example, if the traveller felt time is no enough to let him/her to go to travel agent to enquire any airlines' air tickets prices and seats and date and time air plan departure available time to concern the traveller's destination choice. Then, he/she will be probable to choose to buy electronic-ticket (e-ticket) from internet. If he/she has computer to link internet to gather any airlines' flying date and time and seat available information at home easily. Hence, it seems that one time pressure traveller will be probable to choose e-ticket purchase at home in preference. If the airline can provide online e-ticket purchase option to the time pressure traveller. Due to the pressure time traveller feels closer to departure, the negative impact of number of airline options is not as strong when he/she can view the airline's website to find the flight date, time and seat available information to purchase e-ticket to pre book the date and time to departure the traveller's country and to arrive his/her travelling destination information from the airline's website channel at home or anywhere any time conveniently. Hence, travel agency can bring a positive relationship between airline number of options and pre-booking airline that immediate possibility. When the time pressure traveller hopes the airline can build the good interactive relationship between number of options and decision time limit (number of days till planned travel effort on e-ticket purchase probabilities. So, if the airline website can let the traveller to predict when date and time is accurate available to arrive whom frequently destination choice country as well as the e-ticket's real price , it is not e-ticket predictive price and the real seats number available, it is not the estimated seats number available on the departure time and date to the travelling or arrival country destination. Then, all of these online information to the airline, which will raise the e-ticket pre-booking purchase chance to let the e-ticket buyer to make whose final e-ticket purchase choice decision to win its e-ticket competitors easily.

Consequently, a real time e-ticket information can attract any time pressure e-ticket buyers to choose to buy its e-ticket (electronic airline ticket) more than visiting travel agent's paper airline ticket option when the travel feels hurry to buy airline ticket to travel in short time.

Reducing time pressure consumption
methods

How can sellers persuade consumers to choose to buy their products or consume their services in time pressure environment easily? It is a valuable research topic to concern how to know how consumer individual decision making to spend his/her available resources (time, money and efforts, or consumption relate aspects) as well as how any why he/she chooses the preference brand to buy its any kind of products or consume its services, when he/she chooses to buy the brand of products or consume its services? Hence, marketers need to obtain an in depth knowledge of consumer buying behavior.

In any buying process, time factor will have about 10 % to 40 % to influence consumer decision. When the consumer feels hurry to consume, e.g. planning to go to travel, when he/she needs to choose to buy which airline's air ticket and what day and time is the right air ticket pre booking purchase decision right time choice; or enrolling which school to be chose course to study decision, e.g. how long time is needed to be choose which school is the most suitable to provide the most suitable courses studying choice change; purchase warm clothes to wear in winter, when is the suitable time to choose to buy the cheaper warm cloths to prepare to wear in winter, e.g. Jan to Mar., April to June, July to Aug. month; when is the most suitable time to buy another new house to live, when the property consumer(buyer) has lived present house for long time, e.g. three years or more. All of these issues will include time factor to influence the consumer feels when he/she ought choose to buy the kind of product or consume the kind of service. However, the other factors will also include to influence his/her decision, e.g. family, friend relationship factor, advertising factor, social status factor, cultural difference factor, personal psychological need level or satisfactory level factor, young or old age factor, income level factor, economic environment factor, material enjoyable need factor etc. factors.

However, time pressure factor will be the consumer individual intrinsic (internal) psychological feeling factor, and it is the consumer individual intrinsic feeling to judge whether when he/she ought spend some money to buy the kind of new product or the kind of consume service (what time is the most reasonable or the most suitable time) to make purchase choice decision. However, when the consumer feels hurry to make purchase decision. So, he/she will not hope to spend more time to gather more information to compare and evaluate which one is the right brand of product to choose to buy or the right service to consume among different brands of products or services. Otherwise, if the consumer has more time or he/she can make the decision to buy any brand of product. Then, he/she ought spend more time to gather more information to compare and evaluate which one is the most suitable product choice to buy or which one is the right service choice to consume. So, time pressure factor will have some influence to any consumers to make decision about what time is the suitable time to buy the kind of product or consume the service. For example, heater product is usually when winter weather time, the heater products need number ought increase in winter weather time or season. But, it is possible that the heater products need number won't increase in winter season / weather possible, when one country , there are many householders or families , they have one heater number at least at home. Then, it is possible that these householders or families won't have consumption desires to buy one more heater product to use in winter at home, because they have had one heater to use at home in winter. So , when the country has have many customers number, they are using the kind of heater products at homes. Most people own at least one heater number factor will have possible to influence enough time available to cause they do not feel hurry to buy any heaters to use at homes, so, their do not feel time pressure to buy any heaters in short time. Because they do not plan to buy the kind of product to use at home in short time when they have one heater product at least to use at homes in present.

Hence, it brings this question: How to attract or persuade the customers, they are using the kind of product to let they feel time pressure to make decision to buy another new or same brand of product to replace to use? The product's better quality , long durable time useful, brand loyalty and past good purchase experience factors will influence him/ her to feel time pressure to need to buy another new product in short time. So, when the consumer feel time pressure to make decision to purchase, he/she will choose when is the most right time to gather information, search, select, use and dispose of another new product to replace the old product in the short time.

Hence, the brand of product needs have good product motives, may be raised to the consumer's impluse, desires, considerations which make the buyer purchase the brand's new product to replace the present using product in order to achieve whose satisfactory needs to emotional product motives and rational product motives both. Moreover, persuading or encouraging the consumer feels he/she has real need to buy the kind of new product or replace the present old product (s), the brand of product marketer needs let the consumer feels these any one of nature of motive to raise his/her purchase decision desire in time pressure environment. The natures of motive may include: When the consumer feels desire for saving money, he/she will choose to buy it when the brand of product falls down, when he/she feels fear to be sickness, retirement, he/she will choose to buy insurance policy, when he/she feels pride, or high social status knowledge, he/she will buy premium product , e.g. gold, expensive watch, car , when he/ she feels fashion need, he/she will move house to live from rural to urban, or rural people imitate urban to learn to do their fashion living behavior, when he/she feels possession need, he/she will feel need to buy antiques for its future unique worth satisfactory feeling in possible, when he/she feels health need, he/she will choose to buy health foods, join membership in health clubs, when he/she needs to enjoy comfortable feeling, he/she will feel need to buy micro-oven, washing machine to use at home, when he/she feels love and affection need, he/she will buy gift items to give to whose friends or families for presents in their birthday or lover day etc. special days to let they to feel happy. So, when the marketer can touch the consumer individual different nature of motives to satisfy his/her personal purchase feeling need and it can know how to influence them to feel that they have these any one of purchase motive needs in short time. Then, they will be persuaded to raise time pressure to make purchase decision to buy any kind of products in short time.

However, instead of attractive good product quality method can attempt consumers to make time pressure consumption behavior. The another method is brand loyalty building method, which can be attempted to encourage or persuade consumers to feel consumption desire need to make decision to buy the brand of any products in time pressure consumption environment. For example, when the consumers feel the brand is loyalty and it can build good image to his/her feeling , and this time pressure factor can influence this brand of any products which has high discount price to attract the consumer individual attention , e.g. familiar brand high class cars, the good confident house agent's high class houses, and the expensive and infrequently buying items, come under this category. When their prices are fallen down to sell cheaper , e.g. twenty per cent discount or more than twenty percent discount sale price than the other similar competitive brands' any products' normal prices. Then, it is possible to let these expensive items' consumers have high involvement and high feeling need in time pressure consumption environment. Because they assume that this discount sale price will be short time sale price, e.g. after three months or next month etc. short time discount sale price in short time period. Then, these expensive items' prices will be raised to the normal sale price, even higher price. so, they have time pressure feeling to feel that it is right time to make consumption decision in order to avoid to lose these low price purchase benefit in this non-predictive cheap discount price purchase items. so, if the expensive item marketer can build long time good brand loyalty relationship to consumers. Then, it will have much influential effort to persuade consumers feel consumption desires need by its any extensive items in the non-predictive short term discount period, due to they do not want to loss this large discount purchase price chance. So, short time discounted sale price, it is another method to persuade consumers to choose to buy the brand's any products in short time pressure consumption environment.

The another persuading time pressure consumption method is that it can let consumers to think more habitual buying the kind of products. products like stationery, groceries, food etc. fall under this category. For example, when the consumer fees the brand of any products ,he/she has habitual purchase experience, of he/she feels that the brand's any products won't sell in market temporary, even he/she can not buy it to use again. Then, it is possible to influence him/her to feel immediate purchase need to buy a lot of product or food number to keep to use or eat later in the time pressure environment, e.g. the food consumer buys the brand of any breads to eat in supermarkets habitually, but in this moth, he/she watchs TV advertisement to be acknowledge this brand of any breads won't be bought from any supermarkets as soon as possible. Hence, it is possible to influence him/her to plan to make choice to buy a lot of number of this brand of any breads in order to keep the enough of this brand of breads number to eat later. So, this brand of any breads sale loss in supermarkets that will cause the habitual food consumers of this brand of breads, whom make consumption choice to buy a lot number of this brands any breads in short time suddenly. Because they are eating this brand of any kinds of breads habitually. They feel much eating need to lot number of this brand of any breads in short period, because it can satisfy their habitual taste needs of this brand's any kinds of breads. So, brand loyalty and habitual consumption to the kind of product or food , which will result simply from the habit and it can influence the consumers feel consumption need to buy the brand's any kinds of products or foods when they feel that they may not buy it again or they can not earn discount advantage after the short time. So, any one of these sale strategies will have possible to raise the consumer individual consumption desire to the brand of products in the short time pressure consumption environment. Also it needs to spend much time to gather information in order to make purchase decision, because the brand had built confidence to consumers when they feel this brand's any products or foods are better to compare the similar brands' any products or foods habitually. So, time pressure consumption environment will persuade them to feel consumption desire to buy this brand's any products or foods in short time. When, they feel that they can not buy any more for this brand's any kinds of products or foods or discounting price in this final short purchase time.

In conclusion, these factors can influence consumer behaviors to be changed to feel time pressure need to do purchase decision making behavior from enough time gathering information available feeling behavior. They have these same views, e.g. habits and routines are very influential, particularly for behaviors repeated daily in a semi-automatic fashion. The consumer's past purchase experience to the brand's products, positive or negative emotion to the brand's products, and the brand's familiar, recognition are strong influence , the information available , it is the consumer's mind and the relative important information given to let the consumer knows form different advertisement medias matters for decision making, great between pieces of information and can be influenced by personal psychological timing limited pressure, the consumer's comparison to differences in price or other characteristics, many pursue value (or in bargain), and compare to alternatives or past knowledge, consumer personal greater value on the immediate future and heavily discount future costs or savings to the brand of product, feeling simple and easy decision making process to the product , it can lead the consumer to avoid to spend long time to make purchasing decision and the consumer will easy to choose to buy the product when he/she feels have a loss value if he/she does not decide to buy the product in the short time. SO, it seems that when the marketer can motivate the consumer's consumption desire to feel saving money, promote health, avoid waste time and less nervous workload to gather information for comparison and evaluation alternatives aim. It is seen favorably by the consumer personal time pressure purchase decision making and sense of justice influence factors.

However, sociologists have categorised the motives for consumption behaviors in the short time by the fundamental consumption decision making needs or wants which they satisfy, e.g. having a clear understanding what benefits, characteristics, economic value to the brand's any products , feeling consumption decision making process is a leisure activity. These drivers for consumption behavior will either bring positive or negative to influence the consumer personal emotion, either owning enough time available or time pressure environmental impacts can be seen to influence whether the consumer feels he/she needs how long time to be spent to make comparison and evaluate alternatives in order to make final purchase choice in whom decision making process. Hence, the consumer himself/herself time pressure consumption decision making feeling, it can bring positive purchase choice influence, when the marketer can build brand loyalty to let many consumers to feel in the market. Otherwise, if the marketer can not build brand loyalty to let many consumers to feel, but consumers feel time pressure to compare and evaluate its any products to other similar brands of products in the competitive market. Then, its products may be not the preference choices the many customers among the different brands of products choices. So, building long time brand loyalty relationship to satisfy consumers' needs, it will bring positive preference purchase choice to raise the sale effort to the brand of any products when consumers need to make purchase choice in time pressure consumption environment, e.g. seasonal discount sale period, products or foods shortage supply period, without any forever sale possibility in market. Hence , it seems that brand loyalty building factor will influence any brands of products /foods /service sale or provison number to be raised or reduced in possible. Also, it can explain why and how it has close cause and effect relationship between time pressure consumption environment and the brand loyalty building to the brand of products/foods/services to any marketers nowadays.

What are the in-store and out-store
factors influence supermarket
fast moving consumer decision

It is one interesting question: How can the brand of product seller influence the supermarket/store fast-moving consumers' more visual attention when the supermarket/store visitor is hurry to make decision to choose to buy which brand of product in time pressure environment? Supermarket/store fast-moving consumers do not usually spend much time to say in any supermarket shelf locations to choose numerous similar alternative brands of products. However, I assume the fast-moving supermarket/store consumer's decision is dependent on the interaction between the supermarket different shelf location sale environment and the mind of the consumer. So, the eye tracking explores this rapid processing that lacks conscious access or control to any supermarket or store consumers.

It brings this question: How product packing and placement (as in-store factors) and recognition, preferences, and choice task (as out-of-store factors) which will influence the supermarket / store consumer individual decision making process through visual attention. In split-second decision making, the ability to recognize and comprehend a brand of supermarket/store product can significantly impact preferences. Hence, how the supermarket/store consumer's eye truly sees what whom mind is prepared to influence how much consumption desire to choose to buy the brand's product in short time decision making process when he/she stays in the shelf location, it has less than ten or more than ten different kinds of brands products or foods to let the visitor to choose in the supermarket or store.

Brand owners and product developers will feel responsibilities to overcome promotion or advertising or communication challenge in order to let consumers to know their products are launched on the market. However, it is not until the product reaches the supermarket shelf that has good quality to the effort is judged whether it has how much sale number every day in the supermarket. The judges are the consumers themselves how to make decision quickly through the personal time pressure environment with minor package information processing in the supermarket.

What does it take to be consider an option to influence the consumers' minds on visual attention in point-of-purchase decision making ? The supermarket's in-store activities and the consumer personal out-of-store activities will influence how his / her visual attention to the brand of products in the supermarket / store any shelf locations when he/she is walking to pass any shelf locations. So, it seems that any supermarkets or stores brands of products sale number , it has relation to every supermarket or store visitors' visual attention throughout the point to point (shelf to shelf) decision making process in the supermarkets / stores. So, how much does the supermarket's visitors' time spending to obtain attention to the brand of produc? it will have possible to influence the brand of any products' sale number in the supermarket/store. Hence, in this limited timeframe, the consumer enters a decision making process that is in itself influenced by in-store and out-of-store both factors.

I shall explain what is supermarket / store space quality factor, e.g. top level versus floor level to different shelf variable height, weigh , or shelf space location factor as well as the product price elasticity and price-quality relationship to the brand of products both factors to influence every consumer decision making in supermarket/ store. The in-store factor is more influential factor to compare out-of-store factor to influence consumers' decision in supermarket. For example, where the shampoo brand products are locating to be put on the shelf , it can influence the point to point behavior of shampoo product habitual buyers. If the buyer habitually chooses the shampoo brand products in the shelf location. Also, if all of the shampoo brand products are moved to another shelf locations to display its different kinds of shampoo products to cause the habitual buyer needs to spend much extra time to find where the another new shelf location is displaying the brand's shampoo products.

In this situation, information processing has a heightened decision making role as the buyer needs to spend much time to find where the brand's displayed shampoo products' shelf location to make non-habitual decision making between options. For habitual decisions, the consumer's visual attention is reduced to measuring visual search. However, when the brands of any shampoo products are moved to another new shelf location to display its different kinds of shampoo products. So, the act of another shelf new location search , it will influence the habitual shampoo buyer's visual attention to consider the brand of any shampoo products which are usually used to wash to his/her hair habitually. When he / she can find the other new brands of shampoo products are displayed on the old shelf displayed location of the brand of shampoo products. Hence, the traditional shelf displayed location to the brand of products, when the brand of products are moved to another new displayed shelf locations. This in-store factors that will influence traditional consumers through visual attention concerns to this brand of products more or less.

So, supermarket traditional shelf displayed variable location to the brand of products factor, which will have influence to the traditional consumers' visual attention to do either buying the brand's products or buying another brand's products to replace it, when the traditional consumer feels difficult that he/she needs to spend extra longer time to find whether where is the traditional useful product's displayed shelf location. Then, it will be possible to influence the traditional consumer's traditional purchase decision to the brand's product, and he/she will choose to buy another brand of product to replace when it can be displayed to the shelf location to attract the consumer's visual attention more.

It is one important in-store shelf displayed factor to influence the traditional fast-moving consumer individual purchase decision making behavioral change in any supermarkets or stores when they feel hurry to do personal time pressure consumption decision to make purchase final decision in the point to point counter purchase (the brand's of products are moved from the traditional shelf location visual attention moves to the strange shelf location visual attention) in supermarket time pressure consumption environment.

Hence, in supermarket time pressure consumption environment, in -store and out-of-sore both factors can influence fast-moving consumer individual purchase decision making. The in-store factors can influence product packaging, product placement components as well as the out-store factors can influence choice task, preference and brand recognition components. So, it is common to influence supermarket consumers choose do personal time pressure purchase consumption decision of visual attention purchase behaviors. The different brands' products are displayed to different shelf locations in order to cause shelf displaying products' different decision making effect.

However, instead of shelf displaying location factor, package will also influence consumers' decision making, due to the influence of minute differences in packaging design on visual attention. When, the supermarket consumer feels the brands are not familiar or unfamiliar. Then, he/she will spend more time to evaluate and verify the unfamiliar brands' products whether which one is value to buy in her/his decision making process. He/she will feel visual attention need in order to evaluate in set of brand alternatives to make conscious demand mind cognitive effort by involving working memory. So, if the product's package is attractive, even the consumer is unfamiliar the brand's any product choices which are displayed on the shelf location in the supermarket. The brand's attractive package factor can influence the consumer to raise whom visual attention. Then, the attractive package factor can increase much visual attention chance to many consumers when they are walking to pass through the unfamiliar brand's any products' shelf displaying location considerably. So, it explains when attractive package factor may solve the visual attention problem to fast-moving consumers when they are visiting one strange supermarket to find anywhere unfamiliar brand's products' shelf displaying locations. Because they are the non-traditional consumers to the unfamiliar brand's products, they won't be influenced to choose either buying or not buying the unfamiliar brand's products. When the unfamiliar brand's products are moved to another new shelf displayed location. So, if the unfamiliar brand has attractive package to let the non-traditional consumers feel visual attention when they are passing through the strange shelf displayed location. Then, it can raise purchase chance to the non-traditional consumers target number when they are staying in the strange supermarket.

In conclusion, the brand of products' shelf displaying location and package factors may bring much influence to any traditional or non-traditional consumer behaviors in supermarket or store time pressure consumption environment.

What consumption is most
influenced in preference choice
by time pressure

What kinds of services or products are most influenced to consumer behavioral change by time pressure? Can time pressure factor influence more preference to other factors, such as age, culture, income level, habitual shopping, family or friend relationship etc. factors to influence consumer behavioral choice to these kinds of services or products in consumption market? I shall indicate some kinds of services or products consumption models to explain how time pressure can influence consumers to choose to consume its services or buy its products.

Firstly, for theme park entertainment industry example, has it time pressure to cause any theme park visitors, e.g. Walt Disney entertainment theme park to influence them to feel time pressure to enjoy their emotions to play any entertainment machine facilities and it brings negative emotion to choose the entertainment theme park entertainment consumption activities.

For Walt Disney entertainment theme park example, every visitor needs to pay a fixed ticket fee to enter Disney theme park. So, however, he/she chooses to play how many number of entertainment activities facilities, e.g. only one entertainment playing facility, or more than one entertainment playing facilities. The Disney visitor needs to pay the same ticket fee to enter Disney. So, it will cause the visitors feel unfair , they do not choose to play any entertainment facilities or play only less number of entertainment facilities. Because they need to pay the same ticket price to same to the visitors, who choose to play many entertainment facilities number in Disney. So, it brings this question: Does the Disney visitor feel time pressure when he/she chooses to play many number of entertainment facilities , but he/she will not enjoy to carry on other activities in Disney, e.g. shopping, visiting cinema to watch movies, walking around the whole Disney anywhere to view scene activities. Because US Disney entertainment theme park is very large . It has not only entertainment facilities to attract visitors to play. It has many places are value to visitors to visit or enjoy the other free charge entertainment activities , such as visiting Disney gardens, visiting ocean park, visiting Disney cinema to watch free movies, view scene or seeing free charge ocean animal performance shows , going to Disney shopping centers to shopping, visiting Disney library to read books, visiting Disney ocean park to view different kinds of beautiful fishes non-entertainment machine facility playing activities. All of these activities are value to any Disney visitors to choose to play or visit, instead of entertainment machine facilities activities. So, if one visitor hopes only to spend one day in US Walt Disney entertainment theme park. He/she will feel hurry to choose to play any machine entertainment facilities, or he/she won't choose any machine entertainment facilities to play in Disney because he/she also hopes to play other non-machine entertainment facilities activities, e.g. visiting garden, visiting ocean park, visiting library, visiting cinema to watch free movies, visiting garden to play free charge boats water entertainment activities, watching ocean animal show performance etc. different kinds of entertainment activities, even walking around anywhere fun and excite places in Disney theme park. Hence, the Disney visitor will feel time pressure to choose either playing any kinds of entertainment machine facilities or visiting different places in the whole one day in Disney.

Hence, time pressure factor may influence any one of Disney visitors how to choose any entertainment activities to spend time in Disney. It will bring this question: Because the Disney ticket price is fixed fee, can the Disney visitor will feel unfair to cause negative emotion, if the Disney visitor feels time pressure to choose to play any kinds of machine entertainment activities or doing other non-machine entertainment activities in the Disney visitor's limited timeframe, during he/she stays in Disney? So, it seems that time pressure psychological factor will may influence some Disney visitors to feel unhappy, negative emotion, when they feel their entertainment activities choices are wrong or doing wring entertainment decision making in his/her limited timeframe. Consequently, time pressure factor will influence some feeling time pressure Disney visitors won't choose to enter Disney again. Hence, time pressure factor can have much influence to theme park visitors' behavioral change, instead of whether the entertainment theme park's machine entertainment facilities are attractive or enjoyable playing or how many entertainment facilities are supplied to let visitors to play in the entertainment theme park. So, entertainment theme park service provide need to consider whether their ticket prices are reasonable to let visitors feel, if they do not want to reduce theme park visitors number seriously.

The another example is restaurant food service industry. Can time pressure influence food consumers to choose the restaurant to eat? Instead of food taste, price, seats available providing, restaurant location, public transportation facilities available etc. factors, which can influence the food consumer individual choice to the restaurant.

Is time pressure another one main factor to influence food consumers choice to the restaurant? In what situation, food consumers will feel time pressure to influence whose preference restaurant choice? I assume that the restaurant 's price is reasonable, public transportation facility is convenient to catch to go to the restaurant, food taste is acceptable to the food consumer. Although all above these factors are accepted to the food consumer . But when the food consumer feels hurry to hope to find one restaurant to eat and he/she hopes to spend less time to sit down to eat in the restaurant , e.g. less than one hour. Then, the food consumer will compare all the restaurants are near to whose working place or school , if he/she is one student or one working person. Because he/she needs to eat lunch to go to school or go to office to work. So, the restaurant's food taste, price is not the main factor to influence him/her to choose to eat. Otherwise, whether the restaurant needs him/her to spend how long queue time to wait, or/and the restaurant needs how long cooking time to let him/her to eat, the restaurant needs him/her to walk how long time to arrive the restaurant. All of these factors concern " efficient cooking time, queue waiting time service performance" issues to the restaurant, which are the main evaluation requirements to influence the feeling time pressure food consumer to make decision whether he/she either still ought follow the better food taste, cheap food price factors to be preference decision or he/she ought follow short time queue time waiting or without queue time waiting, fast cooking waiting time factors to be preference restaurant consumption decision.

Hence, it seems that a feeling time pressure food consumer, he/she ought choose the restaurant to eat in preference when it does not need him/her to wait long queue time and wait long cooking time. Otherwise, when the food consumer does not feel hurry to eat, he/she ought choose the restaurant, it can provide good taste food, cheap price in preference to eat.

Hence, time pressure personal feeling will influence students or working people food consumers' preference restaurant choice when the restaurant can provide short time queue waiting or without queue waiting and fast cooking time service preference to satisfy their needs.

However , in some situation, time pressure can influence consumers to choose the service, even its price is expensive than other services. For example, public transportation tool choices service. When one passenger has need to find one kind public transportation tool to catch from the place to another destination, but the destination is far away from his/her location. He/she hopes to catch the kind of public transportation tool to arrive the destination about one hour. Although, his/her location has cheap public transportation tools to choose, e.g. bus, train, tram, ferry, underground train. But, he/she feels that all of these public transportation tools need to spend longer time to compare taxi to arrive the destination. Although, these public transportation tools can be possible to arrive the destination with one house and they must charge cheaper fee to compare taxi. But, however the passenger hopes to arrive the destination in the shortest time. The most important influential factor is that the passenger feels personal time pressure to need to arrive the destination fast and taxi public transportation tool is believed the fast transportation tool to arrive any destination to compare other general public transportation tools , when it has no traffic jam external environment factor influence. So, time pressure factor will influence passenger to choose taxi transportation tool in preference. Also, it seems that when the place often has many time pressure passengers are living. Then, the place's taxi business will be possible better than other locations. Hence, it implies that time pressure factor will bring need or demand number to be increased to some services.

Time pressure also influences how consumers choose to buy the kind of product, when he/she feels that the kind of product will be old fashion or it is not popular to use in society. For example, computer product, the traditional desktop large heavy weight computers will be possible to be replaced to use at home or office or any building places. Due to the laptop small light weight computers , it can be brought to anywhere by the users easily, even it can be brought to catch public transportation tool to use, it can be brought to restaurant, library, shopping center etc. different public places to use conveniently. Due to some working people feel hurry to use computer to do their tasks, e.g. typing one document in short time. If they are not working in office and they have no computer on hand. They will worry about that they can not finish their tasks to give their bosses in limited time on the working day.

Hence, laptop computer will be one good chocie of task tool for busy working people when they need to often to use computer to finish urgent tasks in any time. Hence, it seems that the feeling time pressure working people will choose laptop computer in preference more than desktop traditional computer working tool. Due to the feeling time pressure workers, they feel that they can not finish their daily tasks in office. So, they will feel to need to use laptop computer task tool to help them to do office tasks . When they are catching transportation tool to go home or office time or lunch time , or holiday time. So, laptop computer product is more popular to time pressure working people target consumers.

Laptop computer products can also increase the feeling time pressure student consumers' needs. Because when one students feel home time is not enough to use computer to do their homeworkers at homes. When some students finish all lessons in schools and they need to catch public transportation tools to go home, in this catching public transportation time, they will be possible to hope to use one laptop computer to do their homework. So, one student who often feels time pressure to do whose homework, he will feel need to buy one laptop to carry it to anywhere, e.g. library, garden, school etc. different places. Then, he/she can do whom housework at any places in any time conveniently. Hence, it seems that their laptop computer products will be time pressure consumers' preference task tool.

In conclusion, the different factors influence consumer behaviors. Time pressure factor may be one main factor to influence consumers to choose to buy the kind of product or consume the kind of service in preference. So, when th consumer feels time pressure to influence him/her to do preference choice to consume the kind of service of buy the kind of product. It is possible to occur to influence he/she does irrational economic choice decision. Hence, time pressure factor can being positive or negative both consumption emotion to some kinds of services or products . Hence, the increasing or decreasing number of consumers to some kinds of products or services, it has absolute relationship between of them. So, any product sellers or service providers can not neglect the importance of how time pressure factor influences consumer behavior in our nowadays society.

Time pressure impacts consumer
behavioral effect

I shall indicate cases to explain that how time pressure environment factor impacts consumer behavior as well as what effects will be brought by time pressure consumer behavioral cause. Instead of above discussions concern how customer personal time pressure psychological factor influence, whether hoe time pressure environment factor will also influence consumer behavior. What are the difference between time pressure environment factor and time pressure consumer personal psychological factor? I shall explain as below:

Firstly, the impact of life satisfaction is caused by time pressure on consumers responses. Can effective advertising can impact of life satisfaction when the consumer feels need to buy the kind of product in any time pressure environment? Can effective advertising bring direct impact on sales when the consumer feels need to buy the kind of product in time pressure environment? Effective advertising may being advantages, includes customers feel easy to accept of price increases, favorable publicity, and reshaping market segmentation.

However, when the customer feels need life satisfaction in time pressure lif environment. The time pressure life environment ought impact on the consumer responses on advertising. Hence, when the consumer needs to live in the time pressure life environment. The over-commercialization of advertising ought impact the consumer chooses to buy the brand of product, when the seller has attractive advertising to bring purchase incentives to influence consumption desire to the time pressure environment influential consumer. For example, when the summer season will change to winter season, the ice cream consumers begins to feel weather will change to cold weather. Because many people feel more cold in the beginning. This is seasonable time pressure environment feeling, it may influence many ice-cream likers feel ice-cream may be possible shortage in hot weather or summer season, due to many ice-creams will be bought in summer weather to cause supermarkets in possible. So, if the brand ice-cream can make attractive advertisement to persuade ice-in cream number will be reduced in the coming winter season beginning. So, it may influence many ice-cream likers choose to buy this brand's ice-cream in preference in summer. Because they feel fear none of any this brand's ice-creams can be sold in supermarkets in summer. Because they feel this brand's ice-cream , it's problem to let they can buy any different kinds of ice-cream taste to eat from any supermarkets in summer season. Hence, it explains why effective or attractive advertising may increase sale number, when consumers feel the brand's product number will be shortage or reduced from the seasonal time pressure external environment factor influence.

Secondly, I shall discuss what is the relationship between the effects of product popularity and time pressure on consumer responses? When a brand is popular to let many customers to familiarize in society. Does it increase time pressure to influence consumers choose in preference? Time pressure remaining to product popularity concerns how much sale number is raised to persuade consumers to choose to buy a preference for ecommerce online shopping. It seems to be one time pressure online sale environment. The effects of the ecommerce online shopping environment has relationship between pressure and product popularity on perceived risk and purchase intention.

In ecommerce online sale environment time pressure is operation at the time remaining for consumers to sign up the online seller' website and property popularity is operation to the number of products already sold at the moment when consumers visit the web page. Hence, when on online consumer has intention to buy any products from internet. He/she will attempt to type the product name, then he/she will find some webpages which can provide the different brands of product photos, their prices information to let the consumer to compare whether which brand of product price is more reasonable, better quality , good product image from the web pages' advertisement information to let him/her to evaluate. Hence, any product web page will influence how every online customer feeling is good or bad to the web page's any brands of products. If the consumer feel the web page has many high product popularity indicators, it may bring a high consumption desire to let the online customer to evaluate the web page all products in order to compare which brand of product is the best to choose to buy in time webpage view pressure consumption environment. Otherwise, if the consumer feels the web page has high product popularity indicator , it may bring a less consumption desire to let the online consumer to evaluate any of the webpage products to choose to buy. So, online webpage advertising information will be one time pressure online ecommerce consumption environment.

I assume that online shopping consumers won't like to stay to view on any webpage long time. It is possible that they choose to click more web pages to hope to find more different familiar and unfamiliar both brands of products information in order to make more accurate comparison and evaluation from more different kinds of brands of products in order to make the most accurate online shopping decision. Hence, any brands of products online webpage information will be one time pressure limited sale environment to consumers feel that they need to make the most accurate online purchase decision in short time. Moreover, it seems that if the brand of products which can be showed on the popular product webpage, the it will have much sale chance to let online purchasers familiarize in order to increase sale opportunity more easily.

Finally, I shall explain what is the meaning of external time pressure consumption environment is the long time queue waiting consumption environment. I shall explain how to achieve one simplistic queueing system to solve long time queue waiting problem to bring consumers' negative emotion influence to choose to consume the service or buy the product in preference.

For entertainment service example, e.g. queueing at the cinema counter to buy one ticket to watch the movie , or queueing at the music hall to buy one ticket to listen the music performance show activities. The audiences' ticket purchase aims to sit down in the cinema or music hall to enjoy to listen and see pretty music performance or watch the attractive movie comfortable within one to two hours entertainment time. If the movie or music performance show is attractive, the cinema or music hall will have many audiences accept to spend long time to queue to buy the ticket. However, if the cinema or music hall needs audience consumers to queue long time to buy the ticket, e.g. one house , even more than one house queueing time to wait to buy the ticket to watch the movie or listen the music performance show. Then, the long time queue waiting problem will be possible to cause a lot audiences number to be reduced, because they feel that they need to spend much time pressure to queue to by the ticket to listen the music performance show or watch the movie.

However, of these unacceptable too long queue time audiences can have another/ other cinema(s), music hall(s) to buy the same price , even more low price of movie ticket or music performance show ticket in short time. Then, they must leave the present cinema queue and go to the another cinema or music hall to buy ticket to watch the same movie or listen the same music performance show. So, long time queue is one external time pressure environment to influence consumer's preference choice to the service provider, when they feel it has another service provider does not need them or these audiences need to spend same long time queue time to wait to buy the ticket in order to enjoy the service, e.g. listening music performance show, watching movie.

Hence, in a high time pressure queue situation where decision makers, e.g. audiences have less time than needed (or perceived needed). It is very likely that they feel the queue waiting time stress of copying with themselves queue waiting time maximum limitation. So, if the movie ticket purchase audience feels that he/she will need to spend more than half hour to queue and half hour is himself/herself the maximum acceptable queue time level. So, his/her queue long time pressuree negative emotion feeling will influence him/her to leave the cinema to choose another cinema. He/she feels that ir does not need him/her to queue more than half hour in order to buy the ticket to watch the same movie in the another cinema, he/she can feel more comfortable to watch the movie. So, long time queue will influence some audiences choose another service provider to replace it in possible short time, when they feel waiting in a queue is irritating, frustrating and hence costly.

What is a simplistic queueing system and how it can solve above queue problem. For a grocery store queueing counter case example, for one Apply brand computer shop example, the day's most busy queue time , there are about between fifty and hundred Apply brand potential computer buyers numbers every hour in the day. They need to queue to enquire the salespeople concern to any useful opinions to let them to know in order to make purchase decisions. But, the Apple brand computer shop lacks enough salespeople to answer their enquiries concern any computer purchase challenges. Every computer enquiry potential purchaser needs to spend at least half hour , even more time to queue to wait the salesperson to answer his/her enquiry in the counter queueing line. Hence, the feeling long time queue enquiry waiting consumers will feel time pressure to queue. Then, they will choose to leave the Apple brand computer shop's counter queue line. Consequently, the Apple brand computer will lose many potential computer buyers on the busy day.

The most simple solution is that it can increase the salespeople number in the most busy enquiry time every day. Hence, when every computer potential enquiry customer can contact every salesperson to listen whom opinion concerns his/her any computer enquiry issues in order to let he/she feels that they every one can provide excellent sale service computer issues enquiry explanation performance to satisfy his/her enquiry need to let himself/herself to feel in the short enquiry time. Due to they do not need to spend long queue time to wait every salesperson's feedback or opinion to solve their enquiries in the computer shop. Because they do not feel pressure to spend long time to queue to wait the computer shops every salesperson's opinion. So, they will raise satisfactory feeling to the Apple computer shop's every salesperson individual sale enquiry service performance.

Consequently, the day's computer sale number will be possible to raise after the salespeople can spend much time to solve their enquiries effectively and efficiently.

● The reasons cause consumers feel
time pressure

What factors can cause consumers feel time pressure to but the product in the personal time limited dominated consumption environment? It is one interesting question: Why does the consumer feel time pressure to make short time purchase decision making? I shall indicate some cases to explain this possibility as below:

First, I shall indicate household purchaser time pressure consumption behavior. Consumer house buyer behavior, some house buyer will feel personal time pressure to choose the different houses to make house purchase decision in short time. For example, if the house developer has a 30% discount house price to sell only in the short three months. So, after this three months, all house purchaser will need to pay the original house price. If the house developer's houses prices are between US dollar one million to two million every house. For one million house price after 30% discount , the house buyer only needs to pay seventy million. For two million house price after 30 % discount, the house buyer only needs to pay one hundred and fouty million. So, expensive product's financing factor will influence the buyer's consumption time pressure, such as the house discount price case, due to the house developer's houses prices are very expensive. However, if any house buyers can make decision to buy its houses in three months. Then, they can pay les 30% of the houses prices. Such as the original price one million house, the house buyer can pay less thirty million amount or the original price two million houses prices. The house buyer can pay less sixty million amount. So, the large discount financing amount may be attractive purchase method to influence many house buyers feel time pressure to decide whether they ought choose to buy the property developer's houses in these three months. It is one short term cheap house financing price to let many house buyers feel time pressure to make house purchase decision from this house developer in these three months . Hence, short term high discount price to expensive product financing factor will influence consumers feel it is right time to make pressure consumption decision.

Hence, such as this three months house discount price case, when the property buyer gain this property developer's knowledge of three months house discount price message. This sudden three months house discount price message will be one attractive knowledge of factor to impact the potential property buyers' house purchase desires to be raised in three months time pressure house purchase consumption environment. So, it is one feeling sudden time pressure consumption desire good example for this three months large discount attractive houses price to influence house buyers to make house purchase decision from the house developer in these three months. Consequently, house developer will have possible to raise the large house sale number , if this 30 % house discount price can let many property buyers feel it is one worth purchase price in these three months. So, they will consider that they can not pay less 30% discount price to buy this house developer's any houses after three months. So they need to make house purchase decision in these three months short term time pressure house consumption market for this property developer.

So, this time pressure financing advantage will only bring benefit to this property developer, this time pressure financing advantage won't bring benefit to other property developers, because all property buyers feel need to make property purchase decision in these three months suddenly, due to this property developer can provide a special 30 discount price to any property final decision making to choose to buy its houses in these three months temporary short time. It seems that three months short time can cause final house purchase choice time pressure to any potential property buyers. They expect to gain high discount price to buy any expensive houses. So, these expensive house potential buyers will feel need to make final expensive house purchase decision to choose to buy this property developer's expensive houses in these final three months period. So, time pressure can occur in any short period, when the seller can provide any special sale promotion to persuade consumers to feel need to make sudden time pressure that purchase decision is they hope to earn special sale promotion consumption in the short limited sale period for the seller.

Hence, consumer personal time pressure feeling, it can be predictive to any time occurrence psychological consumption, feeling, such as the property developer's sudden high per cent discount price to expensive house less burden factor to influence the expensive house buyers feel that whether they ought do choice house purchase decision in these short term three months , because the house developer's non predictive and sudden attractive expensive houses reducing prices strategy. So, this property developer's short term three months high house discount price time pressure consumption strategy may persuade or attract , even encourage many potential expensive house buyers choose to spend lesser amount to buy this property developer's discount houses, either is paid by house mortgage bank loan lending payment method or installment payment method or on-time all payment method. So, the different house payment choice buyers will be influenced to make immediate property purchase decision in these three months time pressure period from this property developer's expensive discounted house number influence.

However, in this house market time pressure consumption environment, the property developer's expensive house supply number may also have influential effort to excite the expensive house buyers' house purchase consumption desires, for example, if the other expensive house property developers' between US one million and US two million of every property price's these houses in the country's property marker total supply number is one thousand property unit number. The potential property buyers , they plan to buy these amounts of expensive houses , the property buyers estimate three thousand buyers number at least. Hence, it seems that these expensive house buyers' demand id more than three times to expensive property supply number.

Moreover, the other property developer's expensive property developers ' expensive house prices have no any discount in this three months periods, and some property developers' expensive house prices tend to increase 1 to 10 per cent in these three months period. Hence if the property developer can supply at least three thousand property units number between US one million and US two million sale price and all of these expensive houses are reduced 30 per cent discount to sell in these three months .

Consequently, it is possible to persuade all estimated three thousand expensive house potential buyers choose to buy this property developer's houses in these three months in possible. So, it explain that why this property developer's expensive discounted house supply number will influence these property buyers' preference choice. If this property developer has only one thousand expensive houses to be supplied by discounted 30% sale price. Then, it will cause shortage of expensive houses to satisfy these three thousand expensive house buyer estimated number in the country in three month discount sale promotion period.

Consequently, this property developer will lose two thousand these prices of expensive house potential buyers number in all these three months discounted sale period . I assume that all these three thousand expensive house property buyers will be influenced to make choice to buy its all discounted expensive houses in these three month time pressure discounted sale period. So, it needs to do data gather concerns how many of thee expensive house potential house buyers number in its country in order to avoid discounted expensive houses supply number to cause shortage supply challenges and bring these expensive house potential buyers lose number in these three months period.

In conclusion, it explains why that supply number will influence this property developer's sale number in these three months sale period. Consequently, time pressure sale strategy and supply number has close relationship to influence the seller's sale number in the time pressure sale period.

Secondly, I shall discuss how does environment time pressure factor influences consumer behavior? Does time pressure influence consumer donating behavior? I assume that external environment time pressure factor can influence consumer changes whom original purchase decision making. What circumstance's time can influence consumer individual to feel time pressure to consume. For example, when the consumer expects have one hour to choose whether which brand of product to buy among the different kinds of products. The circumstance is changed suddenly. It influences the consumers feel that they has only 10 minutes to make the final purchase decision.

Why does the consumer feel enough brand of product? What external circumstance factors influence he/she feels only 10 minutes time to make the final purchase decision suddenly? For travel fair time limited external environment influential pressure travelling consumption case example, the international travel fair can indicate that time limited pressure has positive significant influence on traveler perceived value and purchase intention in short time. In addition, perceived value is served as a mediating factor between the relationship of time limited pressure and feeling travelling entertainment purchase intention to the travel fair visitors. It has a beneficial reference for planning a travelling show or fair marketing strategy.

One attractive travelling fair/show can promote the country's different attractive travelling destinations to let the travelling show's visitors to know. It can particularly influence the visitors' long time travelling planning , it can be shorten be short time travelling planning, e.g. after one year's travelling planning can be influenced to make immediate focused on choosing the country's travelling decision if he/she feels the country has more attractive travelling destinations, he/she prefers to go to travel in short time, e.g. within 6 months . So, when the travelling exhibition fair/show can provide the country's beautiful scene photos to let the visitors to view. Then, it will bring effective time pressure feeling to let some travelling visitors feel travelling needs immediately in the travelling exhibition show/fair . This travelling exhibition show/fair can bring the time limited pressure benefit. It is as an external environment factor that can influence the travelling visitors' travelling desires to be raised , when they can view many beneficial scene photos of the country' different undiscovered travelling destination . Then, it can increase their travelling desires to the country in possible.

I shall explain why travelling exhibition show/fair can play an important role in travelling consumer perceived quality and travelling country destination choice decision making to influence travelling visitors feel time limited pressure. However, perceived value has been show to be a value has been shown to be a value of perceived quality and perceived sacrifice to cause travelling visitors feel more interesting to choose to travel the country when they can view the attractive beautiful scene photos in the travelling exhibition show/fair.

A successful travelling exhibition show/fair can bring time limited process increases , the travelling visitors pay more attention to key travelling destination features and positive travelling information from the scene photos and travelling destinations introduction. So , the country's attractive travelling destinations scene photos and clear travelling introduction to different destinations information will be important message to let the different countries' travelling visitors to know when they spend a limited time to enter the travelling exhibition show/fair to view the different scene photos . If the travelling visitor feel very satisfied to the country's travelling exhibition show/fair. Then, this travelling exhibition excite whom travelling interest to choose to go to the country to travel in short time, when the travelling visitors are influenced to feel the country has many beautiful destinations where they feel have travelling interest in the limited time pressure travelling exhibition show/fair environment. If the travelling exhibition show/fair needs they to pay enter fee and it has only two hours or less time to permit to stay in the travelling exhibition show/fair.

Hence, if the time pressure limited travelling exhibition show/fair can let the travelling visitors feel attractive and enjoyable view feeling when they look every the country's any scene beautiful photos and indication how to the different travelling destinations and explains why the country's travelling places are value travelling destinations to let the exhibition visitors to know, when they do not know or discover these any one of value travelling places in the country before. Then, this limited time staying travelling exhibition show/fair will bring positive time pressure to influence some travelling visitors feel interesting to visit the country's unknown or discovery travelling destinations in short time. So, all attractive travelling exhibition shows/fairs are one external environment time limited positive pressure factor to excite some travelling visitors' travelling desires in short time in possible.

Instead of travelling exhibition show/fair can bring external environment positive limited time positive pressure to excite travelling visitors' travelling consumption desires, the another external environment positive limited time positive pressure case is that mobile coupons of limited mobile phone sale number or discount mobile phone call payment plan in short time case. How and why mobile coupons can excite any mobile consumption and/ or mobile phone call user choice to the mobile phone sale company or mobile phone call service provider.

An effective mobile plane useful limited time beneficial purchase strategy can encourage some mobile phone consumers to choose to use the brand mobile useful phone call service plan immediate if the mobile phone call service plan is attractive to the mobile phone call consumer . For example, dynamic discounts strategies are used by marketers to send scarce message which lead to higher consumers' mobile phone purchase intention. An utility increasing discount strategy provides mobile phone call users with an increasing discount over time (e.g. 30% discount for in-store consumption for 30 minutes, after which the discount increases to 40 % , an utility discount strategy provides the same discounts for mobile phone call users over a specific promotional period (e.g. 40% discount from 9AM to 5 PM) phone call using time. An utility decreasing discount strategy offers mobile phone call users with a decreasing discount over time (e.g. 40% discount for in -store consumption for 10 minutes, after which the discount decreases to 30%).

However, these three different discount strategies for bargaining have different impacts on outcomes. However, they have same influences to lead mobile phone call users feel time pressure to do choose whether this mobile phone call using plan is suitable. If the mobile phone call user feels this mobile phone call using plan is suitable to use, then this mobile coupon promotion strategy can influence mobile phone user feels limited time pressure to persuade him/ her to choose to use its mobile phone call service under different time limitation, quantity limitation and discount strategies on the mobile phone user's mobile phone call plan using intention.

Furthermore, I hypothesize that the brand of mobile phone quantity, limited scarcity message that gives a perception that the brand of any kinds of mobile phones are limited for purchase, it will have a positive impact on mobile phone consumers' perceived value of mobile products, leading to a greater tend to make mobile phone purchase decision immediately. Hence, mobile coupon is one type of price-incentive promotion. In various price incentives, discount strategy is a mode of price negotiation between the mobile product consumer and the merchant, such as the mobile phone seller , mobile phone call user and mobile phone call service provider.

However, mobile coupons offer discount under a time constraint to induce perceived scarcity. Scarce commodities are more attractive than those with plenty inventory due to the in special and uniqueness of the former perceived by the consumer. However, scarcity has both forms. They include quantity scarce can let consumers feel need to buy the product in short time. Otherwise, due to stock shortage or low inventory to influence they can not brought the kind of product. Time scarcity means products are for sale only for a designated

    May time dominate consumption

final purchase decision making

    Whether can time limited pressure dominate consumer individual to make more rational purchase decision? Can the consumer make more rational decision , when he/she has enough time to make final purchase decision? I shall explain why and how the consumer can make more rational decision when he/she has enough time as well as I shall explain that without time pressure environment. It may dominate consumers to make more rational or more accurate decision making.

I assume that it is the final time limited pressure day to nee the consumer to spend more nervous do time final purchase decision among the different kinds of similar products choices, e.g. air conditions . If the consumer decides that the day is the final purchase decision to choose to buy one air condition among these different brands of similar air conditions in the super store. So, if on the that day, he/she can not make any final decision to choose which brand of air condition to buy on that final consumption day in the super store when the super store visitor sees the final air condition consumption day advertisement in this year in this super store . Then, he/she won't buy any air condition again if he/she can not buy on that day in this super store.

The another time dominates immediate purchase behavior is that I assume that one common air condition can not be bought in short time later if all air condition consumers can not make decision to buy any air condition in this super store. So, his/her personal time limited pressure can dominate whose final or condition purchase decision in this super store on that day. If the store has many different brands of air conditions to lead him/her to spend long time to compare which is th best worth to buy in this super store. Then, it will let him/her to feel difficult to make the air condition final purchase decision in the store on that day. Otherwise, if the super store has less different brands of air conditions to need him/her to spend less time to compare which is the best worth to buy in the store. Then, he/she may make the final air condition purchase decision making more easily on that day.

So, the final air condition purchase day of the super store, the super store's air condition final day's time can dominate the air condition buyer to make air condition purchase decision immediately. Due to he/she feels that all of these day brands air conditions can not bought from this super store after that day. So, he/she needs to make the air condition purchase decision making in this super store on that final air condition purchase day in this year. Because it is the final air condition purchase day in this super store of all sir conditions products. If he/she can not make the choice to buy any one brand of air condition in this store. Then, it is possible that he/she will lose this store's final cheap price air condition purchase benefits. However, if this super store has too many brands of air conditions need him/her to choose. It will cause him/her to spend more time to choose. Consequently, it will cause he/she feels difficult to compare which brand of air condition is the best and he / she does not choose to buy any one in this super store.

Hence, this super store ought have less number different brands of air conditions to let every air condition consumer to choose in order to let they can make final air condition purchase decision on this air condition cheap price purchase final day. So, less different number brands of air conditions will dominate the consumers to spend less time to make purchase decision immediately and easily on that final sale day in this super store. Hence, it seems that the super store's final air conditions sold day time will dominate many air condition visitors to make purchase decision when they visit this super store in summer season on that day in this super store. Because all this super store's air condition consumers do not expect that they can not buy the best quality of air condition in this super store final sold day , due to air condition stocks number shorten challenge is not supplied enough on that final cheap purchase day in this super store. Consequently, that time pressure will increase to influence them to make the final air condition purchase decision in the final sold day' s short time, before this super store closing time on that day. Their time pressure feeling comes from the super store 's air condition number shortage supply in possibility. It will dominate them to make the final air condition purchase decision in this super store in short time.

The another time dominates immediate purchase behavior case is that I assume that one common picture painter(actor), he finds one architect to help him to build one house. The architect only needs to follow his house picture to build one house. The common picture painter tells him that he will give him building expenditure and building profit after he helps him to build the house profit after he helps him to build the house successfully. After six months, the architect made one decision, he did not demand the famous picture painter paid him for the building service fee. But, he needed him give the house picture to him to replace the building service fee. Because the picture painter feels that he didn't need to pay the building service fee to him to buy the architect's building service in these six months building time. Hence, he accepted his offer to give his common house picture to the architect for his reward.

I assume that this six months time dominate the architect to make the final building service fee decision either acceptance the common picture painter customer's building service fee or acceptance his common house picture replaces the building service fee. However, the architect believes that this common house picture can have higher selling price to compare his building service fee income. Consequently, I assume that his evaluation is right, this house picture selling price is more than three times to compare his past six months' building service income. So, it proved that his choice is right, because he could earn more than three times of his building service income after he decided to accept the common picture painter's this house picture to attempt to sell it in the picture auction market. It seems that this six months long house building time can dominate these both buyer and seller's purchase and selling behaviors, such as this picture painter and this architect. When the architect has this six months enough time to let the picture painter to change his building service offer decision from building service fee payment to his common house picture offer exchange. This architect can achieve his intention to let him to accept his free house picture sold product exchange offer more easily. Otherwise, if the architect can not need six months to build this house, he only needs three months or less time to build this house, then it is possible that the picture painter won't accept his this house picture offer to replace his building service fee easily. If he considers that whether his this house picture's selling price has possible to sell higher price to compare this building service fee for this house picture. He will choose to sell this house picture himself. Hence, due to the picture painter can not sell this house picture in this past six months. So, in this six months period, the house painter can not sell this house picture in picture auction market. This six months period can dominate his low market worth selling feeling to this house picture as well as it can influence him to make this house picture exchange decision to replace his house service fee.

The picture painter will ask himself, ought the house picture painter need to wait how long time to sell this picture in auction market, because he does not know whether the architect needs how long time to build this house? So, this house building time can dominate the picture painter's acceptance of the architect's this free house picture product exchange offer, which is easier acceptance or difficult acceptance . In this six month' house building period between the architect service provider and the picture painter house buyer. Hence, the house building time can dominate the house building provider and the picture painter's house building buyer both house picture free exchange purchase change behavioral choice between of them influentially.

The another time dominates consumption behavior case is that time rich or time poor factor, e.g. one fast food famous restaurant , its success is not only due to its fast food good taste factor, its restaurant location whether is close to the time poor people's offices, it is one main factor. Because this fast food famous restaurant only choose to build its restaurants to close to offices in any large cities in different countries. Hence, the franchisees need to pay expensive franchise loyalty income to buy its franchise in order to it can supply fast foods to the franchisees to sell, but they also need to pay expensive rent to this fast food franchiser, due to their fast food restaurant locations has been chose to locate in the main cities in different countries from the fast food famous restaurant's location decision. Hence, whether long or short time fast restaurant rent period to the franchisees , which can dominate the fast food restaurants' royalty and rent income. For example, if one fast food franchisee only sign one year contract to buy the fast food franchisor's loyalty to help it to sell its fast foods only one year, because it does not ensure how many fast food consumers will choose to buy these fast foods to eat, due to its price is decided by the fast food franchisor. If the cities have other fast food restaurants to let them to choose, they may find other fast food restaurants to replace it to eat fast foods very easily. If this fast good restaurant is not the most famous and it operates only short time. So, it can not earn more fast food franchisees' confidence to accept to pay long time rent to operate its fast food restaurants in cities and pay long time royalty fee to it. Otherwise, if the fast food restaurant had operated its restaurant for a long time period to raise its fast food loyalty's to let many different countries' fast food eaters to familiarize or acknowledge its fast food brand in popular. So, long fast food operation time can confirm that it has many fast food eaters, they prefer to choose to eat its fast foods. It can increase the franchisees' confidence to choose to rent its fast food restaurants and pay royalty to it in preference. Hence, the fast food franchisor's restaurant operation time whether it is long or short time, this franchisor's fast food restaurant operating time pressure factor will dominate the fast food franchisees' choices to decide to pay how long rent sand franchise royalty income to rent its restaurant to do the franchisee's fast food business in the cities locations in different countries. So, it seems that the fast food franchisor's business operation time can dominate the franchisees' choice.

In special , in fast food industry, time rich and time poor consumers behavior will dominate their fast food choices. Time rich people feel they have enough or too much time when time poor people feel time is a major constraint in their daily life. The growth of the fast food business, and the increase eating of fast food are indicators of this trend. At the same time, shorter working hours increased wealth and less pressure on domestic routine have opened up new segments of leisure consumption. But, " free time" in certain areas has not for many people, lead to an increases feeling of time richness.

So, it explains that why many fast food consumers who feel not enough time to work daily. They are time poor working people usually. So, instead of fast food taste factor influences consumer number. The people who feel time rich or poor, e.g. employment rich or poor lunch time to the employee, it will dominate the employee chooses to go to fast food restaurant in preference. So, the fast food restaurant can supply rich time to let them to eat lunch in short time, if the employee has less time to eat lunch or more tasks need him to do on that day afternoon. Hence, feeling time rich or poor to the people factor, which will dominate some consumers' choices to some kinds of businesses, such as fast food industry, or for public transportation tool choice case example, one time poor passenger feels need to go to the destination in short time. The time poor passenger will prefer to choose taxi in preference, then it is possible train or underground train, next it is tram, tain, it is bus or ferry public transportation tool choices. Otherwise, for one time rich passenger, he has more time to go to the destination. The time rich passenger will prefer to choose the cheap public transportation tool , such as bus, ferry, underground train, ferry, train. The final choice is taxi. So, passenger's time pressure will influence whose public transportation tool choice.

● Time pressure dominates consumer psychological factor

What are the factors of time pressure dominate consumer purchase psychological behaviors? How any why do this time pressure psychological factors dominate consumer behaviors? It is possible that time pressure can dominate consumer mind and behavior either choose to buy the product/consume the service or not buy the product/ consume the service. Every consumer's final purchase decision, he/she is influenced how to make by himself/herself personal psychological limited time pressure . It means that he/she will have one time maximum standard to demand himself/herself to make the final purchase decision in whose individual psychological time standard (the consumer's individual psychological limited consumption time). So, it seems that ever consumer's final decision how he/she chooses to buy the product or consume the service, his/her consumption behavior will be dominated by whose psychological time limited consumption pressure.

So, time pressure issue seems evolutionary psychology, it looks at how consumer behavior has been affected by psychological adjustments during time pressure . It seeks to identify which consumer psychological traits are evolved through adaptations, e.g. time pressure consumption adaptations to choose the final purchase decision in the final time limited consumption pressure environment, e.g. the consumer expects this day is the final day to choose to buy what kinds of the product. If he/she can't make final purchase decision on the day, he/she will choose to buy the kind of product later, even he/she does not choose to buy the kind of product in the first or again, that is the products of natural selection, or the supermarket visitor case, he expects to choose which kind of food to eat within final 15 minutes, if he/she can't make the final decision to buy what kind of food to eat within final 15 minutes in this supermarket , or the restaurant eating consumer case, he is queueing to wait to enter the restaurant to eat. He/she expects the final queue waiting time is 15 minutes maximum. If after this 15 minutes, he/she can not be permitted to enter this restaurant, then he/she will choose to leave this restaurant and he/she will find another restaurant to replace it. So, it seems that any consumer will have himself/herself consumption limited standard time to decide whether he/she ought choose to buy any products or consume any services in any consumption environment.

Hence, the cause of consumption time pressure dominates consumer behavior, it is based on these hypothesis: Every consumer has demand characteristic and time pressure can dominate how he/she make final decision to buy or not buy any product or consume any service as well as any consumer needs have time pressure consumption demand because he/she does not expect to spend more time to choose what kinds of products to buy or what kinds of services to consume. He/she expects to make purchase or consumption final decision in short time.

IN fact, consumers will be encoded to influence how they make final purchase decision. There are three main ways in which product information can be encoded. They include: Visual (product picture) ; for example, the consumer stores the memory by visualizing it as on product image. Aconstic (sound); here the consumer stores the information as a sound , this explains why some consumers sometimes get the brand name(words) that sound the same mixed up when they try to remember them. Semantic (meaning); here the object is stored in terms of what it means rather than as an image or sound, e.g. when the brand of toys can let many children feel fun to play. Then, when many parents feel familiar to the toy brand, they must remember this toy brand company is selling any kinds of toys to let children to play. So, famous brand can let consumers familiarize what products that it is selling. Such as the toy brand company can let parents feel its toys are fun to let their children to play. All these sensory information can dominate consumers make final choice purchase behavior to buy its product or consume its service in preference in any time limited pressure environment, if the brand can give positive information memory to let many customers to remember.

So, it seems that consumers are dominated to choose which kinds of products to buy or which kinds of services to consume by positive or negative emotion, time pressure in any consumption environment immediately. It is one time pressure consumption environment theory factor, it can influence consumer behavior is changed in any consumption environment time. Consequently, it explains that why time pressure can dominate consumer behaviors in possible. Also, any product seller or service provider needs to consider how to manage consumption time process to be longer to cause its consumers doe not choose to buy its product or consume its service consequently.

Methods avoid consumers
feel time pressure

In business society, it seems that any consumers will feel time pressure to cause their purchase decision making process changes in any consumption situations, when they feel time pressure either by themselves or third parties influence, e.g. not buying any thing, not consuming any service, irrational making consumption final decision etc. consumption behaviors. How to reduce their time pressure to avoid they do above consumption behaviors. I shall indicate some consumption situtations to explain how to avoid their reducing consumption , due to time pressure factor influences as below:

Firstly, I shall indicate supermarket consumption environment example. In general, supermarket visitors will expect to spend less time to visit any supermarkets to make choice to any foods. They will stay short time when they expect to buy less foods, even, they will stay more short time when they expect to buy more less foods in any supermarkets. So, any supermarkets will need to calculate their clients' limited time pressure how to influence their foods consumption number. If the supermarket visitor expects to spend maximum 20 minutes to buy any foods in the supermarket. Then, he may choose some different kinds of foods to buy, e.g. ice cream, fruit, bread, jam, fish etc. different kinds of foods, Otherwise, if the another supermarket visitor expects to spend maximum 10 minutes to buy any foods in the supermarket. Then, he may choose less different kinds of foods to compare the first one, e.g. fish, jam, ice cream only or bread, fruit , jam only. So, the second one supermarket visitor will buy less different kinds of foods, because he expects to spend 10 minutes maximum , his shopping spending time is less 10 minutes to compare the first one supermarket visitor. Because different supermarket visitor personal time pressure will limit him/her to choose more or less different kinds of foods to buy. However, time pressure will not influence every kind of foods number because every kind of food purchase number will not be influenced to buy more or less , due to the supermarket visitor personal time pressure variable factor influences his/her foods purchase number. Otherwise, the different kinds of food choice will be influenced to choose to either buy or not buy , due to every supermarket visitor personal time pressure is different.

Hence, supermarkets can focus on how to avoid any kinds of food purchase choice loses , due to supermarket consumer personal time pressure influences. In fact, in supermarket every shelf, it usually has many different brands of every kind of foods to let supermarket visitors to choose to buy. For example, the kind of jam food number has many brands are placed on shelf to let them to choose, e.g. there are more than 10 different brands of jam food are placed on one shelf. It will bring one choice problem. IF one supermarket visitor expects to choose one brand of jam within 5 minute, then he finds the shelf has more than 10 different brands of jam are placed on the shelf. Then he will feel time pressure to cause difficulty to choose the best brand of jam to buy from these 10 brands of jam. It will bring the negative emotion if he feels that all of these 10 brands of jam taste and price has no more difference. Consequently, these 10 brands of jam choice will cause he can not make the final jam purchase decision within this 5 minutes individual time limited. Anyway, if there are only 5 brands of jam are placed on this shelf, then the 5 minutes time limited consumer will has less brands of jam choices, it will influence him to do more easy choice to buy one kind of brand jam food from the shelf. It is one limited time pressure of psychological choice factor to influence any consumers feel to do any brand of food choice more easy in short time. Hence, I recommend supermarket shelf ought place every kind of food brand maximum to 5 brands , it is the best food brand number to every supermarket's shelves to let any consumers to choose different kinds of foods to make the easy food choice way in supermarket food market.

So, in super store market, it is similar to supermarket market. Super stores' main products are cloths, shoes, bags, stationaries, electronic products, e.g. fans, air conditions, televisions, radios, warmers, washing machines, dry machines, computers etc. However, super store visitors will like to spend more time to stay in any super stores, due to they feel to need more time to make purchase decision in order to make the most right choice to buy these any products. They usually expect to stay half hour , even one hour or more time in super stores. Their time pressures are depended on whether what kinds of products that they expect to buy in the super store. For example, if the super store visitor expects to buy one laptop computer. He will expect to make purchase choice decision within half hour, even more time. Otherwise, if the super store visitor expects to buy stationery, e.g. pen and rubber and pencil, he will expect to make purchase choice decision within 10 minutes. So, when the super store visitor expects to buy the product is more expensive, then his time pressure time will be longer than the super store visitor expects to buy the product is cheap, such as stationery and laptop two kinds of products.

However , due to super store 's expensive and cheap product consumers whose time pressures are different. So, brands choice number will have much different between them. For laptop example, due to superstore visitors can accept to spend longer time to make laptop purchase choice. So, one shelf can place 5 to 10 different brands of laptops , another shelf can place 5 to 10 different brands of laptops to let them to choose. Otherwise, for stationery example, due to superstore visitors can not accept to spend longer time to make stationery purchase choice. so, one shelf can place less than 5 brands of pens, the another shelf can place less than 5 brands of pencils or another shelf can place less than 5 brands of rubbers , another shelf can place less than 5 brands of rulers to let them to make purchase choice in short time.

Secondly, for restaurant eaters example, when one restaurant has many eaters choose to enter this restaurant to eat its food, then it only chooses to let some eaters to enquire ticket number to queue to wait. Of course, some eaters will not like to wait too long time, so they will leave the queue to choose another restaurant to replace it in possible. For example, in afternoon eating time, these are two busy eaters, the student feels hurry to go to school or the working person feels hurry to go to office after lunch, although the restaurant service staff had given him one ticket to let them to queue to wait. However, their expected queue waiting time is within 15 maximum, but there are many eaters are queuing and their ticket numbers are small numbers. So, they feel that they must not enter this restaurant within 15 minutes themselves limited queue time. Consequently, their late entering this restaurant after 15 minutes issue will influence that they will choose another restaurant in possible. So, the restaurant long time queue will cause some eaters choose another restaurant in busy time. I recommend that the restaurant can limit every eater's eating time, e.g. it calculate every eater's restaurant entering time and it limits every must leave the restaurant within half hour in busy eating time. It can post notice to let them to know in the front door, e.g. Every eater needs to leave our restaurant within half hour, otherwise, you will need to bring your food to leave please. So, every eater know that they need to eat all food within half hour, otherwise, they need to bring their food to leave this restaurant. Then, this restaurant can increase more seats to let many queue waiting eaters , they do not queue to spend long time to wait to enter this restaurant. Consequently, many queue waiting eaters will choose to enter this restaurant, due to their queue waiting times are not exceed their time pressure limited time.

The final case is cinema queue . In general, any cinemas will have many audiences need to wait to buy tickets to watch movies. However, if the cinema has many audiences , they need to spend one hour, or two hours , even more than two hours to queue to wait to buy the ticket to watch any movies in the cinema. If some audiences' expected queue waiting times are within one hour. So, if these audiences' expected queue waiting time are more than one hour. Then, they will choose to leave this cinema and choose other cinemas to replace it in possible. How to avoid these time pressure audiences losing number increases in cinema busy time? I recommend that this cinema ought increase ticket purchase counter service staffs number , e.g. opening more three to five ticket purchase counters number in order to let these one hour time queue time waiting audiences can purchase ticket to watch their movies within one hour. So, opening urgent ticket purchsase service counters number issue is depended on whether there are how many audiences are waiting to buy ticket in the cinema in the time. However, it is only one best way to avoid the cinema audiences number loses in cinema busy time.

Time press how influences video playing game consumer purchase behavior

I shall explain that why it has relationship between the video game student consumer individual learning time and the working people individual working time both can influence video game playing consumer individual video game choice behavior. I shall assume that the different kinds of video game content difficult or easy win competition and entertainment spending on playing time factor will have more influence how the student or working person individual choice of what kind of video game purchase. Otherwise, every video game price and brand and video game entertainment design content will have less influence to every video game consumer individual purchase choice.

Why do the every video game's learning playing time and the playing time is spent to satisfy the feeling of winning game both factors will be the main factors to influence the feeling busy learning student or feeling rest working personal target video game playing consumer individual kind of which video game software purchase choice? Why do feeling busy learning students or feeling rest working people will be prefer to choose to buy the kinds of need spending little time to learn to play to achieve the easy winning of the video game content aim in short time?

Nowadays, the different brands of video game products have different prices, various entertainment design contents and the easy or difficult win content feeling to be promoted to sell to satisfy the students or working people video game players' entertainment needs. However, time pressure will be one important factor to influence students of working peoples' video games choices. I shall explain that the time pressure factor how will influence the feeling busy learning or feeling rest working video game players or video game content software consumers to choose to buy the kinds of video games software which can let them to feel to spend little playing and learning time and they can feel easy to win the video game competition in short time preference in this electronic entertainment video game industry.

Nowadays, video game target customers, they are young students and adult working people in common. When , the student does not need to go to school and he/she stays at home, he /she will like to play video game after he/she finishes to learn just a moment usually or the adult working person finishes jobs on the day, after he/she ate dinner, he/she will also like to play video game at home. So , video game can be one kind of entertainment product to let they feel enjoy to play when they re staying at homes.

Video game can be one kind of entertainment culture or entertainment behavior at home to them in popular. A player's ability to perform within a game entertainment is important, and players tend to knowledgeable about their achievements and failures within any game world. So, when one student hopes to get pass grade in school examination. He will choose to spend little time to attempt to win the video game content competition in short time because it can let him to feel that may increase his confidence to pass the grade in the school examination later in possible when he ensures that he had won the video game content competition. He believes that he can be trained to raise whose judgement and mind and analysis ability in his playing video game proceed. Instead of playing video game can increase student learning confidence, it can also increase the working people's confidence, when the working person hopes to be promoted or increased salary later from his supervisor's appreciation. He will attempt to spend little time to win the kind of video game content competition in short time. He will have more confident to achieve to raise his working performance to let his supervisor appreciation if he can learn how to win the kind of video game competition in short time.

It seems that whether the player needs to spend how much time to learn how to win any kind of video content game competition , this " spending learning time of winning any video content game competition in time pressure playing environment feeling factor will influence the student or working person 's video game content purchase choice. If the video game design is more complex or difficult to let the player to feel to learn to win the game competition as well as it also needs them to spend more long time to learn to play and win the kind of video content game competition. Then, it has possible to influence the hard learning students or hard working people video game consumers, they do not choose to buy any kinds of need spending long learning and playing time to win the kinds of video content game competitive software products. So, it seems that the spend how much playing and learning time to win the video game content competition factor will bring time pressure to let the hard working people or hard learning student video game consumers choose to buy the video content game software products are easy to learn to play in preference because they expect to pass grade or appreciate easy, if they feel that they can learn how to win the video game content competition in short time as well as they do not spend much playing time to win the kind of video game content competition and they will reduce their learning time at homes.

I shall explain why price won't be the main factor to influence video game players' purchase choices in preference. Some video game software sellers feel reduced sale price can attract many video game buyers' choice in preference. It is one wrong mind, due to video game software price is not too much high, it is one kind popular cheap entertainment software product. So , the kinds of similar entertainment content design video game products , their sale price difference between the kind of most expensive , the highest price video game software and the kind of the cheapest , the lowest price video game software won't be difference very much. Their price difference level may be US 410 to US$50 or even less than US$50 level. So,, one video fame entertainment player won't feel that the kind of similar content design of video game software's higher price which will influence he chooses to buy another cheaper similar of kind video game content design software product to replace to the prior higher price one. Because their price difference are not too much or video game software entertainment product is not on kind of expensive product to let them to feel. So, it seems what video game software price won't influence the video game players' prior one of preference choice, it is not easy to be replaced from later cheaper one, when the video game player feels like to play the kind of high price of video game content software before.

Can the video game content influence player individual purchase motivation in preference? In fact, there are many different kinds of video game contents to let players to choose. This free-to -play business model that has rapidly speed to achieve games services to general . So, some students or working people players can free download some kinds of video game software to play from online channel. It will be attractive to the no paid video game players. Hence, free download video game content will influence the paid video game players' purchase decisions for in -game content are not only affected by people's existing general attitudes, consumption values, and motivation , but also by the design decisions and the needs built into the game by the developers. Because the paid video game players won't like to buy the similar content video games, which can be free download to play from online or internet channel. They will feel unfair or not worth or loss if they choose to pay to buy the similar video game content entertainment software, after they discovered that they may be free download this kind of similar video game content to play from internet.

It will bring this question: Why will time pressure influence video game player chooses to download free video game to play in preference? When one student feels that he has no enough time to study, he won't choose to to any video game shops to do video game software comparative behavior to compare which one's price is lower, game playing content is more attractive, brand is familiar in order to make final purchase decision in preference. If he discovered that there has one kind of video game content, which can be free download to play from internet or online channel . So, when the student feels that he needs have much time to study on the day. How will choose to attempt to find some kind of video game contents from computer tool which has the attractive entertainment content , it can let he to feel enjoy to play and it is free download from mobile or computer. Then, he won't choose to spend non predictive time to visit any video game shops to make purchase decision on that day. So, time pressure will be one factor to influence some video game software consumers to feel whether they ought either visit any video game shops to make purchase choice or download some free video game contents at homes for the feeling no enough learning time student players. Even time pressure will also influence adult working people video game players, when the working person feels tries after his full day busy working on that day. Then, he will want to stay at home to rest . Although, he expects to visit any video game shops to choose which video game software product(s) to buy on that day, but when he discovered that there are some video game contents which are attractive to influence him to do free download behavior from internet at home. Also, he feels very tried and he will choose to stay at home on that day. If he can find some free video game contents are attractive to influence he chooses to do free download video game contents behavior and replace visiting video game stores behavior on that day. So, free download video game content entertainment activity will be one attractive promotion video game software method to assist the video game sellers' new video game products to let many feeling time pressure learning or working video game players to know from internet channel. Consequently, online free entertainment video game content download playing choice will influence many video game shops will lose many feeling time pressure video game players number every day in possible. Also, it means that the lazy students or disliking learning students or no job people or (less working hours) part time working people, they will be the main target video game customers, due to they accept to spend much time to visit their video game shops to choose any kinds of video game software to buy in preference.

● How can video game advertisement method influence feeling time pressure and feeling without time pressure video game software consumer purchase ?

In fact, video game sellers can choose new media channel to advertise their new video game software products, e.g. computer online advertisement channel, instead of video game pictures in shops, magazine, newspapers, television, radio ,cinema, public transportation tools poster traditional advertisement channels. However, computer online advertisement channel can attract many feeling learning time pressure of students consumers and feeling lack of enough rest time working people consumers to let them to choose to view their video game software advertisements from online websites at homes conveniently.

It is easy to understand , due to these feeling lack of enough learning time student video game players and feeling lack enough rest time working people video game players, they go back home after they finished learning in schools or they finished jobs in workplaces on that video game purchase planning day. After they eat their dinners, they may turn on computers to search information from internet. Suddenly, they discover some attractive video game contents photos or images are advertised from the video game seller's website or public yahoo website , even they can choose to buy any one of these video game software from online shopping channel. Then, they will feel convenient to buy any one of these video game software from internet channel. SO, online video game advertisement will be the feeling time pressure video game players' first time contact channel at homes or the fastest advertisement contact channel to compare visiting video game store post advertisement, television , radio , magazine contact advertisement channels, when they are staying at homes.

Due to internet is popular to be used to search any information for consumers. So, the traditional magazine, newspapers, television, radio and visiting video game stores advertisement channels won't be more attractive to the feeling time pressure video game consumers . They will choose to find any information from internet at homes in preference , when they have at least one computer to use at home, they can click website to search any information from internet easily.

The most important factor is that they can feel to spend little time to search information from internet to compare spending more time to find anywhere places whether they has magazines or book stores to sell video game magazine and newspapers publishers, radios and television won't inform them when they have video game advertisements to let they know whether what new video game software will promote to sell as soon as possible when they buy newspapers or turn on radios or televisions at home.

Otherwise, internet will be easy to let the feeling pressure video game software consumers to know when whose liking new video content game software(s) will be promoted to sell from internet advertisement easily. Also, the feeling time pressure video software consumers can choose to buy their liking video game software (s) from online shopping channel in possible if the video game seller can provide one website to let him/her to pay visa to buy and then it can deliver the video game software(s) to his/her home immediately or tomorrow or later time when the buyer's home located in overseas or far away from the video game seller's warehouse and their software are needed to be delivered by air plane transportation.

So, the feeling time pressure video game players won't need to leave their homes to spend more time to visit any video game stores to make final video game purchase decision any time. Hence, online advertisement and shopping channel will be one good sale promotion method to any feeling time pressure video game players nowadays. It will influence the traditional visiting video game stores' video game consumers' purchase behaviors to change to online purchase behaviors at homes conveniently, because they avoid to waste much time to visit video game stores as well as avoid to waste much time to choose any video game products in different video game stores, when they are staying in different video game stores. Visiting video game purchase behavior will need they spend whole day time to make final purchase choice, even it is possible that they can not make any video game software purchase decision after they visit many video game stores on that day.

Otherwise , online game advertisement channel can let them to feel to spend little time to search any new video game contents from every web page as well as every web page can show the new video game content images or photos or pictures to let every online users to see clearly when he/she sits down to turn on computer to search any kinds of video game content information to view at home in short time.

In conclusion, online video game advertisement and online shopping channel can attract many feeling time pressure video game players' consideration when they need to search any kinds of new or old video game contents information and it also changes their purchase decision to online shopping from traditional visiting video game store shopping behavior. Video game industry's advertisement method , sale method is the kind of video game playing content's easy or difficult feeling degree , spending how much playing time to win the competition in the game entertainment environment factors will influence the feeling time pressure video game players' final purchase decision making choice behavior to any video game software publishers nowadays.

Time pressure consumption or production situation explanation

Will one consumer feel difficult to make consumption choice or one employee feel pressure to work when the worker works in the company's high pressure productive environment or the consumer makes difficult purchase choice in high pressure consumption environment? Will time pressure bring motivation to the consumer purchase decision or the employee working efficiency? It depends on some factors to either cause time pressure working environment or raise the employee individual efficiency , or time pressure consumption environment can either encourage the consumer purchase decision or discourage the consumer purchase decision . I shall explain as below: What does efficiency mean? Due to economic problem is a scarcity of resource, efficiency is concerns with the optimal production, consumption environment. For time pressure consumption situation example, e.g. supermarket shopping counter check out purchase queue waiting time pressure, cinema purchase ticket queue waiting time pressure, restaurant queue waiting booking table time pressure etc. different consumption pressure time waiting situation. For time pressure working situation example, e.g. supervisor's demand tasks finishing on time before the employee leaves the office on the day, then the supervisor's demand will cause the employee feels time pressure to do all tasks on time, otherwise, he needs to work overtime, even no extra allowance compensation to his extra time loss, or the employee needs to do another employee's tasks , due to he is absent on the day. However, this situation can be called economically efficient production or consumption if: no one can be worse off, no additional output can be obtained, without increasing the amount of inputs, production proceeds at the lowest possible per unit cost. For these economic efficient consumption situation example, the consumer has much time to wait, the shop has less different styles of products to let them to spend time to choose in the shop's shelf.

However, these definitions of efficiency are not exactly equivalent, but all they are caused by the idea that a system is efficient if nothing more than be achieved given the resources available. On time pressure working environment influence aspect, Time pressure working environment may bring efficiency, but time pressure working environment may also bring inefficiency, e.g. employing workers who are not necessary for the productive process. For example, a firm may be more concerned about the political implications of making people redundant than getting rid of surplus workers, or lack of management control, if a firm does not have supervision of workers, then productivity may tall as workers talk it easy, not finding cheapest suppliers, a firm may continue to source raw materials from a high cost supplier rather than look for cheaper raw materials to be supplied to let workers to work in one short time task finishing environment. Then, they may feel short time task finishing pressure to bring inefficiency production result. I shall indicate efficient production and efficient consumption situations as below:

For building a new airport working time pressure situation example, how to evaluate that it is one efficient productive situation. When a new airport may lead a greater increase in social benefit than social cost. It seems that an efficient productive situation in time pressure working environment. The time pressure can excite or encourage workers hard to work and the won't feel pressure to work to cause inefficient performance. Therefore, these is a net gain to society.

However, those people living near the new building airport will lost out. Therefore, this is not an improvement. However , if the people living nearby were compensated for extra noise, when the workers need to use equipment build the new airport in the pressure building time when they feel lack of enough equipment supplies or lack of enough workers to cooperate to work. Then, it is possible to have a negative improvement inefficient production. So, how to evaluate whether the new airport builders feel time pressure to finish this new airport building project before the due date or not. It can depend on whether the people living near the new airport often listen noise or not. In a without time pressure working situation, the workers do not need often to cause noise in their airport production process. If they feel no time pressure to finish this new airport building project before the finishing due date. Their working behaviors ought not often cause noise to influence themselves nervous or emotion to be poor to work, or feeling workload to bring the inefficient performance consequence to finish this new airport after the due date in possible. It ought seem that they won't feel time pressure and they have confidence to finish to build this new airport before the due date. If the employer has enough workers number and equipment supplies number to let them to do this new airport building task. Otherwise, if they need to often cause noise. It implies that it has no enough workers number and equipment number to let them to build this new airport before the due date. They feel time pressure to finish this new airport building project. So , the employer ought increase workers and equipment to reduce their worry about on building this new airport project before or one due date finishing, if the employer hoped that they can perform efficiently.

For avoiding feeling time pressure on consumption situation example, when the product can be allocated efficiency, then consumers will feel less time pressure consumption psychological influence. This occurs when products and services are distributed according to consumer choice preferences. It means that the seller can make more accurate preferable choice prediction whether consumers will choose to buy what kinds of styles of products or characteristics of services provision in preference. So, they won't need to spend more time to do choices to decide whether which styles of products or characteristics of service provisions whom hope to buy or consume in preference.

In one allocative efficient occurs when the price of the product or service is same to the marginal cost. A more precise definition of allocation efficiency is at an output level where the price equals the marginal cost of production . This is because the price that consumers are willing to pay is equal to the marginal utility that they get. Therefore, the optimal distribution is achieved when the marginal utility of products equals the marginal cost. For example , when firms in perfect competition are said to product at an allocative efficient level, monopolies can increase price above the marginal cost of production and are allocative inefficient. So, if the product is sold in the monopolies market environment. Many the similar product sellers raise sale price to sell similar styles of products to let consumers to choose to make purchase decision. Then, will influence them to feel their choices to the kinds of similar styles of products in the time pressure product choice consumption situation. Otherwise, firms are in the perfect competitive consumption environment. Consumers can feel their similar product prices are not difference too much. Then, they will feel less time pressure to make which kinds of product choice of purchase decision in preference. They will spend less time to make final purchase decision. So, whether the kind of product market is monopolies or perfect competition which will influence consumers feel more or less time pressure consumption generally. Consequently, consumer time pressure feeling and the kind of product 's market environment, they have close relationship to influence consumer purchase decision making behavior.

What is dynamic efficient production environment? This refers to efficient over time. Dynamic efficiency involves the introduction of new technology and working methods to reduce costs over time, e.g. letting workers feel that productive time can be reduce to produce the same level of tasks. Then, they can avoid long time pressure to influence their working performance. With this mind, we can define dynamic efficiency as an aspect of economic efficiency that measures the speed or the rate at which the production possibility curve moves from one static equilibrium point to another within a given period. For Ford Motor company efficient production predictive method case example, in the 1920 year, the Ford Motor factor were very efficient for that particular year. However, compared to later decades, we can not say that the production methods of the 1920 year were efficient. On other words, it is important for firms to make best use of given resources. But, they also need to develop greater use of resources over time. Hence, Ford Motor can let workers to avoid time pressure feeling to produce its any motor vehicles i their productive process in 1920 year. When its new productive technology is adopted to be used to manufacture any kinds of its more vehicles in factory. Also, it can raise their productive efficiency to manufacture any motor vehicles in 1920 year. However, although Ford Motor can make best use of given resources to assist workers to produce any kinds of motor vehicles efficiently. The vehicle buyers' driving needs or new design motor demands are increasing. They need new different kinds of Ford Motor design to be provided to let them to choose. So, Ford Motor also needs to develop greater use of more resources over time, due to the more different styles of new design motor vehicles are needed. So, the new kinds of productive resources are needed to be develop in order to adopt to vehicle buyers' needs. If Ford Motor can not find or discover any new productive material and it can not innovate any new kinds of productive methods to be taught to let workers to learn how to manufacture the future new designs of Ford Motor vehicles efficiently. Then, they wil be possible to feel time pressure to work, due to they can not adopt how to manufacture the future new design motor vehicles, when they are not proficient to apply the future new productive technology to manufacture any new design of motor vehicles.

This is one good example to explain high technological manufacturing resources and techniques and method can let workers to reduce time pressure to manufacture in their manufacturing process, but if the manufacturer can not improve its manufacturing technology to let its workers can continue adapt how to apply the new different manufacturing method to manufacture the future new design or innovative products. Then, they will be possible that they feel time manufacturing pressure and raising inefficient manufacturing performance, due to the manufacturing technology or productive technique can not be improved and training to them to raise skillful proficiency. So, these productive workers will onle reduce time pressure to manufacture in short time, if the manufacturer can not improve any new kinds of manufacturing techniques and teach them how to apply the future new manufacturing techniques to work efficiently. .Then, their performance will be ppor in possible when they feel long time pressure o work in the long time pressure working environment. Hence, it has relationship between new technique improvement and long or short time working pressure and performance.

Distributive efficiency can raise consumption desire and it can reduce consumer individual choice time to make purchase decision in short time. Concerned with allocating products and services provision according to who needs them most . Therefore, requires an equitable distribution . Distributive efficiency occurs when products sale and service provision are consumed by those who need them most. Distributive efficiency is concerned with an equitable distribution of resources because of the law of diminishing marginal returns .

The law of diminishing marginal returns states that as consumption of product increase the product users tend to get diminishing marginal utility. For example, if a family already has three cars, but gets a fourth car, this fourth car will only increase this family net utility by a small amount. If by constrast someone on a low income is able to get their first car, the marginal utility will be much higher. Therefore, to be distributive efficient, society will need to ensure an equitable distribution of resources. For car sale case example, if the car seller has distribution of resource, such as different styles of car kinds sale number efficiently, e.g. the high quality expensive car number manufacturing number is less than the low quality cheap car number. Then, there are many low income people may have enough time too pay to buy the cheap car in the car sale market. Then, it is possible that the car company can sell more cheap cars in short time, due to many low income people do not need to spend long time to consider whether they ought buy or not buy any first car, even another car or other cars for their family to drive. They will not feel purchase time pressure to make final car purchase choice, due to there are many common low quality cheap cars number are supplied to be sold in the country's car market immediately. So, when the car company can concentrate on manufacturing many low quality cheap cars to prepare to sell. Although, its high quality expensive car number reduces, and it will increase its high profit earn in possible in short time only. Otherwise, in long time benefit aspect, many low quality cheap cars sale number will increase many low income car buyers nu,bers when they find the car manufacturer can have many different style design of low quality cheap cars to let them to choose more than other car competitors in the country's car sale market.

In long time, it will reduce time purchase choice pressure to its car consumers, when many car buyers believe this car company only it has many different styles of design low quality and cheap price cars to let them to choose to buy to compare other brands of car companies in whose country. Then, they won't feel need to spend extra much time to choose other brands of cars to compare this car company's cars. It implies that the country car buyers only consider to spend less time to choose this brand of any cars to make car purchase decision in preference. They won't feel time pressure to consider other brands of any kinds of style cars purchase choices often habitually.

So, this brand cars have built choice habit to many low quality and cheap car buyers in this country. So, when the seller can build long time brand of any this car company's any car products choice habit to let many buyers this brand cars are preferable choice, then they will prefer to spend short time to make purchase decision for this company's any cars . Then it can sell any low quality and cheap cars to compare other brands of car companies more easily.

How robots shorten working time and consumption decision time

What does human network job mean ? Why may human network job be popular? Why human network job behavior may influence economy ?

Nowadays internet is popular to use. We can apply internet to find data , search any new things, even earn money. Why does internet

may become huma network job source. For example, e-publish may be one kind of new human network job. Any authors may apply internet

channel to help them to sell electronic or paper books from e-publisher web store. They may apply facebook, you tub etc. any online

channel to promote themselves new books to let new readers to know whether when they may buy themselves favourable new topic books to read

from electronic publisher web store.

Thus, future electronic publisher industry may help any authors to build internet network platform to help them to sell and promote

ot advertise their any one new electronic or paper book topic to let global any one reader to choose to buy their any new topic books from electronic publisher web store easily and conveniently. However, it implies that electronic network platform author may be one kind of future new human network job in our societies.

How electronic network platform author job may bring economy benefit in macro economy view? A person can have few friends, contacts and still be very influential if these few

friends and contacts are themselves highly influential, e.g. one author must not need to know any one reader in global society. When they like to choose any electronic books from electronic internet network platform. They may become the author's any one topic book buyer, when they feel the author's any one topic book is fun and attract they make decision to buth the strange author whose the topic book from electronic book publisher's platform web store conventiently in short time. Although, they are strangers, they do not know themselves , but the reader can understand what it way that made Google from writing platofrm to create new creative mind and typing network job method to replace traditional hand writing book method for global authors. It will be one kind of new human network writing job.

Hence, global any one reader can apply an innovative search engine , such as google.com to find whether whom author personal new topic books are value to read from internet.

Then, the electroniuc publisher's web store may be new book store platform sale network to help the author to sell many electronic or paper books from electronic network platform

in short time. So, internet may be future new network plaform to help global any one author to create network writing job absolutely. Furthermore, internet may be popular social media

to help any one author to build goold relationship between his/her readers. It is one kind of new network, human network job. New authors do not need to buy many paper books to prepare to put in any one book shop warehouse. Their every book can print on demand to reduce out of book stock in any one book shop. They may choose to sell either electronic books or paper books both from any one book publisher web store. So, electronic network platform may be one kind of good writing channel to help human authors to create income and it can also help authors to bring new creative mind and new topic fun content books to let readers to know and buy to read from electronic publisher network platform.

Why does human behavior may be one kind of new human network job to bring global economic advantages. ALthough, it may be free income or without inocme, but the person does the network behavior, his/her behavior may be bring advantages to influence many other people's health. For this case, when a worker in a coffee shop in an airport gets a vaccination aganinst the flu, it does not only helps him or her stay healthy, but also helps the many travellers who might otherwise have been inflected if that workers caught the flu. So, the externality , the result implies the vaccination of even a part of a community conveys benefits to the whole community. For example, governments pay special attention to the vaccinations of school children, teachers, health mothers, and the elderly, categories of people particularly susceptible not only to catching, but also to transmitting a disease.

It is not accidental that governments are heavily involved with vaccination . When there are externalities, free market, fail to persuade individual incentives with society's
their the worker's decision of whether to get a vaccine ends up attracting whether other people get sick. The workers might not fully take all these other people's potential suffering into account when making her or his vaccination decision.

As Stanford University does many suggestions, understand this and tries to help them make the right decisions and so providers free flu vaccines for its staff and students.
Small pockets of unvaccinated individuals can allow a disease to gain a spread more widely well-being. For example, parent weighing the costs and benefits of a vaccine for their child is not always thinking of the consequences of that vaccination to other people. THese are markets in which subsidizing or regulating behavior can make everyone better off. Because the reason for requiring that a child be vaccinated before enrolling in school is not just to protect that child, because each child's vaccination affects others via potential contagions.

Robots take our jobs behavioral and economy influences

Robot job behavior brings economy influences

If one day robots can replace human to do simple, even complex jobs. They will bring what influences to our global societial economy.The popular economic refrain declares that the
global middle class is dying and robots will soon take our jobs, e.g. shopping center customer service jobs, library service jobs, cinema ticket sale jobs, restaurant kitchen cooker jobs,
even, bus drivers, taxi drivers etc. public transport driving jobs, accountant, doctors etc. professional jobs. Whether it is beautiful or petty matter if our future societies have many human jobs can be replaced to do from robots. Businessman must may reduce to employ employees and reduce to pay salary or wage, when robots can be replaced to do their employees tasks. But, societies must bring unemployement rate rises , due to societies will have many people loss jobs when their employers choose to buy robots to serve their clients or do any office tasks or customer service or cleaning etc. tasks.

In micro economy view, employers may save money in long term, but in macro economy view, it will cause unemployment ratio rises , even crime rate rises when there are many people lose
jobs in societies. These models of doom, though, fail to account for the hundreds of businesses riding the waves of change in their industries when robots may be invented to replace human to do many simple , even complex tasks in our future societies.

WE may image that one small factory needs to manufacture fishes canes to sell to supermarket, the small , cheaper stuff and higher margin parts of the fishes manufacture industry. Before, this factory needs to employ many human factory workers need to help every fresh customer makeing the perfect fishing gear, designed for performance, durability, and cost in order to achieve to manufacture every fish cane in whole fished processing manufacturing stages. Every worker needs to spend about 15 to twenty minutes to finish every fish cane , till to delivery to any supermarket to sell. If this fish canes manufacturing factory can apply manufacturing robots to help them to finish any one working tasks , every robot can only spend five minutes to finish whole fresh fish cane manufacturing process. Thus, every robot can help this factory save 10 to 15 minutes time to finsh every fish cane manufacturing process. IN fact, time is money, because when every robot can help this factory to reduce 10 to 15 minutes time to compare human worker. Then, this factory can finish about 20 fish canes in one hour if it can use robot to help it to manufacture fish canes. Otherwise, if this factory still use human workers to help it to manufacture fish canes, then it can finsh about 3 to 4 fish canes in one hour. SO, the manufacturing efficiency ensures that robots must help this fish manufacturing factory to raise fish canes number more than human workers. So, in robotic behavioral economy view, manufacturing robots must help this fish canes manufacturing factory to raise fish canes manufacturing number and deliver increasing number to supermarkets to prepare to sell every day. Robots can help this fish canes manufacturing factory bring manufacturing time saving, rising manufacturing efficiency, improving performance and reducing wages expenditure long time advantages in micro economy view. However, manufacturing robots can also bring disadvanages to society, e.g. increasing unemployment ratio, increasing crime rate,

this factory workers will lose jobs and income, they need earn social welfare from government and increasing government finance pressure in short time, even long time in macro economic view.

Stanford University graduate program in economics, Scott lecturer explained that "in demand and supply economic theory for robots supply and demand case, robots supply number increasing may influence human workers demand number decrease. It sometimes calls " the efficient frontier".

No specific human beings were mentioned in any of economics classes. As robots supply and demand in market case, They (robots) may be purely theoretical " agents" who reached to the most reasonable sale prices in order to persuade any one businessman buyer to make manufacturing robot buying decision whether robots can help him / her to bring how much saving time , saving money, saving cost, improving performance, efficiency economic benefit before he/she plans to reduce workers number when he/she decides to apply robots to replace human workers in his/her factory or office or any service department, e.g. cinema ticket sale service, shopping center customer service, shopping center cleaning , supermarket customer service etc. service or sale tasks. When robots can replace human to do any one of these tasks in any organizations. So, robots may be human worker agents who reached to prices the way robots would react to a software

command. There was nothing that explained why some people thrived and others did n't or why truly brilliant, hardworking people could fail when much lazier folks succeeded." Having been admitted to the Stanford University graduate program in economics, Scott lecturer hoped to get his answers there.

How robots influence our future social changing? Using the right technology can be a boon to your business in this economy. For internet example, it is easier than ever to find well-matched customers all around the world, to stay in contact with them, and to more quickly design the products they want. If you focus solely on being cutting -edge, though you risk letting the technology

take over what should be very robust relationships with your customers , employees, and colleagues. IN nowaddays society, technoligical advances and cutomation, personal

relationships in business are more crucial than ever. I mean that robots can not replace human to serve clients to let them to feel more comfortable and passion more easily. For shoe shop case example, if the shoe shop apply one robot to serve its clients to replace human shoe salesperson to serve its shoe customers. Robots ensure that they can not persuade every shoe potential buyer to make shoe buying decision more easily when robots need to contact every shoe potential buyer. The reason is simple, because robots can not touch any one shoe buyer individual emotion very easier.

If the shoe buyer needs the robots to help him/her to choose any right shoe styles when he/she can not feel himself / herself can make the most right shoe style choice decision. The robots can not replace human shoe salesperson to make shoe style choice judgement more easily. They must need longer time to analyze whether which shoe style may be the most suitable to the shoe buyer. Otherwise, human shoe salesperson may attempt to make the most right shoe style choice decision to help any one shoe buyer to chooce the most right style shoe because he/she owns shoe style sale experience, shoe style knowledge, the most important reason is that they can feel every shoe customer individual emotion to touch whether he/she will feel comfortable or happy when they attempt to help every shoe customer to seek the most right shoe style in every shoe customer whole shoe searching processing. Othwerwise, serving robots are only one machine, they can not touch or feel every shoe customer individual emotion whether he/she feel comfortable or unhappy or happy when they need to contact them in whole shoe searching processing. Hence, I believe that some tasks robots can

not repalce human staff to do very easily. Otherwise, robots may bring disadvanatges to let any one businessman to loss his/her customers, due to robots can not touch every customer

emotion to compare human staff in service tasks more easily. Robots serving customer behaviors may cause money lose and customers number lose to the shop in micro economic view.

Intellectual human economic behaviors

What does intellectual human economic behaviors mean ? I believe that when we choose or decide to do intellectual behaviors, then our societies will be influenced to bring economic growth in consequence.I shall attempt to indicate pollution case to explain how and why eithet our intellectual or foolish behaviors may bring economic growth or recession in consequence as below:

On one hand, for air pollution social case aspect example, if we only consider to buy cars to drive for working aimr or holiday leisure aim. Then, our societies air will be polluted. Our health will be influenced to bad. Our car driving behaviors may cause global environment air pollution serously. In long tiem, global air pollution will bring our bodies health to be bad. Although, ourselves car driving behaviors may bring our driving travelling leisure enjoyment and comfortable feeling in short time, also we so not need to pay public transport fare often, but we need to compensate ourselves health economic intangible loss due to air pollution , when cars number increases, dirty air will cause ouselves health to become bad.

In the result, we will need to pay more medical expenditure when we are old age, due to ourselves bodies will become bad, due to we breathe global dirty air every day, due to ourselves cars pollute air in long time, e.g. 10 to 20 years, even 30 more without limited air pollution environment. So, driving cars behavior may be one kind of human foolish behavior and our foolish behavior may bring ourselves future long time medical expenditure absolutely.

One the other hand, water pollution social aspect, if we often keep much rubblish to pollute sea, oil exploration porcessing pollute ocean , ships gas pollute ocaen, then fishes will eat polluted food and drive dirty water, due to global ocean is polluted.

In fact, because human only to conside how to buy boats to carry on leisure enjoyment activities, or catch cruises to travel on the sea. Also, oil manufacturers only consider researching anywhere to find new oil exploration places to manufacture oil product, when their oil exploration processes pollute ocarn . Consequently, global fishes drink polluted warer or eat polluted food. They will have poison. SO, human will have high chance to eat poison polluted fishes, due to fishes are poison or are polluted.

So, human is doing foolish activities, we only hope to find oil exploration places to pollute ocean or we only spend money to buy ticket to catch ships to travel anywhere in global ocean. All of these human foolish behaviors will bring pollution to global ocean. On consequently, we will need to compensate to eat polluted or dirty or poision fishes, ourselves bodies health will be bad. In long time, we need have high chance to pay medical expenditure when we are old. So, pollution case may be one good example to explain how and why human foolish behavior may influence ourselves future need to compensate serious medical loss.

All of these human foolish behavior will bring pollution to global ocean. On consequently, we will need to compensate to eat polluted or dirty or poison fished , ourselves bodies health will be bad. In long time, we will have high chance to pay medical expenditure, when we are old. So, pollution case may be one good example to explain how and why human ourselves intellectual or foolish behaviors may influence future long time economic loss or economic growth or recession in micro and micro economic view.

On another water pollution aspect hand, if we often keep rubbish to sea, oil exploration processing pollutes ocean and ships' gas pollute ocean, then fishes will eat polluted food and drink dirty water, due to fishes will eat polluted food and drink dirty sea water because the global ocean is polluted seriously.

In fact, because human only consider how to buy boats to carry on any leisure water activities, or catches cruises to travel on the sea. Also, oil manufacturers only consider any where to find oil exploratin places to manufacture oil products from ocean, when their pol exploration processes can plooute ocean. Consequently, global fishes drink polluted water or eat direty food. They will have poison. So, human will have high chance to eat poison fishes. Otherwise, such as pollutin case, it can infuence inflation or deflation. Consequently, the reason indicates supply and demand theory. If air pollution is serious, then we will consider health issue, global cars demand number may be influenced to reduce, when global cars number demand will reduce, global car prices and supply number will need to change to fall down in order to attract or persuade global car consumers choose to make car purchase decision. Hence, global car manufacture number and car price will be influenced to reduce, due to global air pollution issue. Consequently, deflation will occur because when the country citizen usually does not spend much extra saving money to buy car expensive goods. Money value will be low. Otherwise, if global cair pollution is not serious, human considers to buy cars to enjoy driving leisure lives. So, global car demand is influenced to increase , also global car price will also influenced to increase.

Consequently, gobal human will choose to buy cars to drive. Due to we accept to spend extra saving to buy expensive car goods. Car sale price and supply may be influenced to rise up. Money value is influenced to reduce. Inflation may be influenced, due to global car consumers number increases, we would not have extra money to spend easily. Car expensive goods expenditure influences our spending habit to avoid to make car purchase decision more easily. So, human intellectual or foolish activities may bring inflation or deflation consequency in possible indirectly in macro economic view.

On conclusion, above pollution case explain that how and why human intellectual or foolish economic behaviors may bring inflation or deflation consequency as wll as economic growth or recession consequency as well as any goods demand and supply increasing or decreasing consequency. It implies that human behavior may have indirect relationship to influence any goods demand and supply number to either increase or decrease result as well as any goods price will be influenced to increase or decrease in micro and macro economic view.

The relationship between social change and human behavior

Why does economic changes may influence human individual behavioral change? I shall attempt to indicate shopping behavior and staying at home behavior to explain their case and effect relationsip as below:

Human behavior can be influenced by economic change or economic change can be influenced by human behavior? Why does recession may influence consumers reduce shopping desire? In social recession suitation, it is possible that many people lose jobs suddenly, due to businessmen lose many customers. They need to make decision to reduce employees number in order to continue to keep businesses. Consequently, many firms (organizations) their employees may lose jobs. When they have much time, due to lose jobs, they will feel to avoid to spend too much time and money to go to shopping often. Many losing jobs people, they will often stay at homes.

So, they will reduce time to go to shopping, then non essential products won't their preferable choice purchase products. Hence, recession will change many losing jobs people their shopping or consumption desires to avoid to buy non essential products often . Usually when economic boom, many people have jobs to do because consumers number must increase when many people have jobs to do. Then, many people can accept to spend money to buy non essential products often. Many people feel spend time to go to shopping can satisfy their purchase of any kinds of new products useful psychology or desire. So, recession is one good example to explain it can influence many people do not like often to leave homes to go to shopping easily. Many people like to stay at homes, becaue they feel worry about spending too much shopping time when they leave homes. Their staying home time is one good negative shopping behavior example. So, economic change may influence human individual behavior changes , they have direct cause and efect relationship in behavioral economic view.

May human behavior influence economic change? Is it possible that human behavior may bring the country social economic change in macro economic or micro behavioral economic view ? I shall indicate publishing industry example. Do you feel that if there are many students feel learning is very important when they read many books or many of students feel interesting to read or they have reading new books in habit, then it is possible that the country will have many students like to spend time to go to any book shops to choose the books, they feel that they can help they learn new knowledge. Then the country will increase students number, they often spend time to visit any one book shop every week. Their visiting book shops behavior which may become their habits. So, the country will increase students number, they often spend time to visit book shops. Also, it implies that visiting book shops behaviors may be their behavioral habits.

So, when the country has many students often spend time to visit book shops , their visiting book shops behaviors may help any one book shop to raise books sale chance. So, the country's student individual often visiting book shop behaviors, their habitual visiting book shops behaviors must may assist help any one book shop to increase books sale number absolutely.

Consequently, any one book shop , its books sale bumber must be influenced to increase to increase because the country will have many students like or feel need visit book shops habit in order to choose any suitable books to buy to read at home in order to raise themselves learning effort. When the country has many bok shops often have many students visit their book shops, then their books sale number may be influenced to increase. It explain why student individual visiting book shop behavior may help any one book shop sale number increases also.

How human productive behavior may influence economic development

May any country which citizen behavior assist themselves country development? It is one cause and effect economic question. I mean that if the country itself citicen can not concentrate mind or energy to choose to do one kind of industry in order to let themselves country can bring the most benefit, then whether the counry itself economy can bring the most serious economic benefit. I shall attempt to indicate these countries themselves indistry choice to explain whether these countries themselves citizen productive behavior may help themselves countries to achieve the largest economic benefits. I shall indicate as below:

New Zealand farmer individual wine productive behavior

For New Zealand country example, this country concerns itself effort is foucs on farming agricultural aspect. So, this country has many farmers concentrate on farming agricultural aspect. May New Zealanders choose to spend time to produce different kinds of wines, e.g. wine or red grape wine is for the people are eating meat, or they are eating dinner.

When these New Zealanders their behaviors choose to do farming or agriculture to grow and produce different kinds of taste of white or red grape wine drinking products job. Themselves grape agriculture behavior will influence these New Zealanders themselves, they can learn how to improve different kinds of grape wine drinking products in order to achieve every kinds of white or read grape wines taste improving aim during their white or red grape producing process.

Why can New Zealander every individual white or read grape wine producers improve their white or read grape wine taste more easily? In behavioral economic view, it can explain that why any one New Zealander white or read grape wine producer can be encouraged or excited or persuaded to concentrate nervous and energy and effort to learn how to improve their white or red grape wine products easily.

In fact, New Zealand is one agricultural food export country. It has good natural environment resource , e.g. land, seed to provide any one farmer to produce themselves any kinds of agricultrual food products, e.g. fruit, or wine food products. Because New Zealanders know themselves country has enough natural resource . So, in common, many New Zealanders choose to attempt to do farming agricultural jobs in order to export themselves any kinds of fruit or meat or wine products to overseas or sell to domestic in order to earn profit.

So, when these New Zealand farmers number has been increasing every year. This country farmers will feel themsleves competition between this New Zealand farmers themselves are serious due to they may feel New Zealanders choose to do agriculture businesses in order to export themselves different kinds of farming food to overseas or sell to local to earn profit.

Hence, when many New Zealand farmers feel that farmers number has been increasing every year. They will feel themselves competition is serious. They must need to spend much time and nervous and effort to research what method is the best how to produce the best taste of white or red grape wine products in order to let local or overseas wine buyers to choose to buy his/her producing white or read grpae products to drink.

Hence, in competition psychological view, may influence many New Zealand white or reaad wine producers had been beginning to change their learning behavior on researching what method is the best in order to produce the best quality of taste red or white wine products to sell in order to attract overseas or local white or read grape wine drinkers to choose to buy his/her wine products. Their behavior will focus on learning how to raising or improving white or read grape wine taste method more than only focus on producing a large number white or red grape wine products. They believe wine quality is more important to compare wine producing number. So, New Zealand wine producers themselves wine producers behaviors have been changing on concentrating on researching wine quality method aspect more then wine producing number aspect in behavioral economic view.

America high technological productive behavior

For America example, US is one high technological country, it owns many high technological knowledge talent inventors, e.g. computer science inventors. Hence, US must attract many diferent countries owning high technological computer inventors choose to go to US to develop their computer science profession career. Also, it seems that when many computer science inventors or professions choose to go to US to develop themselves computer science new career. In behavioral economic view, due to their leaving themselves countries choice, which may bring influence themselves country job behaviors need to be changed. They must need to adapt US new live. Because they will forgive their past computer science job. These computer science professionals need to spend time to adapt US new lives. They " past computer science job behaviors" will need to be changed to their new US any computer employer's new computer science job model.

Because their traditional computer science jobs needed to be forgot in their themselves countries. They will feel their old computer science job knowledge and behavior needed to change in order to let their US any one new of computer company employer feels satisfactory to accept their new working behavior in any one US computer organization.

So, on the other hand, many US computer company employer will feel that they must need time to accept any one new overseas computer science professions their working behaviors, their working attitude daily, because these foreign comouter science professional, their past computer working behaviors and working attitude must be different to US domestic computer science professions.

In behavioral economic view, these overseas computer science professions, their working behaviors and attitude must be needed to change in order to adapt any one US new computer company itself domestic or local computer science professional stafs themselves daily working behaviors and attitude because these overseas and local computer science professionals must need to team work together.

In behavioral economic view, it is only one way that foreign computer science professionals must need to change themselves past country traditiona daily working behaviors and attitude in order to cooperate with these US local computer science professionals in teams more easily.

Consequently, if these foreign compute science professionals can change their past working behaviors and attitude to let any one US local computer science professional feels to cooperate with them easily in short time. Then, the US computer company itself whole computer professional teams themselves efficiencies will be influenced to raised or improved by the changing past working attitude and working behaviors of these foreign computer science professionals. So, in behavioral economic view, only if US any one computer company hopes itself computer teams themselves efficiency can be raised or improved when it decides to employ foreign computer science professionals and US domestic computer science professionals. They need to work in teams together. They must need to let these foreign computer science professionals to know how to change their working behaviors and attitude to let their domestic computer science professionals feel easy to work together. Then, the US computer company itself whole team efficiency must be rasied or improved easily in short time.

● China share market investing behavior

For China share market example, economic development depends on financial market. Because if many Chinese have interest to invest to carry on shares buying and selling activities in orde to learn how to earn shares interest and share profit when the China shareholder can make decision to sell himself/herself shares in the the high price, then he/she can earn money when he/she can sell the China company's shares in the high sale share price position.

If China has many Chinese like to spend time to carry on investing shares activities. Themselves shares buying and selling behaviors will influence China has many companies can increase fund from many Chinese shareholders in order to have enough money to expand or develop themselves businesses in China in long term.

Consequently, when China can have many Chinese like to attempt to carry on buying and selling shares investing behaviors in China share market. Themselves buying and selling shares behaviors can help many Chinese companies have effort to increase enough money or capital in order to continue to do their businesses in long term absolutely. So, it explains why when many Chinese become shareholders , they can assist China will have many companies continue to develop their businesses if many Chinese like to carry on shares buying and selling investing behaviors in long time in China financial investment market nowadays in behavioral economic view.

Why has any individual country have many people invest share behavior which can influence the country's macro consumption desire?

I shall apply shares market buying and selling investment behavior to explaiin why shares investment behavior which may impact the country's overal consumption desire as below:

In behavioral economic view, I assume that when the coutry has many people have interest to attempt to carry on shares buying and selling investment behavior, then their frequent shares buying and selling behaviors which may bring negative consumption desire or shopping desire of these shares investors their consumer behavior.

The reason is simple, when the country has many share buyers number suddenly been increasing rapidly. Consequently, these large group share investors must need to spend much time to research any kinds of company shares variations, whether when their share prices will rise up of fall down in order to achieve buying the company's shares in the lowest price and selling the company's shares in the highest price level in order to earn profit.

Basic on this reason, they must need to spend much extra time to research share prices changing behavior every day, e.g. one working person will wait to leave his/her job, after he/she can spend time to gather data to research the day's share price changing behavior after dinner. So, the working person's right time may be his/her share price market research behavior. Before he/she may spend his/her night time to go to shopping after dinner, but nowadays, he/she will fogive to do his/her shopping behavior before dinner or after dinner at hight sometime. He/she will make decision to spend much night time to turn on computer to click on share market website to research his/her share purchase choice to investigate whether his/her share price whether it rises up or falls down at the moment in order to make his/her share buying or selling decision at ever night time.

I mean the when the country has many people are share investors, their shares investment behavioral spenging time which will influence many shops lose customers at might often because the country will have many people feel need to spend night time to turn on computer or watch television to investigate share price variation. So, the country will have many people / share investors choose to stay at home in order to carry on share price variation investigation behavior, they need to listen share market update news from radios or watch the share market update news from computer or TV at home every night. Consequenly, they must reduce times to leave themselves homes at night. So, their shopping behavior also will be reduced. Because these share investors feel need to spend time to investigate share price variation news at homes which can bring economic benefits (high opportunity benefits) when they choose to forgive to leave homes to go to shopping times (opportunity cost) every night.

On conclusion, it seems that when the country has many people are share investors, then their share price investigating behavior may bring negative shopping emotion at night. Consequently, the country's any one shop may lose many customers from this share investor consumer group in behavioral economic view. Hence, when the country's share investors number had been increasing rapidly, it will influence any shops lose many customers from this share investing customer group at night frequency in short time, even long time in behavioral economic view, because their shopping desires or shopping emotion will be brought negative feeling when they make decisions to spend much time to listen radios or watch TV or computers share price update nes at night. Hence, share market will bring negative impact to influence consumer shopping desire or negative shopping emotion in behavioral economic view.

Can technology influence human shopping behavioral change?

Nowadays, technological development has reached mature stage, whether technological mature stage may bring positive or negative shopping emotion influence to global consumers. I shall aplly internet inventin or ecommerce shopping channel tool to explain whether internet technology can bring postive or negative influence to global consumer behavior in behavioral economic view.

Internet is a good technological tool, it brings e-commerce business chance. In fact, commonly, global has have many businessmen choose to use internet channel to carry on their products transactions between global online-buyers and their electronic websites. So, global many shoppers had begun to feel online shopping is more convenient to compare visiting shops shopping. Their shopping behaviors have been changed from internet technological tool. Global has many shoppers choose to buy any products from any overseas or local businessmen their web stores. They only need to spend time to find any businessmen their webstores to choose the most suitable products to pay visa to buy from their webstores. at homes. So, in general, global had have may shoppers had changed their shopping behaviors from visiting shops to visiting webstores at homes often.

So, it seems that internet technological tool had influenced global many shops disappear, but internet webstores will be replaced their actual shops on streets. Some of businessmen either they choose webstores to replace shops or choose websotes and shops both or still keep shops only. Hence, internet tool influences global businessmen have three kinds of products sale channels to let globa local and overseas consumers to choose how to buy their products. However, in fact, many of global shoppers, youngers and olders had begun to accept to buy any products from webstores. They feel to spend time to leave homes to visit shops , their shopping behaviors will be wasted time to not essential part to their daily lives. Hence, since internet technological invention, it had changed many consumers their traditional visiting shops shopping habit to change to buying products from webstores channel.

However, on the one hand, internet creates webstores ecommerce shopping channel to let global many consumers do not need to leave homes to go to shopping. It brings negative visiting shops shopping emotion to global general consumers nowadays. But on the other hand, it also brings positive visiting internet webstores shopping emotion to global general consumer nowadays. So, it seems that global many consumers feel that they often do not need to spend much time to go out shopping. Many global consumers feel convenient and enjoy to choose any products to buy from different internet webstores, when the online buyer chooses the most suitable product, he she only needs to pay visa card to buy the product from the online seller's webstore conveniently at home.

Hence, online shopping can bring economic benefit to online buyers, e.g. avoiding walking time or spending transport fare to visit the shop to go to shopping, shortening or reducing shopping time to do another important matter.

On conclusion, global many consumers began feel online shopping can bring more economic benefits on shortening shopping time, avoiding transport fare spending aspect. So, online shopping will be popular shopping behavior for future long time. It may encourage global many shoppers can make rapid shopping decision in short time in order to carry on any products buying transaction to global any one online shopper in short time easily in behavioral economic view. So, global many businessmen had begun to build themselves one attraction webstore in order to persuade different countries consumers to choose to click themselves webstores from internet channel to buy any kinds of products in short time easily.

So, internet technology had changed consumers traditional shopping behaviors to build positive online shopping emotion as well as raise online sellers' any products sale chance easily in behavioral economic view.

Why and how human behavior may influence the country's economic growth or recession?

When one country has many people choose to do the same matter for one period, whether their behavior may influence the country's pvera; economic growth or recession . I shall attempt to indicate cases toexplain their relationship as below:

For flowing rubblish behavioral case example, do you feel that when the country has many people often flow rubblish on the streets, instead of their flowing rubblish behavior may bring streets dirty? But, their flowing rubblish behavior may explain that this country has people may have enough money to buy food to ear, or enough cloths to wear, enough bottles of water to drink, even they may have enough money to buy new television, radio, refrigeraters , washing machines, desktops or laptops electronic home products from old to new to use in order to satisfy their living needs. So, when they flow old electronic home products, their flowing old home electronic products behaviors may seem that they have enough money to buy other new home electronic products to replace old home electronic products to use at homes.

However, it seems thaat this country ought have many people have jobs to do. So, many of them, they can easy to make purchase decison to flow any old home electronic products and buy any new home electronic products to use

. Because this country has many people have jobs to do. So, they can often not use old home electonic products to become rubblishs to flow on streets after they had bought any kinds of new home electronic homes.

In fact, it also implies that this country's economy grows rapidly. So, many businesses can glow up rapdly. When they expanded their businesses, they must need to increase employees number in order to let they help themselves to raise productivity or serve their clients absolutely. So, when the country has many businesses can grow up, it seems that its economy must be better or it is improved to compare past. Due to many different kinds of home electronic products had been often bought to use by this country people in this period. So, this country's any streets can be observed that expensive electronic home products were flowed on streets anywhere. then, this country will have many electronic home products sellers can sell their home electronic products very easily. When this country has many people can find any kinds of jobs to do easily. So, due to unemploymen rate had been decreasing.

In behavioral economic view, as this many electronic home products rubblish country case, we can observe this country may have many people have jobs to do. So, consumption number has been increased long time. So, cheap food, or expensive home electronic products may be rubblish on any streets. This country's people , their flowing rubblish behaviors may be explained that many of people have enough jobs to do, so they have ability to buy any good taste food to eat or buy any kinds of expensive electronic home products to use. So, this country's economy may be improved for this long period. So, in behavioral economic view, when this country can have many electronic home products rubblishs are flowed on anywherer in streets frequently. It seems that this country will have many people have jobs to do, so it causes they often change old home electronic products or replaced them easily, when they have enough income to spend to buy any kinds of new home electronic products to use at homes easily. Moreover, their flowing old electronic home products behaviors also indicate that this country has many people their salaries may be increased in possible from their emplyers. When this country can have many different kinds of home electornic products are sold. It means that this country's electronic home products needs or demand had been increasing, due to many people have jobs to do and income increases to excite their living of needs also improve. Consequently, this country may seem have better economic improvement. We can observe from this country's electronic home products rubblish increasing income in theis period.

On conclusion, this country ought experience economic growth at this period. So, " flowing expensive electronic home rubblish increasing number " may seem that this country's economic growth is rapidly in this period, due to many people have jobs to do as well as salaries increase in this period.

Technology how impacts human behavior changing?
Technology how influences human behavior to bring changing? For example, online share purchase and sale transaction from smart phone brings share investor can do share buying or selling transation in any where and any time conveniently, non manual driving auto vehicle, bring car owner feels comfortable and spends free time to do other matter, e.g. reading, listening mucis in himself or herself car freely. electrical energy vehicle can help car owner to reduce air polluton and it can brings the drivers do not feel drive long time in any journeys in order to avoid air pollution for environmental protection responsible car drivers in our societies. Thus, they will drive long time in any journeys when they can drive electronic energy cars to replace oil energy cars.

However, online technology can also bring consumers can choose to stay at homes to buy any things from seller individual online webstore conveniently. Such as online technology can bring shoppers do not need to spend much time to visit shops to buy any things. They can choose any kinds of products from any online sellers individual online webstores conveniently at homes. Online technology excite busy consumers can make purchase decision easily as well as it can help online sellers sell any kinds of products from internet easily.

In behavioral economic view, technology can change human behavior to be improved, it can let human feels comfortable, more free time ro use, rapid making any decisions, such as apply smart phones to make share purchase or sale transaction decision, online shopping decision, even travelling any where decision in short time, when the traveller finds the most cheap hotel accommodation room price and air ticket price frm any travel agent online tourism webstore, then the potential travel customer can follow the online hotel accommodation price and air ticket price data to make decision when to buy the air ticket from the airline travel agent or make decision when to prebook which hotel accommodation room to go to the country to travel from online travel agent tourism webstores. So, technology can encourage global any country travelers to make anywhere to trvel rapidly. If the traveler can find the country's general hotel rooms and airline tickets prices had been decreasing more sightly. The traveler may make travel decision to choose the country to travel in short time, then he/she can prebook the country;s any hotel room and airline ticket to pay by visa fraom the country's any hotel and airline travel agent webstores., before one week, even one month or more easily. Hence, online technology can also encourage traveler individual frequent travel times to be increased, due to global travelers can find any hotel rooms and airline tickets prices from internet conveniently at homes. They do not need to spend time to visit any airline travel agent to enquire travel choice country's hotel rooms prices and airline ticket prices. They can compare global travel of countries choices ' all hotels rooms and airline agents air tickets prices to make prebook airline seat and hotel room decision before one week, one month even six months early.

On conclusion, online technology can encourage global travelers can make travelling any where and when traveling time desicions easily. It can excite tourism industry develops in long time. Also, such as electricity cars invention can encourage environment protection car owners do car purchase decision easily, because they can choose to drive electronic energy cars to replace oil energy cars in order to avoid air pollution occurs easily. So, electronic cars can increase electronic car purchasrs number, due to many of environmental protection attitude of car owners can choose to drive electricity cars to bring air cleans, even non -manual driving cars can encourage lazy driving and free time driving car owners to choose to buy non-manual (artificial intelligent) cars to drive , because they can spend much free time to read, listen music or do any matters in themselves cars, they do not need to drive cars, robotic (AI) auto driving machine is such one non-manual driver to help them to drive themselves cars confidently. So, non-manual driving cars can attract lazy and enjoying free time driving car owners to choose to buy to replace traditional manual cars to drive easily. Moreover, online share transaction can help any share investors to make share buying and selling decision in short time easily. When they can apply smart phones technological tool to carry on share buying and selling activities easily. They can observe any share rising or falling price suitation from smart phones in any where any any time easily. So, smart phone technology can help global any shareholders to make share purchase and sale transaction easily. So, technology can encourage human makes decision in short time rapidly.

How and why employees behaviors may influence economy development?

In behavioral economy view,I believe the country's any organizational employees behavior may bring indirect relationship to influence the country's long term economic development. I shall indicate past manufacture industry social development period to explain their relationship. For many countries' past business activities had belonged to manufacturing industry, such as US, UK past before 1980 year, it focused on steel manufacturing and steel manufacturing related machine products. So, US, Uk developed countries manufacturing industries may be past main country's economic income sources. I assume US , UK past had one million number different kinds of industries. They ought had about seven houndred thousand number organizational businesses were belonged to manufactured industry. They may include:

Steel manufacturing and steel related machine manufacturing, e.g. vehicle manufacturing, home appliances, e.g. washing machine, television, radio, refrigerate cooler, heater, air condition etc. different kinds of different kinds of steel -related manufacturing machine, they were manufactured from US, UK steel machine manufacturers. So, US, Uk the other three hundred thousand number industry may be general service industry, e.g. hotel service, restaurent, cinema, public transport service, tourism lesiure , wine bar, supermarket etc. different kinds of non-manufacturing industries business organizations were operated in UK, US past before 1980 year.

So, in UK, US developed countries industry development history, they ought have high percentage of businesses belonged to steel related manufacturing machine and steel products. Also, in the past before 1980 year, US, Uk business employers , they employed many workers are manufacturing workers. They needed to spend long time to work in factories. They were skillful workers, and they are trained to manufacturing cars, washing machine, television, heater, etc. even steel itself different kinds of steel related products to prepare to deliver to their shops to sell to US, Uk local or overseas clients.

So, I believe that past UK, US ought employ many employees, they belonged to skillful manufacturing workers, manufacture increasing steel machine or steel related machine number of products rapidly daily. So, if UK, US had had many of these manufacturing factories owned high skillful workers, then their manufacturing steel-related machine or steel both kinds of products number must be influenced to raise rapidly. Consequently, their steel machine manufacturing products would been exported to overseas or would been sold to local both markets , they may be influenced to raise sale number. They (these manufacturing workers) needed to be trained to know how to manufactur these different kinds of machine products in the efficient teams and they ought to be trained to raise their efficiencies in order to shorten time to manufacturing many kinds of steel related manufacturing machine or steel itself products rapidly. So , if their efficiencies and manufacturing performance was improved, these US, UK any one manufacturing worker and their teams ought achieve raising productivities significantly.

Hence, when past UK, US manufacturing industry development period, if these two countries' any manufacturing factories could have many manufacturing workers could be trained to be skillful and proficient manufacturing workers. Then, in past every day to these factories workers, they ought help their steel or steel related manufacturing employers to raise any kinds of machine or steel products number in every team. So, when past in the manufacturing industry development, US, UK could have many factories' manufacturing workers themselves steel or steel related machine products manufacturing skill could be trained to to improve to any kinds of these machine or steel manufacuring products quality as well as their products number could be influenced to raise by themselves skillful improvement significantly every day.

Then, what would be influenced to occur to past UK, US manufacturing industry period? In behavioral economic view, when these two manufacturing industry developed countries, such as UK, US , if they had many factories workers can be trained to improve their skill in order to achieve any kinds of steel or steel-related machine products quality could be improved as well as products manufacturing number could be also increased absolutely.

In consequence, past UK and US both countries ought increase themselves any kinds of steel and steel related machine products number to be supplied to themselves local shops to let local clients to choose any one kind of machine manufacturing products to buy easily as well as they could also export to supply overseas any countries to buy their different kinds of steel or steel related machine products to let overseas steel or steel related manufacturing machine product buyers, they can have many of these different kinds of these steel or steel-related different kinds of manufacturing machine from UK and UK these both countries easily to compare other countries.

On conclusion, I believe that past US, and UK macro manufacturing industry income GDP would increase significantly. So, they would have good economic growth performance because when many of these manufacturing workers themselves manufacturing effort could be improved. So, it explained when employees manufacturing abilities can influence economic growth indirectly.

Robots invention whether they can help organizations to raise efficiencies or inefficiencies?

In behavioral economic view, in any organizations, when the organization hopes its worker teams can raise efficiencies , the organization may choose to increase more workers number and/or it can provide training to improve these workets themselves skills in order to raise their efficiencies. For one warehouse example, when the warehouse increases many goods , they are needed to delivered these goods from the shelves to the delivering destination locations. If this warehouse supervisors feel these workers themselves goods delivery speeds are slow, which is possible due to this warehouse's workers number is not enough. So, this warehouse supervisor ought increase workers number in order to increase their goods delivery speed in order to deliver goods from the shelves to every indicated goods delivery destination in order to let any one lorry driver can transport the right kinds of goods and ensure the accurate goods number to transport to any one client home rapidly.

However, if this warehouse supervisor planed to buy several warehouse goods delivery robots to assist these warehouse workers to find the right kinds of goods from shelves and then deliver to the right destination location in the warehouse. So, these warehouse orkers can concentrate on counting the accurate goods number and ensuring the right kinds of goods in order to prepare to let lorry drivers to transport these goods to these goods of buyers themselvers homes rapidly. Consequently, in the first step, robots can concentrate on finding th right goods from shelves and delivers them to the right goods transportation of location destination. Then, in the second step, these warehouse workers can concentrate on counting the accurate goods number and ensuring the right kinds of goods in order to prepare to put them to the lorry. Consequently, when warehouse robots and warehouse workers can cooperate to work together, the most important, robots, can deal on finding the right kinds of goods and deal on delivering the accurate number of goods of job duty as well as these warehouse workers can only concentrte on counting the right kinds of goods number in order to avoid it has none any mistake of wrong kinds of goods and inaccurate goods of delivery number to be transported to the lorry and to deliver to any one buyer's home.

So, it seems that warehouse robots ought help any one warehouse worker to raise himself efficiency and avoid goods delivery of mistake occurrence easily as well as their help to warehouse workers that can let any one goods buyer feels their goods can be delivered to their homes rapidly. Moreover, warehouse robots can also help these warehouse workers to raise efficiencies because warehouse robots can help them to shorten goods delivery time between any one shelf and any one goods delivery destination of location in the warehuse because robots may help them to find the right kinds of goods from the right shelf in the short time. So, any one worker does not need to spend long time to seek anywhere is the right shelf location for the kind of goods when the kind of goods are needed to deliver to the buyer's home from lorry. Warehouse robots can help them to do this aspect of " finding the goods from the right shelf in short time job duty". So, any one warehouse worker only needed tospend less time to do the counting of any right kind of goods number and ensuring the right kind of goods job duty. Consequently, this warehouse 's any one worker, his any one kind of goods delivery time may be reduced, because robots' assistance and they may have more confidence to avoid mistake to deliver the wrong number of goods and/or the wrong kind of goods to any one goods buyer's home.

On conclusion, it seems that warehouse robots ought may help any one warehouse worker to raise efficiency for any one team in the warehouse as well as the warehouse any one supervisor does not need to spend much time to observe any one worker individual performance for " goods delivery job duty aspect" because their goods delivery job duty that had been replaced to do by these several warehouse robots. Robots can achieve the more accurate of right kinds of goods and the right number of goods delviery job performance to compare any one of human warehouse worker themselves right kinds of goods of delivery and right number of goods of delivery job performance. So, when robots can participate to cooperate with this warehouse's any one worker to do their goods of delivery job duty in this warehouse every day. Then, robots can raies any one of supervisor individual confidence in order to let they do not need to spend time to observe any one of worker individual whose goods of delivery job performane. They can concentrate on supervising any one worker whose goods transport to lorry in the final step in order to avoid to deliver wrong goods number and / or wrong kind of goods to any one goods buyer's home every day. Consequently, this warehouse's overall teams of their delviery of goods performance many be improved by robotss' participatin to goods of delivery task as well as this warehouse's oveall teams themselves efficiencies may be influenced to raise by robots' goods of delivery task participation.

www.ingramcontent.com/pod-product-compliance
Lightning Source LLC
Chambersburg PA
CBHW060602120726
48002CB00010B/2779